Pierrot:
A Critical History
of a
Mask

PIERROT
A Critical History of a Mask

Robert F. Storey

PRINCETON UNIVERSITY PRESS
Princeton, New Jersey

Copyright © 1978 by Princeton University Press
Published by Princeton University Press, Princeton, New Jersey
In the United Kingdom: Princeton University Press,
Guildford, Surrey

All Rights Reserved

Library of Congress Cataloging in Publication Data will be
found on the last printed page of this book

Publication of this book has been aided by a grant from
The Andrew W. Mellon Foundation

Clothbound editions of Princeton University Press books are printed on
acid-free paper, and binding materials are chosen for strength and durability.

Excerpts from the poetry of T. S. Eliot are reprinted from his volume
Collected Poems 1909-1962 by permission of Harcourt Brace Jovanovich,
Inc.; copyright, 1936, by Harcourt Brace Jovanovich, Inc.; copyright ©
1963, 1964, by T. S. Eliot. These excerpts are also reprinted by permission
of Faber and Faber Ltd. from the British edition of *Collected Poems 1909-
1962* by T. S. Eliot.

Excerpts from the poems and plays of Wallace Stevens are reprinted by
permission of Alfred A. Knopf, Inc., from the volumes *Collected Poems*,
copyright © 1954 by Wallace Stevens, *Opus Posthumous*, copyright © 1957
by Elsie Stevens and Holly Stevens, and *The Palm at the End of the Mind*,
edited by Holly Stevens, copyright © 1967, 1969, 1971, by Holly Stevens.
Several poems and a verse-letter from Holly Stevens' volume *Souvenirs
and Prophecies: The Young Wallace Stevens*, copyright © 1966, 1976, by Holly
Stevens, and extracts from *Letters of Wallace Stevens*, edited by Holly Stevens, copyright © 1966 by Holly Stevens, also appear by permission of
Alfred A. Knopf, Inc. Excerpts from the poems and prose are also reprinted by permission of Faber and Faber Ltd. from the British editions of
The Collected Poems of Wallace Stevens, *Opus Posthumous* by Wallace Stevens, and *Letters of Wallace Stevens*, edited by Holly Stevens.

Patricia Terry's translation of Laforgue's "Autre Complainte de Lord
Pierrot" is protected by copyright © 1958 by The Regents of the Univer-
sity of California; reprinted by permission of the University of California
Press.

Verlaine's sonnet "Pierrot" from his *Œuvres poétiques complètes*, edited
by Y.-G. Le Dantec and revised by Jacques Borel, copyright © 1962 by
Editions Gallimard, and excerpts from Pascal Pia's edition of Laforgue's
Poésies complètes, copyright © 1970 by Editions Gallimard, are reproduced
by permission of Librairie Gallimard, Paris.

Printed in the United States of America
by Princeton University Press, Princeton, New Jersey
Designed by Laury A. Egan

For Chom

99473

Au clair de la lune
Mon ami Pierrot,
Prête-moi ta plume
Pour écrire un mot.

CONTENTS

LIST OF ILLUSTRATIONS

ACKNOWLEDGMENTS

I am grateful to the museums, libraries, and collectors named above for kindly allowing me to reproduce the works in their possession. I would like to thank, in addition, these copyright agents, photographers, publishing houses, and repositories for supplying the following illustrations or for permitting me to use them in this book: 1, Biblioteca Comunale dell'Archiginnasio di Bologna (photo: Antonio Bonavera); 8, photo: Bibliothèque Nationale, Paris; 9, photo: Musées Nationaux, Paris; 10, The Trustees of the British Museum; 11, Georges Girard, Imprimeur, Paris, and Tristan Rémy; 13, The Boston Free Public Library, Rare Books and Manuscripts Division; 16, The Museum of Modern Art, Film Stills Archive, New York; 19, The Library of Congress, Prints and Photographs Division, Washington, D.C.; 24, photo: Nathan Rabin, New York; 27, 30, 32, S.P.A.D.E.M., Paris (© by S.P.A.D.E.M., Paris, 1978); 29, ADAGP, Paris (© by ADAGP, Paris, 1978; photo: Galerie Louise Leiris, Paris).

PREFACE

My subtitle suggests both the focus and the scope of this book. It is, first, *a* history of Pierrot, not *the* history: no attempt has been made to be complete or "definitive." Pierrot is so plastic and culturally accommodating a figure—and so ubiquitous a mask—that any study making completeness its aim is courting sure failure, especially if it aspires to be anything more than a catalogue of titles, names, and dates. My goal has been to trace the fortunes of Pierrot down the main channel of his development and into one of the two important tributaries of his modern career—the poetry of Laforgue and of the most prominent American poets of this century, T. S. Eliot and Wallace Stevens. I have made no exhaustive effort to uncover "new" material about the origins and early life of the clown but have, rather, restricted myself to a close examination of the recovered documents—chiefly, the relevant *scenari* of the *commedia dell'arte*, the plays of both the "Ancien" and "Nouveau" Théâtre-Italien in Paris, the dramatic literature of the Parisian fairs, the repertories of the great nineteenth-century mimes, the significant *littérature pierrotique* of the last century, and of course the poetry of Laforgue, Eliot, and Stevens. In short, the primary intention has not been to enrich one or more of the isolated areas of our factual knowledge about this fascinating figure, but to assemble carefully the extant pieces of his history in an attempt to gain a "critical" perspective upon both the details and the full panorama of his long life. Among the questions I address are: What sort of character and role does Pierrot have at the different stages of his development? Does he retain a fundamental identity throughout his career? What are the factors responsible for his survival and progress? What is the nature of his appeal to his maskers and his audience?

The second of those two important "tributaries" into which Pierrot's fortunes are swept in the nineteenth and twentieth centuries is, of course, the world of the graphic arts, where he flourishes brilliantly on the canvases of Daumier, Ensor, Rousseau, Picasso, Juan Gris, Rouault, and many other artists. I have refrained from taking up this aspect of his history for several reasons. First, I feel much more comfortable in the realm of words than in the realm of paint, and fear that unless I were to spend several more years before those canvases, educating my eye in the museums, I would be prone to indulge in outrageously (and fruitlessly) naïve speculations about them. Second, I am intimidated by the sheer number of major artists who have seized upon Pierrot as a subject: I doubt whether any but the most superficial treatment of their work could be accommodated in a single history of the figure. Third, and finally, I am loath to relinquish the thematic unity that has emerged from my literary research in order to bring another discipline—and, with it, a completely different perspective—into the discussion. As I hope to show as the book progresses, Pierrot's theatrical and literary history is the record of his vacillations between two dramatic and psychological "types." At one pole stands his Italian predecessor Pedrolino, who, like the Gallicized Harlequin, is a creature of insouciance and activity, a character of almost no psychological "depth," a symbol of comic irrepressibility and unselfconscious verve. He inhabits a dense social world, but, curiously, rarely suffers pangs of social conscience. At the other pole stands Hamlet—a figure of melancholy indolence, a character of inscrutable depth and complexity, a symbol of human vulnerability and mortality, a moralist tortured by conscience—but, just as curiously, an egoist who is profoundly asocial and solipsistic. These two types of humanity (and, consequently, the Pierrots whose definition they circumscribe) live in a universe in which time is conspicuous either by its relentless advance or by its momentary suspension. For the Pierrots of the graphic arts, however, time does not exist. They share a relationship with the artist, the viewer, and the geometry of their canvases that calls up eternal emblematic meanings—meanings that, perhaps paradoxically, acquire their full weight only when the viewer exercises his remembrance of Pierrots past. The art of the painterly *pierrotiste* is always a retrospective one: the very life of his creations is sustained by the vague survival of the popular Pierrot in the minds of their beholders. This need not be, and often is not, the case with the art of the dramatist or poet. In short, the assumptions with which the painter regards his subject would seem to differ greatly from those of the writer; and whatever conclusions any critic tenders about both or either must responsibly reflect those differences. Perhaps the illustrations I have included will someday encourage one or two other *amis de* Pierrot to supply us, not only with his pictorial history, but with an equally welcome chronicle of his life in dance, music, and film. Such, at any rate, must be my hope.

Of the friends and advisors who saw this book through to completion, Professors Robert Martin Adams, John Espey, Gerald Weales, and Wallace Fowlie deserve a special note of thanks. Dr. Adams was, as always, generous in his inspiration and encouragement; Dr. Espey criticized, to my great profit, the early drafts of the manuscript with characteristic sensitivity and conscientiousness; Dr. Weales won my unbounded admiration and gratitude by volunteering to read the entire work in one of its later stages and by offering copious suggestions, both helpfully specific and shrewd; and Dr. Fowlie, while demonstrating an understanding of my subject that I can only hope to have approached, suggested with unflagging courtesy and insight how I might turn all of these "manuscripts" into a book. I am further indebted to the staff of the Henry E. Huntington Library, San Marino, California, for granting access to the library's valuable Larpent collection of play-scripts, and to Mr. Geoffrey Hope, who spent long and, I am sure, exasperating hours checking over my translations. I would like to record here, in addition, my gratitude to the trustees and administration of the University of Pennsylvania for the summer grant that enabled me to prepare the manuscript for publication.

In order to save space and to keep the text as uncluttered as possible, I have omitted full documentation for quoted excerpts from the poetry of Verlaine, Laforgue, Eliot, and Stevens: their poems may be found quickly and easily in the standard editions listed in my Bibliography. I have rendered most foreign-language citations directly into English, but when a quotation is a sizable portion of verse or is prose that is significant for the nature of its language, it is cited in the original language and translated in a footnote. Except where indicated, all translations are my own, and for their occasional errors and awkwardnesses I am—notwithstanding Mr. Hope's expert eye—wholly responsible.

Pierrot:
A Critical History
of a
Mask

I

Origins and Birth

*L'origine de Pierrot n'est-elle pas aussi in-
téressante que tous les arcanes qui ont excité la
curiosité des Bochart, des Pères Kircher, des
Cluverius, des Champollion, des Franck?—
Une histoire bien faite d'Arlequin, de Pierrot,
de Polichinelle, serait des plus instructives et
des plus intéressantes.*—Théophile Gautier
in *La Presse*, January 25, 1847

To move from the etiolated, wraithlike clown who wan-
ders, moonstruck, in and out of the vague, disquieting
harmonies of Schoenberg's expressionistic song cycle to a
quick and capricious buffoon of sixteenth-century Italy,
who darts about a trestle stage in the glare of a bright noon
sun, is to take a large step indeed, in point of both history
and the imagination. But it is a necessary step if we are to
grasp the sometimes elusive and mercurial character of
Pierrot. Created and nourished by the popular imagination, he has survived four centuries of social and philosophical change, managing to adapt to the world in which
he momentarily finds himself with remarkable pliability
and success. For Pierrot was not always infected with the
enervating weltschmerz and hypersensitivity of Pierrot
lunaire, nor possessed of the troubled, dandiacal éclat of
Jules Laforgue's little heroes, nor even succored by the
shuffling tenacity of Charlie Chaplin; rather he had, in the
very earliest days of his career, a comic, engaging poise
and brilliance that bespoke nothing of the beautiful but
vulnerable soul or the pirouettes of a pliant cane.

His career began in the *commedia dell'arte*. This development in the Italian theater of the Renaissance, in popular favor throughout the second half of the sixteenth century and the whole of the seventeenth, lasted, though in decline, well into the 1700's. The *commedia* was improvised theater (comedy was its métier) in which a *scenario* (plot outline) served in place of a script in dialogue. It was performed by a professional company of about a dozen members, each usually fulfilling in play after play an inherited or invented role and seldom straying from the "type" thereby sustained or created. Though the troupes' numbers began to swell towards the end of the seventeenth century when the *commedia* was moving into a kind of decadence, the basic company consisted of two *vecchi* or old men, Pantalone and the Doctor; two pairs of "principal" and "secondary" Lovers; a soubrette; a Captain; and a "first" and "second" *zanni* (comic valets, such as Pulcinella and Coviello, or Brighella and Harlequin). In the "classical" period of the art, all but the serious figures, the lovers, wore masks or correspondingly comic makeup, and each character dressed in traditional costume that was sometimes slightly modified as an inheritor of the role added or changed a nuance of interpretation. Perhaps taking their cues from professional actor-playwrights of the sixteenth century, such as Angelo Beolco (*"Il Ruzzante"*), the *commedia* players particularized the "types" and heightened the comic effects by putting dialect into the mouths of the *zanni* and serio-comic personages. Whereas the Lovers spoke only a pure and mellifluous Tuscan, the other characters, or "masks," conversed, babbled, and intoned in the dialects of their "origins."

It was not uncommon for an actor to bring such a degree of sophistication to his interpretation of a role and to sustain it indefatigably for so many years that he and his character became synonymous in the eyes of his public. Dominique Biancolelli and Tiberio Fiorilli meant Harlequin and Scaramouche to seventeenth-century French audiences, just as Catherine Biancolelli, the talented daughter of Dominique, meant Columbine. This is not to imply, however, that a *commedia* performance was a one-man affair. On the contrary, all evidence seems to suggest that the comic effect for which it was conceived, or—since we are looking at it from the other end—which it was most capable of eliciting, depended for its success upon a delicate balance and harmonization of character relationships, of intrigue devices, and of serious and farcical incidents. To demonstrate this and, at the same time, to try to arrive at a clear understanding of how the character or "type" functioned in this genre, we may look at one of the several hundred of existing scenarios—this one from the only collection published by a contemporary, Flaminio Scala's *Il teatro delle favole rappresentative* (1611)—and briefly summarize the plot from its elliptic, diagrammatical prose. The play takes place on the thirty-second of the fifty days into which Scala has partitioned his *scenari;* its title is *Li Duo finti Zingari* (*The Two Disguised Gypsies*).

Isabella and her servant Pedrolino, both disguised as gypsies, have returned, after much traveling, to Rome. There they find family and friends grieving over their ominously long absence. Isabella's beloved, Flavio, has been overcome by a profound melancholy, and her brother Oratio has been driven mad by her assumed death. Oratio's own intended, Flaminia, daughter of Doctor Gratiano, has had to endure the distress of hopeless love for the madman, and Franceschina, Pedrolino's wife, finds herself daily making flirtatious overtures toward Captain Spavento in an effort to warm her empty bed. So much frustrated passion immediately arouses Pedrolino's theatrical instincts, and he takes advantage of his disguise, donned during his sojourn out of fear of adventurers, to pose as a pander and necromancer. To the eager Flavio, he exhibits Isabella's "corpse," the sight of which moves the duped young man to thoughts of suicide, while to Isabella's father, old Pantalone, he outrageously promises the

carnal delights of his pretty gypsy companion. With characteristic cunning and impudence, he persuades the Doctor, the Captain, and Arlecchino, Spavento's valet, to
dress up in women's clothing; then he boldly pairs the first
two off, assuring each that his mate is a wench, and sends
the innocent Arlecchino to Pantalone's bed. But while
deep in this mischief, he shows a taste for plotting that
runs to more than the pathetic and farcical: he reunites the
lovers Isabella and Flavio and, by thus permitting his mistress to lay off her disguise, "cures" Oratio of his demen-
tia. The cure results, of course, in a second happy
union—of Oratio with Flaminia—and the consternation of
the old men over Pedrolino's pranks melts, at the final curtain, into the joy of conjugal blessings.[1]

We should keep in mind that *Li Duo finti Zingari* exists
only in a bare, skeletal form: Scala's scenario (or a less elegant version of it) was drawn up originally as a kind of
prompt copy, tacked up in the wings during a performance
for the actors' perusal. I stress this in order to suggest that
the latitude with which we can reconstruct the details of a
commedia performance and thereby interpret the effects of
the play upon an audience is unusually great, requiring of
a critic some reliance upon information that lies outside the
play and, therefore, more than usual caution and tact. This
said, we may then ask ourselves: What were those effects?
What was the play-world of a *commedia* production like?

In recent studies of the *commedia dell'arte*, "the social
milieu of the characters," writes Allardyce Nicoll, "has received careful scrutiny and elucidatory comment. From
this the passage is easy to an interpretation of these figures
as objects of satire and hence of the comedy in which they
appear as satirical comedy."[2] But we need hardly quibble

---

[1] The complete scenario appears in Henry F. Salerno, trans., *Scenarios of the Commedia dell'Arte: Flaminio Scala's* Il teatro delle favole rappresentative (New York, 1967), pp. 235-41.
[2] *The World of Harlequin* (Cambridge, England, 1963), p. 150.

with the logic of this proposition to reject it, as Nicoll does, outright. For the moment let it suffice to recall that most of the "types" in this scenario, as well as in the other forty-nine of the collection, were at least twenty-five years old at the time of its publication,[3] and their popularity had by no means diminished during those years. Indeed, the new-born Arlecchino had yet to know his greatest triumphs. Now satire, if it is to be at all pungent or comically vital, must *reveal;* that is, it must strip its victim down to his "essential" character, using most often, and particularly in the theater, a rather rough blade. If, in fact, the aim of the improvised comedy was social satire, its curiously long persistence in the theater would go unexplained. To have "exposed" such a character as Pantalone, for example, in terms of his social role in each play where he appears would have either quickly blunted the intended satirical sting or else wearied the most patient of audiences.

This observation suggests then a second possibility: that the *commedia dell'arte* existed as a showcase for a fixed number of characters, not as they were shown in any satirical light, but rather as they revealed themselves in all their human and serio-comic complexity in play after play, giving pleasure with each appearance by exposing hitherto unknown facets of their personalities.[4] Such a hypothesis immediately proposes that we call up a single character whom we know (or think we know) to possess this near-human complexity, in order to compare him with the *commedia* "type"; and for most of us, that character would be Hamlet. Before we carp at such a comparison, let us recognize that Hamlet and Harlequin "possess certain salient qualities in common." They both evince "the almost unaccountable power of passing over all frontiers"; they both attract and accommodate the most disparate of inter-

---

[3] Of all the masks, the *zanni* had the most uncertain lifespans; but see below, p. 16, for Pedrolino Pellesini's long career.
[4] So Nicoll regards the masks: see *World,* pp. 21-24.

preters—are admired, like Shakespeare himself, by "classicist and romantic alike."[5] And yet a serious comparison is unthinkable, not merely because Harlequin is essentially a "comic" and Hamlet a "tragic" character, but because, as Nicoll points out, they "inhabit utterly different worlds."[6] I think, however, that we can go beyond Nicoll's explanation of their differences—that Hamlet "stands forward before us as a character born of the penetrating imagination of a supreme playwright, expressing himself with that author's passionate eloquence"[7]—and in so doing, arrive at, or at least approach, the essence of the "type."

In a figurative sense, Hamlet appears in no other work but *Hamlet*. Even his most recent appearance, in Tom Stoppard's *Rosencrantz & Guildenstern Are Dead*, is nothing but a replaying of his eternal role. (Mr. Stoppard's play is only *Hamlet* from a Beckettian perspective.) To find him in any place but Elsinore would be a little like coming across Huysmans' Des Esseintes at a cocktail party: it would give us—as, in fact, the Dane's appearance outside Shakespeare's tragedy gives Nicoll—"a measure of discomfort."[8] Our feeling would arise, in the case of Des Esseintes, from knowing that he himself was uncomfortable, that he had been taken from his orange rooms, his bejeweled tortoise, and his *orgue à bouche,* and set down in a room full of (ugh) people. Or—to abandon our metaphor—we would feel uneasy for Hamlet, and more so than for Des Esseintes, because we would be aware that, whatever he might be doing, he would be asking the same question of himself over and over: Is Claudius, Gertrude, Ophelia—no, am *I* worthy of existence? Hamlet is a character whose introspective doubt has become almost proverbial, a character whose reflections about his own moral worth have given him a somber metaphysical dimension that seems to have sicklied o'er the whole world of the play. True, Hamlet can

[5] Ibid., p. 2. [6] Ibid., p. 3.
[7] Ibid., p. 8. [8] Ibid., p. 7.

jape vulgarly with Ophelia or goad Polonius with all the
élan with which the Captain teases Franceschina; but we
accept these departures from his proverbial (and princely)
deportment not so much because Hamlet has a far-ranging
and complex human vitality, but because for Hamlet there
is only one character in his play: himself. He can do, therefore, anything he wants to do. Anything, that is, but what
he wants to do most: escape the unblinking eye of Conscience.

In how different a world do we find ourselves and with
how different a companion when we turn, however, to *The
Merry Wives of Windsor*. For Falstaff, drawn in the true
manner of the *commedia dell'arte,*[9] is sublimely ignorant of
the moral universe; "every moment," as W. H. Auden
writes of him, "is one of infinite possibility when anything
can be wished."[10] And because he lives in this "eternal
present," his creator has trouble confining him to the
world of play (a world that is, paradoxically, impregnated
with temporality and fixed moral values) and can restrain
him to *one* play not at all. "Once upon a time," Auden
writes suggestively, "we were all Falstaffs: then we became
social beings with super-egos."[11] Like Hamlet, he might
have said.

All this has taken us quite a way from *Li Duo finti Zingari*,
not to mention Pierrot, but it is important that we do not
fall into the all too easy error of misconstruing the word
"type." The characters of the *commedia dell'arte*, like
Falstaff, exist in a present "when anything can be wished,"
all living, so to speak, at the tips of their libidos. There
should be no question of Flavio's sincerity when he offers,
on erotic impulse, to kill himself over the "corpse" of
Isabella, just as there is none when Hamlet broods upon

---

[9] Nicoll contends that when Falstaff was introduced into *The Merry
Wives*, "a definite approach was being made towards the commedia
dell'arte method": ibid., p. 22.
[10] *The Dyer's Hand* (New York, 1968), p. 193.
[11] Ibid., p. 195.

outrageous fortune. The difference is reflected in our
choice of verbs: Flavio, meeting experience directly and
with no thought of its historical, that is, moral, implications, *offers* to give his life; Hamlet, rooted in the temporal
present, with Time stretched tight both behind and before
him, buffers the world with his ego and *broods*. The "type"
can be conceived, then, as a bundle of passions, lacking
none of those we commonly attribute to a "deeper" character, but merely expressing them with a spontaneity and
forthrightness conventionally appropriate to his station.[12]
The actors themselves were cautioned against violating
those conventions lest, I would suggest, they turn the
world of the play into a frenetic confusion of unbridled
impulses—in other words, into farce. Andrea Perrucci, in
Dell'arte rappresentativa (1699), for instance, advises the
Lovers to refine their *concetti, soliloqui,* and *raconti*—all
those professions of their passionate attachments—to a
pitch of elegance. Not only must they diligently read
"books written in good Tuscan," but they must also master
all "the figures and tropes of rhetoric."[13] Moreover, their
very gestures must betray no coarseness: in speaking,
"they must not raise their hands higher than their eyes,
nor lower them below their breast."[14] As for the masked
personages, Perrucci cautions strictly against the confusion
of the characters of the Doctor and Pantalone, or, what
would be worse, the lowering of either to the level of the
zanni. "The role of the Doctor," says Perrucci, "must not be
so serious [as that of Pantalone]. . . . The vivacity of his
wit and the prolixity of his speech give him license to
abandon his seriousness, but not to the point of abasing
himself to the role of second *zanni*, which would be an un-

[12] Compare Gustave Attinger's discussion of the masks in his *L'Esprit de la commedia dell'arte dans le théâtre français* (Paris, 1950), pp. 39-43.

[13] Copies of Perrucci's book are extremely rare, but long excerpts from it are reproduced in Enzo Petraccone, *La commedia dell'arte, storia, tecnica, scenari* (Naples, 1927). My quotation is from Petraccone, p. 74.

[14] Cited in Attinger, *L'Esprit de la commedia dell'arte*, p. 40.

pardonable mistake."[15] As Nicoll makes clear, "Perrucci's instructions . . . are not to be regarded as the impractical meanderings of a mere theorist. He was writing with full knowledge of what the commedia dell'arte demanded and of what could be found among its more distinguished practitioners."[16]

With some understanding, then, of the kind of characters that people these *scenari,* we must put them back in *Li Duo finti Zingari* and see what we can make of the play as a whole. A cursory rereading of the plot immediately raises several important questions: Why do Pedrolino and Isabella remain disguised to the end of the play? Why does Flavio not think it curious that Pedrolino is in possession of Isabella's corpse? Why does Isabella deceive Flavio into thinking she is dead? The answer to all these questions is, of course, that there is no answer, but that if things had been otherwise, the play would not exist. Had Isabella revealed her identity to everyone in line 1 of the first act, we might have a newspaper article but we would hardly have a play. So the pleasure that we receive from reading or watching this comedy does not lie in our following a logical unfolding of events, leading to a conclusion that we sense as both inescapable yet pleasurably unsettling: neither the outcome of the intrigue nor, by extension, the ultimate fortunes of the characters really worry or concern us. Here the single question that gives so much teasing delight is simply: What will happen next? And because this is the question that the play presumes to pose, it liberates itself from the logical demands of realism—though this is not to say it cannot trespass freely on that ground—and consequently rises easily above the plane of social satire. For long plays, as the *commedia* productions were, to sustain themselves on such an elementary principle, it was necessary that both the actors and the writers of the *scenari* be gifted with a fertile invention as well as an intuitive sense of rhythm and

[15] In Petraccone, *La commedia dell'arte,* p. 119.   [16] *World,* p. 33.

proportion. The audiences' emotions had to be actively and immediately engaged from scene to scene in order that their reactions to the events transpiring be as naïve and spontaneous as those of the characters on the stage. The pacing and balance of the incidents therefore had to be carefully controlled. A lover's speech of despair, a father's admonition to his son, a suitor's soliloquy of praise or admiration could not continue long enough to tire, nor the comic business, the *burle* and *lazzi*, last long enough to attract all interest from the serious personages. A close inspection of *Li Duo finti Zingari* will show this careful balancing of serious and comic scenes. Indeed, we may even say that, in this scenario, as the comic action becomes more frenetic in the second and third acts, the serious interludes, in which Flavio is shown Isabella's "corpse," acquire greater and more touching poignancy.

These remarks, however, do not explain why the *commedia dell'arte*, as comedy, was so viable a form. In its farcical byplay we can recognize those elements which would have momentarily enlivened any performance; but for an explanation of the comic potency of the plays taken in their entirety, we must look elsewhere. We must look, in fact, to the type as it functions in the plot. It is for this reason that I have selected *Li Duo finti Zingari* for discussion. As a scenario among Scala's fifty, it is neither the best nor even the most representative of the collection; its chief value for us lies in the use to which Scala has deftly put all the characters. As we have noted, the types are rather strictly limited in role and station, and their passions accordingly governed by the comic conventions of conduct that accrue to them. This being so, and these characters, through their repeated appearances in play after play, being so familiar to their audiences, it is likely that the playgoers came to expect certain things in the regulation of the intrigue. And it is this very predictability inherent in the type, I would suggest, that gives the improvised comedy—plotless in the accepted, Aristotelian sense of the word—such comic potentiality.

Whereas the unexpected disruptions of a complete and single action create the delight of many "modern" comedies (posing the question: How will it all end?), here it is the momentary thwarting, the sudden deflecting of the characteristic passions of the types that leaves us in such a state of comic bewilderment at the end of, say, Act II, and with such a feeling of satisfaction at the harmony of the final tableau. In a great number of Scala's plays, this deflection is accomplished by purely fortuitous occurrences: letters are confused (*Flavio tradito*); twins are mistaken for one another (*Li Duo capitani simili*); persons believed dead are taken for ghosts (*La Creduta morta*); blood relationships are discovered among would-be lovers (*La Sposa*); and persons in disguise are taken for anybody and everybody (*Isabella astrologa*). When, however, Fortune seems somewhat sluggish in accomplishing what she should do, her role is appropriated by two very important characters—the *zanni. Li Duo finti Zingari* gives us a case in point. Here Pedrolino's role is not simply to fool those who deserve to be fooled and lend a hand to lovers in distress; if anything, he inexplicably seems to delay the Lovers' reconciliation throughout the play. His function is obviously to keep the play moving, to keep overturning the libidinous drives, whether refined or comparatively coarse, of the other characters. And what he does through capricious design, Arlecchino does through witless inadvertence. As Constant Mic observes, the first *zanni* "instigates confusion quite voluntarily, [but] the second creates disturbance through his blundering. The second *zanni* is a perfect dunce; but the first sometimes gives indication of a certain instruction. . . . *The first* zanni *incarnates the dynamic, comic element of the play, the second its static element.*"[17] In the

---

[17] *La Commedia dell'arte* (Paris, 1927), p. 47 (emphasis mine).

former capacity, the Pedrolino of *Li Duo finti Zingari* represents a force, if symbol is too strong a word, of uncertainty,
of misrule. To the other characters—Calibans all—he is an
Ariel, albeit a fleshly one, whose wings keep coming between the stone and that twenty-first crab.

Into this family of *zanni* Pierrot is born. Although he
does not appear under his own name and familiar costume
until towards the end of the seventeenth century, in
France, in what may be called a second stage of the *commedia*'s development, intimations of that appearance may
be found among the *zanni* of the early years of the *commedia
dell'arte*. A note in the collection of scenarios left by
"Dominique" Biancolelli, Harlequin of the first Italian
troupe in which Pierrot appeared by name, suggests that
Pulcinella was his progenitor: "The nature of the *rôle* is that
of a Neapolitan Pulcinella a little altered. In point of fact,
the Neapolitan scenarii, in place of Arlecchino and
Scapino, admit two Pulcinellas, the one an intriguing
rogue and the other a stupid fool. The latter is Pierot's [*sic*]
rôle."[18] But we are tempted, in our quest for origins, to
look beyond the amorphous and protean figure of Pulcinella[19] towards a *zanni* of sharper outline, one whose
personality is a little better delineated, who can call himself
the father of his child because the eyes and nose are his,
not simply because it has two arms and legs. Some
scholars suggest that Pierrot bears a close family resemblance to three early and related Italian fools, Bertoldo
and his progeny, Bertoldino and Cacasenno.[20] But all
agree, with good reason, that the *zanni* who, in name and

[18] [T.-S. Gueullette, trans.], "Traduction . . . du recueil des scènes que
joseph biancolelli jouoit en habit d'Arlequin," MS. 13736, Bibliothèque de
l'Opéra, Paris, I, 113; cited and trans. in Allardyce Nicoll, *Masks, Mimes
and Miracles* (London, 1931), p. 294.

[19] See K. M. Lea, *Italian Popular Comedy* (Oxford, 1934), I, 100, for a full
discussion of Pulcinella's multiform personality.

[20] See Maurice Sand, *Masques et bouffons* (1860; English trans. *The His-
tory of the Harlequinade* [Philadelphia, 1915]), pp. 183-92; and P.-L.
Duchartre, *La Comédie italienne* (1925; English trans. *The Italian Comedy*
[London, 1929]), pp. 255-58.

personality, stands directly behind him—if he is not, indeed, the "Italian equivalent" of Pierrot[21]—is the Pedrolino of *Li Duo finti Zingari.*

The success of Pedrolino's role and its obvious importance for the *commedia dell'arte* in the last quarter of the sixteenth century and first decade and a half of the seventeenth seem to have owed a great deal to one Giovanni Pellesini, who interpreted the mask throughout his lengthy career.[22] His dress was probably that of the Pedrolini who appear in two woodcuts of the period: one of these, in which the *zanni* reports to his master Pantalone, stands at the head of the first scene of Oratio Vecchi's madrigal play *L'Amfiparnaso* (Venice, 1597); the other, the clearer of the two, is an illustration for G. C. Croce's burlesque poem celebrating *La Gran Vittoria di Pedrolino contra il Dottor Gratiano Scatolone, per amor della bella Franceschina* (see illustration 1). Pedrolino appears in three plays of the "Corsini" collection of scenarios[23] and in all but one of Flaminio Scala's fifty, taking a prominent place in the great majority of them. His function there as "first" *zanni* sometimes gives him a Janus-faced aspect. He may work cleverly in the interests of the Lovers in one play—*Li Quattro finti spiritati*, for example—by disguising himself as a magician and making Pantalone believe that the "madness" of Isabella and Oratio can be cured only by their coupling together; then, in *Gli avvenimenti comici, pastorali e tragici*, indulge his capricious sense of fun by compound-

[21] Nicoll, *World*, p. 88.

[22] Documentation of Pellesini's career begins in the year 1576, when he appears in Florence, apparently at the head of his own troupe called *Pedrolino*. For a detailed account of the movements of this troupe and of Pellesini himself, see Lea, *Italian Popular Comedy*, I, 265-92.

[23] Unfortunately this collection is inaccessible to me, but each scenario is described briefly in Vito Pandolfi, *La commedia dell'arte, storia e testo*, V (Florence, 1959), 252-76; and of the descriptions of the scenarios in which Pedrolino appears—*La Mvla Grande, Il Granchio*, and *Il Prencipe d'Altavilla*—at least one gives indication that he may enjoy here different nuances of character from those of Scala's *zanni*: in *Il Granchio*, he appears to be a father on equal footing with Pantalone.

ing the young persons' misfortunes. But more often than
not, as in the last-mentioned piece, he repents of such mischief and is forgiven by all before the play ends. An engaging figure of quick and volatile wit emerges from these *scenari*, taken as a whole. K. M. Lea has suggested that Scala,
the Flavio of the *scenari* and a producer, director, and agent
of companies, composed his *Il teatro* with an "all-star cast"
of the "chief actors of his day" in mind, "without regard to
the composition of a company at any particular period."[24]
If this is so, then the importance of Pedrolino as a "first"
zanni and of Pellesini as his interpreter during these years
cannot be overestimated.

When the Italian troupes began to penetrate into France
in the mid-sixteenth century,[25] Pedrolino and his fellow
personages were soon accorded noble and royal patronage. Intimacies between rulers and players became not uncommon. In a breach of royal protocol, Henri IV wrote, in
December of 1599, to Harlequin Tristano Martinelli of the
excellent company of the Duke of Mantua, expressing his
desire to see Harlequin and his companion players perform in his *royaume;* and in 1603, Pedrolino Pellesini
figured among the members of a troupe entertaining at the
court in answer to another call from the delighted king and
queen. He played in Paris again in 1613-1614, this time
with Martinelli; but at the age of eighty-seven he seems to
have lost the verve and dash of his younger days—or so it
appeared to the weary Malherbe, who complained of one
of their performances at the Louvre: "gay spirits and sharp
wits are needed [in the theater], and one hardly finds these
in bodies as old as theirs."[26] Understandably, the troupes

[24] *Italian Popular Comedy*, I, 293.
[25] For documentation of their early activity, see particularly Raymond
Lebègue, "La Comédie italienne en France au XVIᵉ siècle," *Revue de Littérature Comparée*, XXIV (January-March 1950), 5-24; and Armand Baschet,
Les Comédiens italiens à la cour de France (Paris, 1882).
[26] *Œuvres de Malherbe*, ed. Ludovic Lalanne (Paris, 1862); cited in Baschet, *Les Comédiens italiens à la cour*, p. 244.

that appeared thereafter did not number Pellesini—or Pedrolino—among their members.

Indeed, during the long period from 1614 to 1660, when a company of Italian players finally settled permanently in Paris, the name of Pedrolino is absent from the records describing the movements and development of the *commedia dell'arte*. But it is unlikely that the mask disappeared entirely, especially among the less distinguished troupes whose fortunes are unrecorded. If nothing else, Scala's published scenarios must have kept the *zanni* alive among *commedia* enthusiasts for a good number of years. Nevertheless, the French theater rather than the Italian was responsible for the continuation of the Pedrolino tradition, in the somewhat altered guise and role of Pierrot, beginning in the year 1665.

In 1658, the Italian Comedians in Paris performed a version of that "wretched Spanish play" (as Goldoni later speaks of it)[27] based upon the Don Juan legend, *Il Convitato di pietra*, which so caught the town's fancy that several other plays on the same theme appeared in the French theaters soon afterwards. The version that concerns us here is that produced by Molière's company, and from Molière's pen, in 1665, called *Don Juan, ou Le Festin de pierre*; for at the opening of its second act, a short scene is played between Charlotte, a young country lass, and her slow-witted swain, Pierrot. "The success obtained by his comedy," suggests the historian of French theater, Edouard Fournier,

again in its turn tempted the Italians. . . . In the early part of February, 1673, a bare fortnight before the death of that great author, the Italians performed in their theater a new plot made up of the best scenes of their old piece, *Il Convitato di Pietro* [*sic*], and, particu-

[27] Carlo Goldoni, *Mémoires*, in *Tutte le opere*, ed. Giuseppe Ortolani (Milan, 1935), I, 176.

larly, of the most amusing passages appropriated by them from the comedy of Molière. This comic medley, made up like the dress of Harlequin, was entitled *Aggiunta al Convitato di Pietro* [*La Suite du Festin de pierre*]. Among the characters transformed and adapted by the Italians in this extraordinary scenic hotch-potch was Pierrot, with his simpleton ways, his naive love affairs and his unaltered name. Little attention was paid to this new-comer, so that, haphazard and, as it were, out of charity, the part was entrusted to a low-salaried member of the company named Giaratone [or Geratoni]. He did marvels. The others had the good sense not to be jealous and thus, in one stroke and by the one success, the character and the comedian alike acquired rights of citizenship.[28]

Fournier's last statement is a little misleading, since there is no record of Giaratone's having been received into the company as an important member until 1684, when he again took Pierrot's role in a play called *Arlequin, Empereur dans la Lune*.[29] But it is true that, from this latter date, he began to appear frequently on the stage of the Hôtel de Bourgogne (whose *salle* the Italians had been occupying for four years under the illustrious title of *Les Comédiens italiens du Roi*) until the closing of the theater in 1697. Fortunately, a good number of the plays and parts of plays that the Italians performed from 1682 up to the year of their suppression were collected and published as *Le Théâtre Italien* by the troupe's last Harlequin, Evaristo Gherardi; and in these we can see several new developments in the evolution of the role that had been appropriated and, as it were, recreated by Giuseppe Giaratone.

It is difficult to say how much of Molière's creation was influenced by the mask of Pedrolino (if we can assume any influence whatever) and how much of Giaratone's was di-

[28] Cited in Maurice Sand, *Harlequinade*, I, 205-206.
[29] See [François and Claude Parfaict], *Histoire de l'Ancien Théâtre-Italien* (Paris, 1753), p. 107.

rectly influenced by either.[30] The name *Pierrot*, as Georges
Doutrepont points out, had obvious, traditional French as-
sociations, quite apart from the *commedia dell'arte*, at the
time of the writing of *Don Juan*. "If we consult our usual
dictionaries," he writes, "we read under the word *Pierrot*:
1. first name or proper name, diminutive of or derived
from *Pierre*; 2. first name or proper name often employed
in literature for a peasant or a keeper of a sheep-pen; 3. a
type of the old Italian Comedy, or a buffoon of pantomime
with a floured face and white costume."[31] We need hardly
go beyond the first two entries to find the source for
Molière's character. Indeed, in this stereotypical, bucolic
role, Pierrot is often alluded to, with easy familiarity, in the
poetry of the period. In La Fontaine's *Le Berger et La Mer*,
for example, we find these burlesque lines:

> *Son maître fut réduit à garder les brebis,*
> *Non plus berger en chef comme il était jadis,*
> *Quand ses propres moutons paissaient sur le rivage.*
> *Celui qui s'était vu Coridon ou Tircis*
> *Fut Pierrot, et rien davantage.*[32]

The rude and clumsy Pierrot who loiters in this verse, set
off against the traditionally elegant pastoral figures, shows
clearly through the naïve *patois* that Molière puts in the
mouth of his own "Piarrot"; and the latter's puerile oaths
(*Ventrequenne! Jerniquenne!*), his stammering professions of
love, and lumpish, peat-like character—slow to kindle and

---

[30] Biancolelli's scenario of *La Suite du Festin de pierre* is of no help here:
Pierrot's name appears only once, and in this unilluminating context:
"*Cette scéne* [sic] *se passe à la campagne. je* [ARLEQUIN] *fais tomber aux pieds de
Spezzafer le cor de chasse dont il sonne, en suite en courant je culbute* PIERROT;
puis je trouve un aveugle . . .": MS. of the Opéra, II, 177; cited in Oskar
Klingler, *Die Comédie-Italienne in Paris nach der Sammlung von Gherardi*
(Strassburg, 1902), p. 154.
[31] *Les Types populaires de la littérature française*, II (Brussels, 1928), 45.
[32] "His master was reduced to watching over the sheep / (No longer
the master-shepherd he had been before) / When his own flock grazed on
the riverbank. / He who had seen himself as Coridon or Tircis / Was Pierrot, and nothing more": *Fables*, IV, 2; cited in Doutrepont, *Les Types
populaires*, II, 46.

slow to burn—all suggest that he is stamped from this very
mold. If, as Fournier points out, Molière gave him "the
white blouse of a French peasant,"[33] then I doubt very
much that we have to look for traces of his origins in the
commedia dell'arte at all.

Some apparent connections may be made, however, between the Pierrot of Molière and that of Giaratone, since
several plays of the Gherardi collection present Pierrot as a
paysan who closely resembles in language and character
the peasant of *Don Juan*. In the *Esope* (1691) of Eustache le
Noble, for example, Pierrot accosts the peripatetic *fablier* to
recount a pathetic tale of friendship betrayed. When Compère Jaquet generously arranges a tryst between his
white-frocked friend and a frisky young lady of his close
acquaintance, Pierrot stupidly "fell into their trap":

> *Alle m'attendi dans la grange*
> *Par un soir qui pleuvoit, et là je la trouvi.*
>
> *Mais dès que j'arrivi,*
> *J'y fu prins, et l'an fit un tintamarre étrange,*
> *Et le tout par Jaquet qui venit en tremblant*
> *Me faire un biau semblant.*
> *Tant y a je l'épouzi par le conseil du drôle,*
> *Qui me juri su sa parole*
> *Qu'alle étoit comme un varre net.*
> *Mais si tôt que j'eus fait un si sot Mariage,*
> *Je m'appercevi que Jaquet*
> *Avoit écramé le fromage.*
> *Le soir je la trouvi ronde comme un tambour.*
> *Quand je li demandi d'où vian qu'alle étoit grosse:*
> *C'est, sditelle, que j'ai mangé trop à la nôce.*[34]

---

[33] Cited in Maurice Sand, *Harlequinade*, I, 206.
[34] "She waited for me down at the barn / One rainy night, and that's
where I found her. / But soon's I got there, / I was caught: somebody
made a lotta funny noise, / And the whole thing was Jaquet's doin's, who
come out, tremblin', / To put on a big show for me. / Thing was, he was
so good I took that little weasel's advice and married her, / Him swearin'
up an' down / She was clean as a whistle. / But soon's I got yoked into
this marriage, / I found out that Jaquet'd / Done skimmed all the cream

This woeful little narrative may be compared profitably, I think, with a short passage from *Don Juan* to suggest the similarity of the two characters, especially in language and temperament. Pierrot is reproaching Charlotte for her cold unresponsiveness towards him:

Non. Quant ça est, ça se voit, et l'en fait mille petites singeries aux personnes quand on les aime du bon du cœur. Regarde la grosse Thomasse, comme alle est assottée du jeune Robain; alle est toujou autour de li à l'agacer, et ne le laisse jamais en repos. Toujou al li fait queuque niche, ou li baille queuque taloche en passant; et l'autre jour qu'il étoit assis sur un escabiau, al fut le tirer de dessous li, et le fit cheoir tout de son long par tarre. Jarni! vlà où l'en voit les gens qui aimont; mais toi, tu ne me dis jamais mot, t'es toujou là comme eune vraie souche de bois; et je passerois vingt fois devant toi que tu ne te grouillerois pas pour me bailler le moindre coup, ou me dire la moindre chose. Ventrequenne! ça n'est pas bian, après tout; et t'es trop froide pour les gens. [35]

Pierrot's appearance as a peasant among the fifty-odd plays and fragments of *Le Théâtre Italien* is restricted to three or four pieces, however, and his main role is that of a

---

off the milk. / That night I found her round as a drum. / And when I axed her how she come to be so fat, / She says it's because I et too much at the weddin' ''": Evaristo Gherardi, ed., *Le Théâtre Italien de Gherardi* (Amsterdam, 1721), III, 195-96. This collection will be cited hereafter as G in the text.

[35] "Nah: when there's love you can see it, 'n' a body'll pull a thousand little tricks on the people they's really in love with. Look there at Fat Thomasse, how crazy she is 'bout Robin; she's always around a-teasin' him, never lets him alone. She's always a-playin' some trick on him or a-smackin' him in the face when he goes by; just th'other day, when he was a-sittin' on a stool, she took 'n' pulled it right out from under him 'n' layed him out flat on the ground. There, you see, that's the way it is when people's in love. But you, you don't even gi'me the time a day; you always sit there just like a block a wood: I could go walkin' by you twenty times 'n' you wouldn't budge to gi'me the least little slap or even say anythin' to me. Goll-darn it, it ain't right, a-tall: you're too cold for anybody'': *Œuvres complètes*, ed. Louis Moland, VI (Paris, [1881]), 329.

valet of the Italian type. Usually he is a servant of the Doctor or a domestic in one of the old men's households. Luigi Riccoboni's early *Histoire du théâtre italien* (1728) shows him in the costume he will wear for the next hundred years: a bit more close-fitting and elegant than Pedrolino's nondescript dress, it is made up of a pair of the same trousers, a long white jacket slightly fluted at the bottom and buttoned up the front, a large ruffled collar, and a soft, flat, white hat set back on his head. He is played, unmasked, with a powdered face (see illustration 2).

In most of the plays, his personality is compounded of that engaging mixture of simplicity and intelligence, of independence and naïve candor that seems to characterize the earlier Pedrolino. Indeed, in a short scene between Pierrot, Columbine, and her older sister Isabelle of *Arlequin, Homme à bonne Fortune* (1690), Regnard comes quite close to reviving that insinuating and nimble suggestiveness that must have rippled through the patter of Scala's *zanni.* Here Isabelle is insisting on her rights as older sister to be presented as the marriageable daughter of M. Brocantin:

ISABELLE. . . . . Is it fair for me to give up my rights to a younger sister?
PIERROT. (*to* COLUMBINE) It's true you're still only a slip of a thing: and I've seen those kinds of goods in bottles bigger than you.
COLUMBINE. I admit, Pierrot, that I'm still a little girl. But if you only knew what I have already . . .
ISABELLE. My dear little child, don't you want to hold your tongue?
PIERROT. Eh, come on, let her speak. (*to* COLUMBINE) Well, out with it: what do you have?
COLUMBINE. I have . . . But I wouldn't dare say it.
ISABELLE. (*to* COLUMBINE) You're right not to, because you're going to say something foolish.
PIERROT. (*to* ISABELLE) Oh, for heaven's sake, let her talk. You're cramming her words down her throat.

COLUMBINE. You won't make fun of me?

PIERROT. No, no, say it.

COLUMBINE. I have a bit of a bosom, Pierrot, seeing as you want to know.

PIERROT. Oh, let's see it, let's see!

COLUMBINE. O-oh, no-o: I don't show it yet. I'm waiting for it to fill out more.

(G, II, 329)

The basic honesty of Pedrolino—an honesty that could sometimes be laid aside when the intrigue began to lag—is reflected in the unequivocal common sense and, at times, injudicious outspokenness of Giaratone's Pierrot. More than once he wisely counsels his masters against their behaving forty years younger than they are. But when he shuffles off his mother wit to take up philosophy, Pierrot is hopelessly at sea. In the following scene from another Regnard play, *Les Filles Errantes* (1690), he gives sagacious advice to a girl under his charge:

PIERROT. (*taking an armchair*) Let me have your attention, Glaudine. . . . Honor is a jewel, but a jewel that tarnishes when you leave it exposed to the air. A young girl is like a bottle of *eau de la Reine d'Hongrie*; she loses her virtue if she's not well stoppered.

. . . .

I am to you as a bridle is to a horse, a staff to a blind man, a rudder to a boat; I am the bridle and you are the horse; I am the staff, you are the blind man; you are the boat, and I the rudder; but a rudder that will keep you from foundering on the rocks of men: because this world is a sea, and winds blow into this foaming water . . . which makes the Reason in . . . this sea . . .

GLAUDINE. Help! help! a drowning man!

(G, III, 24-25)

Significant differences between Pierrot and Pedrolino can be noted, however, and some can be attributed to the

fact that the latter is closer to the type of "first" and the
former to the type of "second" *zanni*.[36] In this subordinate
role, Pierrot often gives evidence of the clumsiness and
ignorance—and, occasionally, absolute stupidity—that are
such familiar traits of that valet. In Fatouville's *Arlequin,
Empereur dans la Lune*, for example, he derides the Doctor's
speculations about the satellite that will figure so largely in
his own meditations two centuries hence: "I won't be such
a fool to agree that the moon is a world. The moon, the
moon, indeed! It's no bigger than an omelette of eight
eggs!" (G, I, 180). Sometimes, though rarely, his blunders
embroil him in intrigues in which he deserves no part.
Pasquariel, in Brugière de Barante's *La Fausse Coquette*
(1694), is entrusted with a letter by his master Léandre to
take to Angélique, a young lady in Pierrot's household.
Pierrot offers to deliver the letter to his mistress; but the
epistle that eventually gets into her hands is one that Pierrot has written to his own willful girlfriend, and Angélique
reads with some surprise that *"when I pretended to love you it
wasn't my heart that spoke, but I loved your fricasseed chicken."*
And he receives the beating that follows with a murmured,
"Cela est juste" (G, V, 311).

He is not unaware of these "faults" of character and, in
fact, he is naïvely grateful for them. He muses aloud to
himself in Palaprat's *La Fille de bon sens* (1692) upon the
Doctor's foolish courtship of Angélique:

A man who's already seen fifty-five to marry a girl of
twenty! And I'm supposed to think he's a great man of

[36] We read in the *Calendrier historique des Théâtres* (Paris, 1751): "This
role [of Pierrot] had its birth in Paris in the troupe of Italian comedians
who were the predecessors of those of today. It happened thus: formerly,
Harlequin had always been a dullard; but Dominique, a man of intelligence and ability who recognized the genius of our nation, which seeks
wit everywhere, decided to inject some into his role, and gave to the
character of Harlequin a complexion different from that of the old *zanni*.
However, to retain the mask of an ignorant valet at the Comédie-
Italienne, the role of Pierrot was conceived to replace the old Harlequin":
cited in Emile Campardon, *Les Comédiens du roi de la troupe italienne* (Paris,
1880), II, 46.

learning after that? Ah, mother and father, how grateful I am to you for never having made me learn to read! Eh, I believe it, science and books make only fools. I've never known anything but the proverbs of old people, and yet I think I'm a cat that you don't pick up without mittens.

(G, IV, 78)

This side of Pierrot's character is not, however, completely foreign to the earlier Pedrolino. It is obvious from most of the scenarios we have that the *zanni* were rarely unalloyed personages; and maybe, as Nicoll ventures, "instead of thinking rigidly of clever and stupid, we should rather regard these characters as akin to Laurel and Hardy, concerning whom it is difficult to determine which partner is less foolish, which more astute."[37] Pedrolino's *lazzi*, those tricks and comic turns by which a plot was farcically enlivened, often suggest, for example, the careless blunderings or lapses of good sense we have remarked in Pierrot. A scene in *Il Ritratto* in which Arlecchino and Pedrolino are both tricked out of their clothing by a cardsharp and left in their underwear provides an obvious occasion for such foolery. Indeed, Maurice Sand, in his early work on the *commedia* characters, *Masques et bouffons* (1860), pulls so many of these *lazzi* out of Scala's collection that the characters of Pedrolino and Pierrot begin to look like mirror images.[38] But as Mic points out, the earlier mask, of "purely Italian invention," exhibits a certain nimble *baroque* quality that Pierrot is without.[39]

In some of the plays of the Gherardi collection and especially in those of Regnard, we begin to encounter, on the other hand, a delicacy, almost a sensitivity in Giaratone's whitefaced creation that is wholly absent from Pedrolino—and apparently from all the other *zanni* of the *commedia dell'arte*. In the early scenarios, Pedrolino's love for

[37] *World*, p. 67.
[38] See Maurice Sand, *Harlequinade*, I, 200-204.
[39] Mic, *La Commedia dell'arte*, p. 45n.

Franceschina sometimes provides the occasion for a farcical scuffle between him and Arlecchino (*Li Duo vecchi gemelli*) or for a burst of jealous anger when he is cuckolded by Doctor Gratiano (*La Fortunata Isabella*). But it never elicits the tenderness, both comic and pathetic, that infuses this scene of Regnard's *La Coquette* (1691), in which Pierrot stands tongue-tied with love before his master's young daughter, Columbine:

> COLUMBINE. A candle . . . Don't you understand I'm asking for a candle to seal up this letter?
> PIERROT. Pardon me . . . but it's that . . . to tell the truth . . . Miss, I'm going. [*leaves*]
> COLUMBINE. It's hard for me to know these days what kind of disease has attacked the brain of this brute: he can't see anymore, he can't hear . . . He must have something loose upstairs. (PIERROT *brings in his mistress's muff.*) You really want me to seal a letter with a muff? I'm asking you for a candle, do you understand? I think he'll drive me out of my mind. (PIERROT *grimaces.*) Oh, here's a new species of madness I've never seen in him before. Since when have you lost your speech? Speak! Answer! Tell me who has you so worked up.
> PIERROT. I don't dare. I feel a storm inside me, here . . . a suffocation of my spirit . . . beating against love. Here: here's a letter that will tell you everything.
> COLUMBINE. But what in the world does this little ceremony mean; I find it rather amusing. Let's take a look at what this letter says. (*She reads.*)
> *As there is not an animal in the world that does not love some other animal, so I love you. I can say nothing more, but remain your very humble servant and faithful admirer, Pierrot.*
> My very humble servant and faithful admirer, Pierrot. Ha, ha! so *that's* what the trouble is, Sir Lover. Truly, I am ravished to have made such a conquest.

PIERROT. Oh, Miss, I know quite well that my merit isn't capable of meriting . . . but on the other hand . . . now the occasion's come up . . . your beauty . . . I'm not very rich, but still and all, I'm a good man.

COLUMBINE. I know that better than anybody; but I beg of you, Sir Pierrot, to choke down your gasps of endearment a little and go take this letter to Lord de la Maltotière.

PIERROT. (*leaving*) Ah! the little crocodile . . . hff!

(G, III, 100-102)

In *Les Originaux* (1693) by Houdart de la Motte, Pierrot's equally hopeless love for Marinette has pushed him to the last resource:

. . . let us die. Die, you say? Yes, my poor Pierrot, who's holding you back? What charm do you find in the world? Fortune allows us a dress of cloth for our body, Love allows the desires of our heart to stagnate within us. When we cry, Marinette laughs; she dances when we tear our hair. It enrages me to think of it: I've become bald since I fell in love. Come, it's done, let us die; let us take a knife to our bowels. What an idiot! I'd lose all my blood. Oh, well, we'll shoot ourselves through the head. Still worse: after that they'd all say I've got lead in my head. What can I do? Ah, damn Love!

(G, IV, 321)

It is this Pierrot, characteristically refined by Watteau to a higher pitch of delicacy, that will fascinate the Romantics: the Gilles-Pierrot who appears in the painting of *Les Comédiens italiens*, for example, standing apart from the other members of the company and radiating a certain naïve sincerity, a being "likeable but strange."[40] Indeed, Pierrot appears in comparative isolation from his fellow masks, with few exceptions, in all the plays of *Le Théâtre Italien*, stand-

[40] Nicoll, *World*, p. 93.

ing on the periphery of the action, commenting, advising, chiding, but rarely taking part in the movement around him. Some of this disturbing static quality we can simply put down to his laziness; and in comparing Pierrot with his *baroque* predecessor we must not underestimate the influence that Giaratone himself had on the shaping of his mask. The authors of Gherardi's collection undoubtedly wrote their plays with the potentialities and comic strengths of the company of the Comédie-Italienne well in mind. But to understand fully Pierrot's character and his role in these comedies, we must take into account other factors that were exerting strong pressures upon the delineation of the "type" and upon the whole genre of the *commedia dell'arte* in France.

The first is that the comedians were playing before an audience that had an imperfect understanding, if any understanding, of the Italian language and its dialects. Consequently, they found it necessary quite early to emphasize more and more the visual element in their plays, a practice which in many cases meant the subordination of the intrigue to scenic effects created by elaborate machinery. Stage apparatus was certainly playing a part in the native Italian *commedia dell'arte* at this time, but it was brought in to animate the lavish spectacles of the "royal operas" and tragedies and was largely absent from the comedies. Yet a verse-letter by Charles Robinet de Saint-Jean dated February 4, 1673, finds him applauding *La Suite du Festin de pierre*, that *"pure comédie,"* for its *"Spectacle"* and *"Maintes machines."*[41] It is also significant that he singles out for praise among all the actors of the piece chiefly the two principal *zanni*. The obvious explanation for the high esteem in which the *zanni* came to be held, as well as the implications this had for the *commedia dell'arte* in France during the third quarter of the century, is suggested by an entry in a journal kept by one Sebastian Locatelli, a Bolognese, during his voyage to France in 1664-1665:

---

[41] Cited in Parfaict, *Histoire de l'Ancien Théâtre-Italien*, p. 413.

I admit I was little amused [at the Comédie-Italienne] because the actors, playing in Italian before people who didn't understand it, were obliged to gesticulate and fall back upon contrivances, changes of scene, and other things of this nature in order to content the spectators. The excellent Zanotti ["Octave"] in the dialogues with his Eularia could no longer charm the public by the finesse of his expressions, the subtlety of his repartees, the piquancy of his sallies and equivocations. You could say the same of the other actors, all excellent. The type who is most relished in France is Tracagnino, because of his tumbles, capers, and other comic inventions.[42]

The Italians began introducing French songs and scenes into their repertory as early as 1668, and not long thereafter, by a comic *coup*, Biancolelli obtained permission from Louis XIV to perform plays in French.[43] The damage that had been done to the old repertory and spirit of the *commedia* was irreparable, however, especially since the two *zanni* into whose hands the intrigue was committed during this crucial period, Harlequin Biancolelli and Scaramouche Fiorilli, had arrived in France almost completely dissociated from that spirit. Fiorilli obtained his greatest effects by mime, and particularly by long silences and immobility; Biancolelli, on the other hand, triumphed by his virtuosity in speech and *lazzi*.[44] The effects these actors had

[42] (Paris, 1905), p. 180; cited in Pierre Mélèse, *Le Théâtre et le public à Paris sous Louis XIV, 1659-1715* (Paris, 1934), p. 35n.

[43] The Comédie-Française protesting the introduction of French into the Italians' repertory, Louis XIV called one representative from each troupe before him to decide the dispute. After hearing the complaint of the celebrated Michel Baron, speaking on behalf of the French company, the king turned to Dominique, representing the Italians. Dominique asked him, "Sire, in which language shall I speak?" The king responded, "Speak as you like." And the clever Harlequin then said with a bow: "I've gained my cause." See N.-M. Bernardin, *La Comédie italienne en France* (Paris, 1902), p. 18.

[44] See Attinger, *L'Esprit de la commedia dell'arte*, pp. 172-80, for a full discussion of this point.

on the carefully balanced plots of the old pieces, which depended for their success upon all the players' working in
close concert, their every gesture subordinate to the intrigue itself, can be easily imagined: the plays of the
Gherardi collection are, for the most part, showpieces for
the "first" *zanni*, the plots sometimes attenuated to flimsy
pretexts for Harlequin and Scaramouche to appear in as
many disguises as they can find costume. Moreover, the
cultural acclimation of the *zanni* encouraged their coales-
cence into consistent, believable entities (here Molière's
influence might have made itself felt), encouraged them to
become personages more closely akin to what Auden calls
"social beings" than to passionately impulsive types.
When such an adjustment would have done insupportable
violence to the character, as in the case of the chameleonic
Harlequin, then a consistency of *interpretation* took its
place. We have a comfortable sense in these plays not of
the *character* under Biancolelli's or Gherardi's black mask
but rather of the performer. But with Pierrot, a super-
numerary upon whom these comparatively simple plots
make no demands that might violate a coherent
personality—hardly make any demands at all, in fact—
actor and type are still one; and part of the great attraction
that the figure exerted on, for example, Watteau[45] can
perhaps be explained by this unity (we might even say sincerity) of conception and interpretation. Harlequin seems

[45] Giaratone's influence could only have been, of course, a "posthumous" one, since the old Comédie-Italienne had been closed before Watteau arrived in Paris. The Pierrot tradition persisted at the Parisian fairs as
well as in the private salons of enthusiasts of the Italian theater after 1697
(see below, Chapter II); but the Gilles-Pierrot of Watteau, as Xavier de
Courville has pointed out, "hides beneath his inert jacket and in his vacant gaze other dreams and other miseries, different from those of the
Gilles of the fair" (*Luigi Riccoboni dit Lélio*, II [Paris, 1945], 198). Since those
dreams and miseries are occasionally shared by the Pierrot familiar to
Gherardi's readers, it seems not unreasonable to suppose that part of
Watteau's very personal vision of the *zanni* was early formed by the paint-
er's own reading in *Le Théâtre Italien*.

always ready to pull off his mask and put his role aside to chat amiably with the Columbines of the *fêtes galantes;* but Pierrot's pathetic white face cannot be unmasked: creator and role are fused into a single character.

A last but very important influence upon the delineation of the "types" at this time is the social and professional satire of these plays. Any satirical intent the *commedia* might have had at its inception was soon lost; but in the plays of the Gherardi collection, the masks, or what now replaces the masks, are not infrequently made the butt of the playwrights' witty thrusts at ignorant but well-heeled doctors, thick-witted fathers, and lovers the fools of books. Only the *zanni* are exempt from these darts, but it is they who throw them. One illustration will serve for many. In *Ulisse et Circé* (1691) by "Monsieur L.A.D.S.M.," Harlequin is suggesting to Mezzetin possible employments for their talents once they have put the Trojan campaign behind them:

HARLEQUIN. We'll be . . . we'll be . . . disciples of Hippocrates.
MEZZETIN. Who are these disciples of Hippocrates?
HARLEQUIN. Men who make their living at the expense of other people's lives.
MEZZETIN. Oh, I understand, you mean hangmen . . .
HARLEQUIN. A doctor, nitwit, not a hangman! A disciple of Hippocrates a hangman! You have to have very little experience of the world to confuse the two.
MEZZETIN. However you want it: I can't make the distinction.
HARLEQUIN. There's still a big difference: one dispatches his man right away, and the other makes him linger on some time beforehand.
(G, III, 510)

This native French satiric impulse is responsible for much

of the loss of authorial sympathy for the type on this
stage.[46] By grafting omniscient shoots of topical wit and
perspicacity upon these *zanni* and thereby localizing them
(to Paris, to 1691, to polite or bourgeois society) the writers
have diminished them as general symbols of human conduct and manners. Pierrot's basic naïveté sometimes allows him to escape this diminution, since he often plays
the role of straight man. Shortly after the scene cited
above, for example, he enters to request Harlequin's in-
formed opinion of Parisian life and manners (". . . Paris!
yes, I've heard a lot of talk about that city; but tell me, since
you've been there: what kind of place is it and how do they
live?"). But, distressingly, the penchant for satire is carried
over into other areas, areas in which Pierrot is not
exempt—into plays where a kind of crude spirit of travesty
prevails. *Arlequin Protée* (1683) by Fatouville, for example,
presents Harlequin as Proteus among a bizarre assortment
of masked personages and mythological figures; but as
Gustave Attinger says, "Harlequin is not *disguised* as Proteus and is not *playing the role* of Proteus; Harlequin *is* Proteus in truth, but a Proteus who has only Proteus' gift of
metamorphosis and whose reactions are Harlequinesque."[47] And further on, he adds significantly, "*Arlequin
Protée* is hardly anything else than *Protée* interpreted by
Dominique Biancolelli."[48] The same may be said for Dufresny's *Les Adieux des Officiers* (1693), where Pierrot, or
rather Giaratone, appears as Mercury; or for Palaprat's
Arlequin Phaéton (1692), where he appears as Epaphus; or
for the several others of this genre.

It may be objected here that all these remarks are based
upon a collection of plays whose editor deliberately suppressed, as Gherardi admits in his "Avertissement," the
Italian element; that this is a collection by French authors
who had an imperfect knowledge of and sympathy for the
uniqué genre of *commedia dell'arte*; and that these plays,

[46] See Attinger, *L'Esprit de la commedia dell'arte*, pp. 167-83.
[47] Ibid., p. 182.   [48] Ibid., p. 183.

whose long scenes in dialogue far outnumber the improvisatory episodes "in the Italian manner," were never meant to evoke the spirit of the early *commedia* or to preserve the spirit of the "type." All of this may be true, but the facts remain that these were the plays "accommodated" to the Théâtre-Italien in order that the troupe "conform to the taste and intelligence of the better part of its audience,"[49] and were the pieces that *tout Paris* admired when they were performed—were in fact the only ones in which the *commedia dell'arte* and its masks survived at this time, on this stage, in any viable form. As Harlequin noted in the *Livre sans nom* (1695): "If we produced only our old pieces our Hôtel would be little frequented. . . . [The old Italian scenarios] no longer draw an audience, and we still put them on sometimes only in order to conserve for us the true taste of comedy."[50]

Though they had been repeatedly warned, the Italians overstepped their satirical bounds in the spring of 1697: their theater was closed and they were forbidden by royal command to play within thirty leagues of Paris. The reasons surrounding the order are still very much in the shadow of contemporary rumors and contradictory accounts,[51] the chief explanation usually being that the troupe had announced a play based upon a novel, *La Fausse Prude,* that had just appeared in Holland and that purportedly satirized Mme. de Maintenon, the king's mistress. Whatever the reasons for the Italians' dismissal, their Parisian exile lasted for nineteen years. Some of the players chose to return to Italy; others found employment

[49] "Avertissement" to *Le Théâtre Italien de Gherardi,* Vol. I, p. VI.

[50] [Charles Cotolendi], *Le Livre sans nom* (Paris, 1695), I, 20; cited in Mélèse, *Le Théâtre et le public,* p. 51n.

[51] See, e.g., Mélèse, *Le Théâtre et le public,* pp. 51-56; and T.-S. Gueullette, *Notes et souvenirs sur le Théâtre-Italien au XVIIIᵉ siècle,* pub. J.-E. Gueullette (Paris, 1938), pp. 21-25.

for their talents in the provinces. Giaratone himself retired
to the environs of Paris,[52] never to return to the theater,
leaving behind him a disembodied mask, fully naturalized
to the French language, culture, and taste. It was a mask
that had managed to retain an essential integrity despite its
divorce from a timeless world, but, now pushed into a narrow Present, was having to gather its sometimes nimble,
sometimes dubious wits to prepare for its abuse in the next
century.

[52] Campardon, *Comédiens du roi*, I, 245n.

II

L'Education Foraine:
The Eighteenth Century

Accourez, Acteurs d'Italie!
Dansez! Mettez-vous tous en train!
Célébrez ce jour qui vous lie
Pour jamais au Peuple Forain.
—Alain-René Lesage, *Le Rappel*
de la Foire à la Vie

It was Brossette who recorded the testy remark by Boileau, apropos of the Italians' suppression:

> Since Molière, there have been no good plays on the French stage: only wretched little trifles that rouse one's pity. I've been sent the *Théâtre Italien*; I've found some strikingly good things in it; there's a bit of salt everywhere: it's a mine of salt *("grenier à sel")*. . . . I feel sorry for those poor Italians; it would have been better to chase out the French.[1]

Such a state of affairs as Boileau describes could not have lasted long. The Parisian theater public, which abhorred a vacuum, was impatient for the reappearance of intelligent comedy upon the stage; and not even the most talented dramatists of the day—Dancourt, Dufresny, Regnard— could provide the Comédie-Française with a complete comic repertoire. As for the remainder of that repertoire, both tragedy and comedy, it was "hopelessly dull."[2]

---

[1] *Bolœana,* in Vol. III of *Lettres familières de Boileau-Despréaux et Brossette* (Lyon, 1770); cited in Courville, *Luigi Riccoboni,* II, 13.
[2] Attinger, *L'Esprit de la commedia dell'arte,* p. 292.

Very soon after the Italians' dismissal, a certain enter-
prising entrepreneur by the name of Alexandre Bertrand
rented the *salle* left empty by the exiled company, organ-
ized a troupe of comedians of his own, and opened the
theater to the public. Eight days later, an order of the king
invoked the seventeen-year-old privilege uniquely enjoyed by the Comédie-Française to perform plays in Paris,[3]
and Bertrand was obliged to vacate the Hôtel. His
temerarious undertaking gives indication of the kind of
energy and industry that was deployed in the years that
followed to reinstate the vital, "salty" comedy that had delighted the Italians' patrons. And to those who know anything of the previous undertakings of this indefatigable
showman, it suggests still more: that the Gallicized spirit
of the *commedia dell'arte,* as it had been suffused through
the much-applauded masks of the Théâtre-Italien, was far
from being dead to the Parisian public; and that the suppression of it would last a very short time indeed.

Bertrand, a director who was taken early with *"le démon
du théâtre,"*[4] had opened an exhibition of marionettes in
1684 at the Foire Saint-Germain, one of the two great Parisian fairs that attracted the crowds each year. In the
seventeenth and eighteenth centuries, the Foires Saint-
Germain and Saint-Laurent were not only busy centers for
merchants but also exciting theaters of diversion and cheap
entertainment. Here among the boutiques of the vendors,
the cabarets and cafés, could be seen dancers on ropes,
jugglers, performing dogs, giants, magicians, dwarfs, acrobats, fortune-tellers, ventriloquists, lions, elephants,
seals. . . . In 1618, we find two traveling comedians solicit-
ing authorization from the monks of Saint-Germain-des-
Prés to give presentations at the fair, probably *parades* (tres-

[3] The privilege (1680) extended to recited plays in French and did not
abridge, therefore, the rights of the Opéra. The Italians, as we have seen
(see above, Chapter I, note 43), trespassed freely upon the privilege with
the indulgence of the king.
[4] I borrow this happy phrase from Maurice Albert, *Les Théâtres de la
Foire* (Paris, 1900), p. 17.

tle farces) in which one actor took the role of Harlequin, the other of Columbine.[5] But the earliest permanent "theaters" at the fairs were most likely those of the marionette artists, on whose stages shrill little Polichinelle held uncontested reign. One Jean Brioché or Briocci is usually credited as the first to create a vogue for these open-air shows. From the early years of Louis XIV's reign, he is said to have begun shuttling his marionettes from their regular domicile at the Pont-Neuf to the Foire Saint-Germain, there to entertain the populace with the topical and scurrilous wit of his *gens de bois*.[6]

Little is known about those early productions at the fairs which employed human actors. The first of these playlets to survive is a "comic entertainment in three interludes" attributed to Maurice Vondrebeck and Charles Alard and performed by their troupe of dancers and tumblers in 1678. A crude mélange of dancing, acrobatics, "transformations," fustian, and farce, *Les Forces de l'Amour et de la Magie*[7] must have attracted, nevertheless, quite a little audience; for in 1679, we find Alard requesting, and obtaining, official permission from the king to accompany his tumbling acts with "a little dialogue."[8] The privilege was implicitly rescinded the next year, of course, when the Comédie-Française was granted exclusive rights to perform plays in French; but the managers of the fair booths having been seized with *le démon du théâtre*, it was to take more than the wooden kicks and metallic squeaks of Polichinelle to exorcise it.

The year of the Italians' dismissal was a very important one for the fairs; for although Bertrand's audacious reopen-

---

[5] Emile Campardon, *Les Spectacles de la Foire* (Paris, 1877), I, xi.

[6] [François and Claude Parfaict], *Mémoires pour servir à l'histoire des spectacles de la Foire* (Paris, 1743), I, xl. Cf. Charles Magnin, *Histoire des Marionnettes en Europe* (Paris, 1862), pp. 130, 145ff.

[7] In Parfaict, *Mémoires*, I; reproduced in Eugène d'Auriac, *Le Théâtre de la Foire* (Paris, 1878), and also in Maurice Drack, *Le Théâtre de la Foire, la Comédie-Italienne et l'Opéra-Comique* (Paris, 1889).

[8] Albert, *Théâtres de la Foire*, p. 13.

ing of the Hôtel de Bourgogne came, predictably, to nothing, his fellow forains Alard and Maurice conceived and put into effect an even more daring scheme. Under the pretext that their dancers, tumblers, and marionettes bore the names and costumes of the old masks, they both declared themselves the legitimate heirs of the suppressed theater. Hardly three months after the departure of the exiled comedians, they opened two new *loges* at the Foire Saint-Laurent and began presenting French scenes from the Italians' repertory. Then began a long and almost uninterrupted series of arrests and suppressions, countered by the slipperiest of subterfuges—a series that stretches from the beginning of the Foire's theatrical history to its virtual end in 1762.[9] Especially during the first ten years of the century, the Comédie-Française was unremitting in its attempts to close down the theaters of its protean enemy. But suppressed in one form, the forains did not fail to rise up in another, their spectacles conforming to every restriction of each new ordinance but always so ingeniously contrived that their professional rivals, the *"Romains,"* were cheated of their spoils.

Denied the privilege of staging "regular" comedies in 1703, the forains knitted together farcical scenes to create plays that were calculatedly neglectful of the unities. Prohibited the use of dialogue in 1707, they turned to monologue, pantomime, and parodies in alexandrined gibberish called *pièces à la muette*. And soon after the Opéra fattened its purse with the forains' purchase of musical privileges in 1708, they created the *opéra-comique* in vaudevilles, a species of subversive participatory theater. With the forbidden "dialogue" of a play versified upon placards (or *"écriteaux"*), which were held up to the audience by two hovering cupids, the spectators gave "speech" to the ac-

---

[9] For a full account of the struggle, see Bernardin (*La Comédie italienne*), Albert (*Théâtres de la Foire*), Campardon (*Spectacles*), the brothers Parfaict (*Mémoires*), and especially Jules Bonnassies, *Les Spectacles forains et la Comédie-Française* (Paris, 1875).

L'Education Foraine   39

tion by singing the words as an orchestra played a popular
tune. When the actors acquired the right to sing their own
verses (1714) and, later, began to tie them together with
snatches of prose, the Théâtre de la Foire moved into one
of the last stages of its evolution.

Not long after the *pièces à écriteaux* began to draw the
crowds, new writers appeared at the fairs to add their talents to these now-popular theaters. Alain-René Lesage,
who had given *Turcaret* to the Comédie-Française, turned
to the Foire in 1712; and he was soon joined by other
writers—Carolet in 1715, Dorneval (a future collaborator)
in 1716, Piron in 1722. The Foire productions of the first
stormy decade had been no mean successes: in 1709, the
Comédie-Française had been forced to close its doors for
lack of an audience; in the next year, Dancourt was com-
pelled to allow the Doctor and Pierrot upon that august
stage.[10] The young T.-S. Gueullette began entertaining his
friends with privately staged *parades* inspired by the farces
of the fairgrounds at about this time.[11] Even a few members of the dissolved Comédie-Italienne—not to mention
Dominique *fils,* son of the famous Harlequin—were finding the Foire audiences as large and appreciative as their
old patrons of the Hôtel de Bourgogne.[12] But it was with
Lesage that the Foire was drawn from the *parade* and farce
to genuine comedy. And it was with his comedy that the
old masks of the Italian theater were infused with new and
invigorating blood.

This is not to imply, however, that it was the same blood

[10] *La Comédie des Comédiens, ou l'Amour Charlatan*: published in *Les
Œuvres . . . de Monsieur Dancourt* (Paris, 1742), VII. See Antoine de Léris,
Dictionnaire portatif . . . des théâtres (Paris, 1763), p. 116; cf. Attinger, *L'Esprit de la commedia dell'arte,* p. 293.
[11] See below, Chapter III, pp. 77-79.
[12] After touring the provinces for a number of years, the son of Biancolelli made his debut at the Foire Saint-Germain in 1710. He performed
at the Foire under the mask of Harlequin until 1717, at which time he
joined the new company of Italian players at the Hôtel de Bourgogne
(Campardon, *Spectacles,* I, 264). For the members of the old Italian troupe
at the fairs, see Parfaict, *Mémoires.*

that had coursed through the veins of, say, Scala's characters, or even those of Gherardi's repertoire. The Pierrot that appears early at the fairs inherits, it is true, the immaculate livery and personable traits of Giaratone's moonfaced creation—his occasional playfulness, his naïve candor, his laziness, his confident sententiousness. But he also inherits the old traditions of itinerant performers and the taste of their publics, a taste for dancing, singing, and acrobatics. "We must not forget that despite the contribution of actors and repertoire of the old Italian troupe, the Foire is above all a theater of *jongleurs*," as Gustave Attinger reminds us.[13] Among the occasional Pierrots of the Foire were some excellent acrobats and dancers: Roger, who made his debut in Bertrand's troupe in 1698;[14] the Sieur Antoni, "the most perfect rope-dancer of his time [c. 1700-1722] to be seen in France";[15] Nivelon, who danced a notable *entrée* as Pierrot in 1740;[16] and Dourdet, who, in 1742, was charged with the composition of ballets for the Opéra-Comique.[17]

Perhaps the most important inheritance of Pierrot in this new century, however, was a theater that, of necessity, was highly diversified, plastic, "malleable." The entrepreneurs, actors, and playwrights of the Foire had to be venturesome and ingeniously accommodating, living, as they did, between the cup and the lip. And of course they had to be more nimble-witted than the competition. In 1716, the régent called a new troupe of Italian comedians to Paris, a troupe that accorded the black-sheep heirs of the old Théâtre-Italien few tokens of cordiality. In fact, the occasional playlets of the early Foire writers, dramatizing the precarious state of their theaters, often depict the French and Italians as allies, *malgré eux-mêmes*, besieging the

---

[13] *L'Esprit de la commedia dell'arte*, p. 290.
[14] Parfaict, *Mémoires*, I, 13.
[15] Ibid., I, 21.   [16] Ibid., II, 146.
[17] [François and Claude Parfaict and Godin d'Abguerbe], *Dictionnaire des Théâtres* (Paris, 1767), II, 339.

nose-thumbing forains.[18] The amoral and impudent gaiety of the old Italian masks provided just enough salt for the quick, evanescent wit of such retaliatory gestures; and the proficiency in song and dance that the types had inherited directly from Gherardi's stage, and originally from the *tréteaux* of Italy, made them naturals for the fair repertoire. Pierrot (probably because of the popularity of his greatest interpreter of the fairgrounds, Jean-Baptiste Hamoche) actually became in 1718 a personification of the Foire in several little plays describing its persecution and death at the hands of its rivals—as well as its grinning persistence and *rappel à la vie*.[19] Again, in 1721, when Hamoche was deprived of the privilege of playing *opéra-comiques*, his Pierrot (representing the Foire) was laid out in a winding sheet; and Gille, eager to step into his shoes, declared himself the successor of the deceased, bringing with him all the constraints of new "privileges" contracted with the Opéra. But Thalia, the faithful muse of the forains, appeared to shame and send the impostor shuffling away.[20]

It is tempting to begin our study of Pierrot *forain* at this date, 1721, when his popularity was beginning to eclipse that of all the other *zanni*, including Harlequin. But the history of the fair theaters, as I have briefly tried to sketch it, suggests that Pierrot had a long and somewhat rocky apprenticeship some time before this third decade of the century. I think it was an apprenticeship of considerable importance.

Let us begin, then, with a look at his appearance at one of the oldest and most persistent spectacles of the Foire—the marionette theater. The disingenuous little actors of

---

[18] E.g., *L'Opéra-Comique assiegé* by Lesage and Dorneval, presented at the Foire Saint-Germain, 1730: published in Lesage and Dorneval, *Le Théâtre de la Foire*, VII (Paris, 1731). This collection will be cited hereafter as L&D.

[19] *La Querelle des Théâtres* (1718) by Lesage and La Font; *Les Funérailles de la Foire* (1718) by Lesage and Dorneval; and *Le Rappel de la Foire à la Vie* (1721) by Lesage and Dorneval: all appear in Vol. III of L&D.

[20] *La Fausse-Foire* by Lesage, Fuzelier, and Dorneval (L&D, IV).

this stage often showed a malicious streak during the middle years of their prosperity, and with a well-placed and vengeful kick from their own *sabots,* they would send (say) Romulus flying from M. de la Motte's tragedy and hustle Pierrot into his wooden-heeled boots.[21] But the parodies in which Pierrot appears throughout the century, both as a stringed actor and as one of flesh and blood,[22] actually tell us little, or at least nothing new, about the development of his own character. So it is not to these that we should turn to see how our simple friend first appeared to the patrons of the Foire, but rather to the "straight" entertainments, those having their own small intrigues, independent of wholesale allusions to other plays and other theaters. The brothers Parfaict, in their ambitious *Dictionnaire des Théâtres* (1756), give us some idea of what the majority of these plays were like, when they preface their presentation of a specimen of the genre with this tantalizing little blurb:

> *Marchand (le) Ridicule,* marionette play, presented by the marionettes of Gillot at the Foire Saint-Germain, 1708. This *parade* of an anonymous author has not been printed: since its style is more sober than that of others and it is not filled with scurrility and coarse equivocations, we give it here in its entirety to acquaint the reader with this species of entertainment.[23]

M. Janbroche, the merchant of the title, appears in conversation with a crony at the opening of scene 1, and we are hastened into the midst of things:

[21] *Pierrot-Romulus, ou le Ravisseur poli* (1722) by Lesage, Fuzelier, and Dorneval (L&D, V).

[22] Pierrot appears as Minerva in Lesage's parody of *Télémaque* (L&D, I) and as Attis in Fuzelier and Dorneval's parody, *La Grand'mère amoureuse* (L&D, VIII). Pierrot also appears twice in *Les Parodies du Nouveau Théâtre Italien* (Paris, 1731-1738), notably in Legrand's *Agnès de Chaillot* (1723), a highly successful parody of Houdart de la Motte's tragedy, *Inès de Castro.* His "presence" is felt in another celebrated parody by Legrand in this collection, *Œdipe Travesti* (1719), in which he is given the role of the expired King Laius of Voltaire's tragedy.

[23] Parfaict and Abguerbe, *Dictionnaire des Théâtres,* III, 304.

JANBROCHE, *to the friend*. Sir: your servant. Would you do me a favor?

THE FRIEND. What favor would you like from me?

JANBROCHE. I'd like very much to ask you to watch over my shop, and especially my daughter.

Obviously a fair-weather friend, the *compère* suggests that Pierrot be put on the job, and M. Janbroche calls out his reluctant valet: *"Pierrot, holà, Pierrot!"*

PIERROT. What is your pleasure, Sir?

JANBROCHE. I must ask you to take my place and be the steward of my house.

PIERROT. Oh, but Sir, I can't beat your steward.

JANBROCHE. . . . to watch over my shop and, especially, to take care of my daughter.

PIERROT. Oh, but Sir, I'd be happy to look out for your shop, but not your daughter. Because that's merchandise like *eau de la Reine d'Hongrie*: as soon as it's left to evaporate, the savor goes with it: a girl's the same. So you'd do well to watch over her yourself, Sir.

JANBROCHE. Go, get going, you knave: go tell my daughter to come speak to me.

His instructions to his daughter are curt and unequivocal:

JANBROCHE. . . . I'm going to leave to go find some fabrics I need, and I don't want anything sold from my shop during my absence.

MLLE. JANBROCHE. That will seem completely ridiculous.

JANBROCHE. That's why they call me the ridiculous merchant. [*Justement.*]

MLLE. JANBROCHE. But my dear papa, how do you want me to send the customers away?

JANBROCHE. My daughter, when some customer comes to ask you for some cloth and says, Miss, have you a nice holland to sell me? you must answer: Truly no, Sir. That way, you'll keep your honor and your reputation.

Meanwhile, in another part of Paris, a young marquis is preparing for his forthcoming marriage. He summons his manservant, Polichinelle, who is busily writing verses in the jakes ("everybody sets to where he can"), and he instructs him to purchase a gentleman's wardrobe from his *"marchand ordinaire,"* M. Janbroche. The obliging domestic presents himself at the shop, greets the young clerk, and asks for what is obviously a popular fabric, *"drap d'Hollande"*:

MLLE. JANBROCHE. Truly no, Sir.
Polichinelle continues to ask MLLE. JANBROCHE *for several kinds of fabrics, and she continues to respond*: Truly no, Sir.

. . . .

POLICHINELLE. . . . Miss, do you have your virginity?
MLLE. JANBROCHE. Truly no, Sir.
POLICHINELLE. . . . Ha! here's the first girl that's told the truth. . . . Has it been long since you lost it?
MLLE. JANBROCHE. Truly no, Sir.
POLICHINELLE. Good, good, so much the better, here's just the job for me. . . . If a nice big man like myself, who's not all eaten up with fleas, asked to lay with you—would you refuse him?
MLLE. JANBROCHE. Truly no, Sir.

In scene 6 occurs the *anagnorisis*: M. Janbroche returns from his trip, and Pierrot rushes in from the wings to deliver his news: "The males are lying with the females!" He tries to calm his master's jerky rage ("But Sir . . . but Sir, let youth have its day"), but the merchant's anger can be assuaged and his honor satisfied only by a public union of the miscreants in marriage. And the play ends with dances to celebrate the wedding.

I hesitate to pick apart this little *chef-d'œuvre*, lest its naïve charm go the way of its heroine's maidenhood. But it is so suggestive in some of its details that it may be fruitful to pull aside the strings of these puppet people and study their vacuous physiognomies for a moment. We may benefit, however, by putting alongside the play one of its closest counterparts with live actors—a *pièce à écriteaux*. This would help us to flesh out our argument (*Fy! tais-toi, Pierrot, tu es une bête*) and make our conjectures about the early Pierrot *forain* much more tenable. Since the audience alone had legal rights to the spoken word in the plays *à écriteaux*, the constraints under which the actors labored (surpassed only by those of the mime pure) were somewhat comparable to the strings, the immobile features, and the constricted domiciles of Polichinelle and his family. We are fortunate to have eyewitness accounts of several of Lesage's *pièces à écriteaux*, reproduced in Emile Campardon's *Les Spectacles de la Foire*; and when one of these is combined with a summary of the play's plot—Attinger has been so ingenious as to do the work for us—we derive a clearer idea of what such a production was like than by reading the succession of verses and stage directions as they appear in a printed version of the piece. The magistrate's report from which this account is taken was prompted by a complaint from another company of forains, who suspected that the play trespassed upon their newly purchased privileges from the Opéra. Following Attinger's practice, the magistrate's extracts are printed in italics, and the plot outline (in roman) is taken from the *Dictionnaire des Théâtres*; Attinger's summarized portions of the outline are between brackets.

HARLEQUIN: ORPHEUS "THE YOUNGER" (1718)

ACT I

The performance begins with several dances on the rope, in which several men and women and children dance one after the other; among them is an Italian who, while dancing on the rope, performs various tricks with two flags that she has in her hands. Then the curtain is drawn and there ap-

*pears a stage which represents a desert and, in the back-
ground, mountains, at the top of which one sees the sun. At
that moment, a Harlequin appears, who by gestures and
pantomimic figures expresses his despair, caused by his pov-
erty and the harshness of a woman whom he loves; and he
tries to strangle himself.* A solitary philosopher, who
lives in this place, arrives and tries to turn him from
his resolution with moral maxims. . . . He persuades
Harlequin to consult the sage Urganda, the Unknown. . . . [They set off towards the mountain, the
abode of Urganda.] *Urganda comes out from the depths of
a cave, accompanied by two young girls, and, seeing Harlequin, she invokes evil spirits; from a cave and the mountains
appear several tumblers, dressed as demons, who perform
several stunts.* [Urganda informs Harlequin that he is
the son of Apollo and of a girl of the Venetian Opera.
She predicts a magnificent fate for him. On the coun-
sel of the philosopher, Harlequin calls for his father.]
They both invoke him, singing his praises in the manner by which the gods are invoked at the Opéra.
. . . *Then the gleam of the sun disappears at the top of the
mountains by the drawing of some curtains, and the sun descends from his chariot to a point some distance below the
flies, not by a counterweight or any machine, but rolled over
a kind of gently sloping stair; and he recognizes Harlequin as
his son.* The recognition made, Harlequin asks money
of his father, who, not having any, presents him with
a lyre, assuring him that he will bewitch all of nature
with this instrument. . . . *Then a tumbler dressed as a
monkey descends from the top of the mountains and performs various stunts; Harlequin attracts him by playing the
lyre* and there is a very amusing lazzi [*sic*] between
Harlequin, the philosopher, and the monkey. *Then
from the top of the mountains some hunters descend a sloping stair, pursuing a wild animal, played by a tumbler who
performs various stunts in his flight. Harlequin subdues
him.* [Harlequin disposes in the same fashion of a

group of officers who have come to arrest him; his lyre charms them, he deals them some blows and runs off.] *This makes up the first act, which is performed as much by the actors as by the spectators, who follow the écriteaux descending from above and on which are written the vaudevilles that compose the piece: the actors gesticulate and by various pantomimic figures express what is on the écriteaux; the spectators sing, and in several places, to tie together the verses, the actors speak a few words; and when the écriteaux descend, 4 violins, a bass, and an oboe play the air of the vaudeville indicated on the écriteaux, which the public sings.*

ACT II

In the second act, a backdrop descends, which changes the scene, and in place of the desert and mountains, appears a large portico, through which one sees a plain. Columbine, who loves Pierrot, expresses her love for him. Harlequin arrives and says sweet things to her; she spurns him, but he tells her that he is the son of Apollo, and that he has the power to charm her whenever he likes. She says she doesn't care; he plays his instrument; she noticeably changes; she softens towards him and finally sacrifices Pierrot, who, despairing of her inconstancy, goes off to throw himself into the river. [They order preparations for the marriage; they lay out the wedding feast,] *at which, to divert those at the table, three tumblers—two dressed as women and one as a Turk—play two different airs upon a guitar, a violin, and a harp, the guitarist singing two or three verses of songs. During the meal, a tumbler dressed as Pierrot comes up out of a trap in the stage,* returning after his death. Seeing his ghost, Columbine utters a loud cry, falls unconscious; they carry her into the house, where she dies. [The Doctor, Columbine's father, persuades Harlequin after a great effort to emulate his older brother, who descended to Hades to seek after his wife.] *A trap is opened in the*

middle of the stage, from which shoot flames by means of
some pieces of paraffin thrown into a stove under the stage;
Harlequin leaps through the trap, concluding the second act,
which, like the first, is performed by écriteaux . . . etc.

ACT III

The scene changes and represents the river bank
where spirits roam about, making haste to pass the
·fatal boat. . . . Harlequin accosts several ghosts and
asks each one which doctor gave her her passport.
One says that she died of regret after losing her husband; another, on the other hand, says that she lost
her life from rage at not being able to deceive hers, so
much was she obsessed with it. After a few other similar scenes, in which manners are amusingly censured,
Mercury, to entertain Harlequin, shows him the
pastimes of the spirits on this shore. Then several
tumblers, representing spirits, perform their exercises,
which consist of a thousand kinds of astonishing
postures. Pluto and Proserpine, hearing that there is a
new Orpheus in Hades, come before him and command him to play his instrument. They are so en-
chanted that Pluto tells him that he is willing to give
Columbine back to him, on the same condition that he
gave Euridice to his brother Orpheus: that he will not
look back at her until she is outside of Hades. Harlequin, true to his family's character, is no less curious
than his brother: he stumbles over the same obstacle,
and, like Orpheus, loses his wife. *Then, to entertain*
Pluto and Proserpine, tumblers dressed as spirits assume
various postures, mounted on the shoulders of other
tumblers; [they] turn themselves into crossbars; then a
group becomes a fountain, then an oak tree. After which, a
tumbler, dressed as Scaramouche, performs various feats of
equilibrium, by which the play ends.[24]

[24] In Attinger, *L'Esprit de la commedia dell'arte,* pp. 299ff. Campardon,
Spectacles, II, 362ff, and Parfaict and Abguerbe, *Dictionnaire des Théâtres,* I,
264ff, also consulted.

We are at first struck by the great differences between these two plays. On the one hand, the complete absence of stage accouterment, the amatory confusion, the unabashed bawdry—all of this suggests the little *fantoccini's* direct inheritance from the *commedia dell'arte*. On the other, the delight in travesty (in both the ancient and modern senses of the word), in topical parody and satire, and in extravagant spectacle is clearly traceable to Gherardi's stage. And in both plays, the influence of the fairgrounds hardly needs comment: the amours of Polichinelle have taken the center of the stage; the *lazzi* of Harlequin have exploded into tumbling and acrobatics. But despite these differences, we can detect, if only by implication, certain similar and almost predictable tendencies in the presentation of character in these pieces, tendencies that arise from what Lesage calls the "particular proprieties"[25] of the Foire theaters. In *Le Marchand ridicule*, it is the simple presence of wooden actors that establishes these proprieties. Incapable of nuance in either gesture or expression, the marionette impresses his personality upon his audience by an extravagance of movement and speech, by the grossness of his character. And in this little play, Pierrot is nothing more than a lazy booby. He still remembers Giaratone's saw about the volatile nature of a woman's chastity, but he has little of that earlier *zanni's* engaging sense of self-importance or his delight in the philosophic play of his own mind. He has, in fact, picked up some of the loutish traits of his cousin Gilles. The Giaratone-Pierrot could quibble rather cleverly with his master; this little simpleton only makes absurd blunders. But we would hardly expect psychological subtlety from a marionette play at the fair, especially when even the puppet plays of the exquisite Maeterlinck seem distressingly clumsy today.

What is more important is that this same exaggeration of manner plays a large part in *Arlequin Orphée le cadet*. No longer does Pierrot brood upon throwing himself from a

---

[25] "Préface" to L&D, I, sig. A5ʳ.

window for love of the coquettish Columbine; he actually jumps into the tide and makes an end on it. But the Pierrot in this play, almost a caricature of his former morose self, does not suffer from the same malady that infects his wooden counterpart. It is the rigidity of the marionette's person that tends to magnify certain poles of his character; here it is the fantastic plasticity of the intrigue that allows the zanni's dominant traits to balloon disproportionately. We have recovered in this play at least one essential element of the commedia dell'arte—the overriding emphasis upon the play as spectacle. But the sense of uncertain suspension that prevailed in that earlier comedy, a suspension protracted by forces of circumstance or the caprice of zanni, to be resolved finally and inevitably by the Lovers' unions—this is gone. And as in many of the Foire productions, the romanesque element "distends the subject."[26] The fates of the characters do not concern us because the characters themselves no longer concern us: they are sacrificial pawns to advance the play. Not only are their burlesque propensities, such as Pierrot's sensitivity, exaggerated and exploited to move the action forward; but also the satiric intelligence that the zanni have inherited from long years at the Hôtel de Bourgogne is brought just as freely into play.[27] Because the public, later the actors, sing their own satire, the wit acquires great pungency and complexity. The rhythms, the musical cadences, the use of melody for analogy and contrast—all these devices tug at the supple outlines of the "types" to stretch them into dichotomous attitudes. The uneasy coexistence that results—on the one hand, Harlequin's buffoonish acrobatics, and on the other, his pointed raillery—smooths out the nuances of his plastic personality; the delicate shadings of his character are

[26] Attinger, L'Esprit de la commedia dell'arte, p. 321.

[27] The only two lines preserved from Arlequin Orphée le cadet, for example, are these spoken by Harlequin: "I don't have any reason to be proud of my birth, seeing as my father doesn't want to recognize me. I'd prefer to have been the son of a kind monk: those fellows have a little bit of conscience": Parfaict and Abguerbe, Dictionnaire des Théâtres, I, 265.

blurred, and he becomes, not Harlequin, but (as the magistrate's report describes him) *a* Harlequin.

In the more sophisticated pieces of Lesage and his collaborators, we discover the consequences of this development for Pierrot. Especially in the plays written between 1713 and 1727, his character seems to lose a good deal of the tenuous coherence and complexity that Giaratone was able to bring to it. In *Le Tombeau de Nostradamus* (1714) and *La Ceinture de Vénus* (1715), both by Lesage, Pierrot appears as a rustic pure, but one whose temperament has been refined by the power of love—and song. When, in other plays, he loses all traces of Gallic rusticity, he sometimes sacrifices whatever little Bergamask sense he had as well. He and Harlequin are conducted to a strange island by two unendearing young ladies in Lesage and Dorneval's *L'Isle des Amazones* (1718), and there they play a scene that would have done credit to Stan and Ollie:

HARLEQUIN. Still laughing, eh? Well, what do you have to laugh so much about, you booby?
PIERROT. It's just that . . . (*he keeps laughing*) Hee, hee, hee, hee, hee . . .
HARLEQUIN. Well, just what?
PIERROT. (Air: *Mirlababibobette.*)
  It's that this Marphise—
    Mirlababibobette—
  I saw her
  Sizing me up *pied à tête.*
Mirlababi, sarlababo, mirlababibobette.
    Sarlababorita.
HARLEQUIN.
  And here we sit yet.
Don't trust her, my friend. She's a crocodile.
PIERROT. Oh, no! no, because I heard her say under her breath once to the other one: This big fellow's ready to eat.
HARLEQUIN. You heard that?

PIERROT. Word for word.
HARLEQUIN. O woe! We're done for!
PIERROT. Why do you say that?
HARLEQUIN. (Air: *Monsieur la Palisse est mort.*)
    My poor Pierrot, alas!
    How well I see that these jades
    Are nothing (in spite of their charms)
    But accursed ogre-maids.
PIERROT, *shocked.* What! you mean that eat human flesh?
HARLEQUIN. Ah! I don't doubt it.
PIERROT, *crying.* Oh, mercy! You didn't have to tell me that! I'm going to die of fright!
HARLEQUIN. (Air: *Les Trembleurs.*)
    Into their kitchen they'll go
    To sever our spines—just so,
    And put us in a boiling pot
    Or stew us *en haricot.*
PIERROT.   I fear the hash.
HARLEQUIN. Me: the souse.
PIERROT.   They're going to make a dainty dish
    Of Harlequin and Pierrot!
                  (L&D, III, 337ff)

Vincent Barberet, in his study of Lesage's work for the fairs, finds these violent fluctuations of Pierrot's character rather unsettling.

Like Harlequin [he writes], Pierrot is assigned the most diverse roles by Lesage, and sometimes the most opposed to his personality. Besides making him a valet, a roasting specialist, a chef, a hash-house cook, an adventurer, he just as frequently dresses him up as someone else. Finally, he also employs him in *pièces à tiroir* [loose successions of scenes in which a number of characters present themselves before a central figure, "sometimes on a summons, sometimes to request a consultation or to obtain some favor"], and in the same fashion as Harlequin. In these latter roles, his character is quite badly defined.[28]

In *Le Rémouleur d'Amour* (1722), by Lesage, Fuzelier, and Dorneval, for example, Pierrot appears as a tool-sharpener whom Love has summoned to his palace to hone the barbs of his arrows. After being presented with several newly sharpened darts, Love flies to Paris, leaving Pierrot alone to receive his suppliants. A penurious fop who is pursuing *"un rebelle cœur,"* a schoolmaster whose students are practicing elocution on his daughter and pretty young wife, a coquette, a Swiss—all these Pierrot advises with worldly savoir-faire. In short, the *zanni*'s usual plodding intelligence has risen to Harlequinesque acuity; and this is all the more surprising when we learn that the play was performed by a company of marionettes. We do not really feel as Barberet does, however, that Pierrot's character has been completely violated, since we have known the Giaratone-Pierrot to manage some clever little things of his own. Rather we feel that Lesage and his cohorts have squeezed him until his head is bulging with wit, that they have taken exaggerated advantage of one aspect of his personality to the neglect of all the others. In *La Boîte de Pandore* (1721), they do the same, but give to the operation an ingenious twist. Pierrot plays a *naïf* at the beginning of the play, an innocent who takes unassuming and unconscious liberties with the young Pandora, whose famous box has not been opened nor its contents scattered into the world. But at the play's end, when Lust, Jealousy, and Pride are winging invisibly about the stage, the *naïf* undergoes a Jekyll-like transformation: his language decays into a bucolic *patois* and he reverts to his unbecoming, cloddish origins.

What we are witnessing in these plays is the disintegration of the "type" into rough, generic lumps. Pierrot's character has begun to fragment, to cleave into the pieces

28 *Lesage et le Théâtre de la Foire* (Nancy, 1887), p. 154.

that Giaratone, by the force of his personality and the un-
demanding naturalism of his role, had been able to hold
tightly together. The improvisatory nature of the Foire
stage is not the only factor responsible for this fragmenta-
tion. Pierrot has also begun to reproduce himself, to multiply into "pierrots," to become as numerous as little Gilles.
We are told, for example, that Belloni, the Pierrot of *Arlequin Orphée le cadet*, was a memorable interpreter of the
mask at the Foire. A member of several troupes during his
career, he first appeared at the Foire Saint-Laurent in 1704
after touring the provinces with a group of players directed
by Joseph Tortoriti, Pasquariel of the old Théâtre-Italien;
and it is generally believed that he acquired his air *pierrotique* from a study of Maganox, a Pierrot of that company.[29] But this able actor was not the only Pierrot of the
fairgrounds. Jacques Bréon was playing the role contem-
poraneously with Belloni, from 1704 to 1720; and the
brothers Parfaict tell us that he was "formed by nature" for
the part: "his face, his eyes, his figure, his voice, and his
gestures—everything expressed the character that he
played on the stage."[30] Nor should we forget the rope-
dancers, Roger and Antoni, who entertained fair audiences during the first quarter of the century with naïve performances in the role.

In 1712, Jean-Baptiste Hamoche arrived in Paris from a
tour of the provinces, made his debut at the Foire, and
after a time became the most celebrated Pierrot of the fair
theaters.[31] This comedian, whose affinity for the role must
have been almost as great as Giaratone's, probably helped
retard the gradual disintegration and coarsening of the
zanni's character. At any rate, we can sense in many of the
plays of the next decade a stronger cohesion and force of

[29] See Parfaict, *Mémoires*, I, 33-38.   [30] Ibid., I, 42.
[31] Hamoche was at the fairs from 1712 to 1718, then from 1721 to 1732,
where "he obtained, thanks to the naturalness and truth of his acting,
great applause and became the favorite actor of the public": Campardon,
Spectacles, I, 391.

personality behind the mask than in any group of pieces
since Gherardi's collection. Of course, several other factors
contribute sensibly to this impression: the first is that
Harlequin begins to lose his formidable status at about this
time, probably because of the absence of good Harlequins
after the Englishman Richard Baxter (1721).[32] Another is
that many of the plays themselves, of Lesage and his co-
authors, are offering better possibilities for the unfettered
development of character. The stories in Galland's recent
translation of *Mille et une Nuits* (1704-1717) are being mined
for inspiration, either casual or direct, to furnish material
for new intrigues; and the plots that result often have
enough autonomous interest to allow them to escape the
generous satirical wadding that pads out so many plays of
the Foire repertoire. A final reason for this apparent rein-
tegration of Pierrot's personality is the addition of new
plays to the repertoire by Alexis Piron. Whereas Lesage
had been content in his earlier productions to keep the intrigue separate from the *zanni's* buffoonery, "the drollery
of Piron explodes on every level."[33] Consequently, Harlequin and Pierrot become inextricably tied up with the
action; the plot, now trading upon their personalities,
demands that they provide enough currency for the trans-
action.

Lesage and Dorneval's *Achmet et Almanzine* (1728) is one
of the first, and most successful, of the pieces to elevate the
amatory intrigues of exotic lovers, abetted by a well-
intentioned valet, to the highest rung of thematic importance in the plot. Here, as in *La Princesse de la Chine* (1729),
La Reine du Barostan (1729), *Zémine et Almanzor* (1730), and
Sophie et Sigismond (1732)—to name the best of the
genre—Pierrot assumes a consistent outline and personable depth. He is invariably the honest, loyal valet of a
hero-prince in these plays; and he often plays the pander

[32] Barberet, *Lesage et le Théâtre de la Foire,* p. 136.
[33] Attinger, *L'Esprit de la commedia dell'arte,* p. 314.

for his master and his beloved. But though he is usually responsible for the direction the action of a play takes, he has none of the omniscient authority of a Pedrolino, sending his charges scuttling about the stage like wind-up toys. It is only by the most wonderful of coincidences or by his master's own astuteness, in fact, that the intrigue is saved from Pierrot's near-tragic blunders.

In *Zémine et Almanzor*, for example, the *zanni* is servant to Almanzor, adopted shepherd son of the king of Astrakhan. A wedding has been set for Almanzor and the king's own daughter, Zémine; and when Prince Alinguer comes seeking the young lady's hand, the king must disappoint his wishes. Smarting from the sting of this unexpected turn, Alinguer then relates a story that Pierrot has been spreading about—that Almanzor is a miser who counts his money in secret every night, hiding inside a closet for which only he has the key. The king flies into a rage, bursts into Almanzor's chamber, and demands an explanation for this disgraceful conduct. When the closet is opened, only a shepherd's dress and staff are discovered: ". . . to keep me in mind of my birth," sings the embarrassed youth, "And to take up again, Sir, / If deprived of your favor" (L&D, VIII, 127). The king then announces another surprising secret—that Almanzor is his true son and heir, and Zémine the adopted child—and the lovers are happily and connubially united.

The Foire repertoire of the insouciant Piron disdains such tragicomic sobrieties. In *L'Ane d'Or* (1725), Harlequin is transformed into an ass by a sorceress's potion; and in the second act, Pierrot and his scullion, Frippesauce, chase him over the stage to put him into a stew. As the valet of M. Agrippain in *L'Antre de Trophonius* (1722), Pierrot and his master come to kneel before Trophonius's cavern for advice on Agrippain's forthcoming marriage. But Harlequin, who has just absconded from the old man's household with as much money as he can carry, is posing as the sage's priest. He delivers a few majestic whacks of his bat on the backsides of the prostrate pair, makes a somersault, then disappears. Pierrot is skeptical.

PIERROT, *rubbing his shoulders.* What mangy kinds of ceremonies are these supposed to be?

AGRIPPAIN. Speak discreetly. Everything is mysterious here. I quite expected something extraordinary; but before one understands, one must . . .

PIERROT. I understand that for the ten swats they gave you, I got twenty, and I'm not here for anything. I swan, Sir, you can go down in that hole by yourself. Be hanged if I'm going down there.

AGRIPPAIN. So your irreverence will spoil the mystery all the more.

PIERROT. So help me, Sir, is that what you think of me? Leave this alone, your Oracle of Tropho . . . of Troupho . . . How do you say it?

AGRIPPAIN. Trophonius.

PIERROT. Yes, of course, I remember: Fotronius. Leave these oracles alone, I tell you, and let me give you a little advice about your marriage. Marinette is a feisty little thing who's not a child anymore. She's come of age: she's taking advantage of her rights and enjoying every minute of it. Take a feel of her pulse. Honest, is this the business of a suitor who's fifty years older than her? I married at thirty: I was only a year older than my wife, who was a little prudish at the time, but anyway . . .

AGRIPPAIN. Let's not speak of age. It suffices that I'm healthy.

PIERROT. And she's even healthier. And now you've got a little braggart with a temper like a demon. You're trapped like a Beaunois: she's extravagant; you're a little tight . . .

AGRIPPAIN. Oh! I wouldn't be stingy with her. Jewels, banquets, gowns, money, she'd have everything she wants.

PIERROT. (Air: *Nanon dormoit.*)
    And you believe
    That, for her, that'll be enough
    To please?
    Outside of high living,
       Clothes, cash,
    You need . . . you need . . .
AGRIPPAIN. I know what you need.
PIERROT. You need what you won't be giving.[34]

"The retirement of Hamoche in 1733," writes Barberet, "was fatal to Pierrot. After this date, we hardly ever see him appear again except in old plays."[35] It is true that Hamoche's retreat probably hastened the gradual disappearance of Pierrot from the plays of the Opéra-Comique; but this is not the only reason for the *zanni*'s dwindling popularity after that date, nor is it the most important. The year 1733 marks another event in the history of French theater and a much more significant one: the appearance of *La Fausse Antipathie* by Nivelle de La Chaussée. And with this first *comédie larmoyante,* or "tearful comedy," French drama took a new and decisive turn. Although the second generation of Foire writers (chiefly Charles-François Pannard and Charles-Simon Favart) were not all in accord with La Chaussée's practices,[36] they each shared to some degree the assumption that underlies his plays—that moral instruction by the comedy should be more a matter of mollifying the passions than attacking vice and ridiculing folly. So it should not be surprising that the Foire stage came to

[34] Alexis Piron, *Œuvres,* ed. Pierre Dufay, IV (Paris, 1928), 74ff.
[35] *Lesage et le Théâtre de la Foire,* p. 155.
[36] In *La Barrière du Parnasse* (1740), for example, Favart made game of the *comédie larmoyante;* but thirty years later, towards the end of his career, he began writing plays in the tearful mode. For a full discussion of Favart's relationship to La Chaussée, see Auguste Font, *Essai sur Favart* (Toulouse, 1894), pp. 172ff.

entertain only fitfully, in the years that followed, those equivocal past masters of folly and vice, Harlequin, Pierrot, and Scaramouche. From the plays proper, Pierrot was eventually pushed into *divertissements* and pantomimic afterpieces following the performances. Soon after Hamoche's departure, there was, in fact, a great vogue for pantomimes at the Foire, and especially those performed by English troupes. Pierrot's character, as it had been accommodated to the rough-edged spectacles of pre-Hamoche days, slips very easily into a type of entertainment that demands what we might call an extravagance of personality. Such a personality as his is invaluable to a mimed play: the audience's immediate recognition of Pierrot's, of Columbine's, of Harlequin's most fundamental traits of character helps to fill in the wordless exchanges, the mute solicitations, professions, and denials in a production of this sort with just the right tonal suggestions. But a cloistered life in the pantomime exacts high payment from its characters; and in the measure that they contribute to its success, they often sacrifice as much of their own selves. Obviously, Pierrot can no longer dispense sage advice to penurious dandies or harried schoolmasters when he is denied both song and speech. The verbal satire that plays so large a part in many of the Foire comedies cannot penetrate the pantomime. As a result, Pierrot's levelheaded intelligence is hewn away, leaving him only Harlequinesque *fourberies* to express the clever side of his character. But since Pierrot has never had the slippery agility of his black-masked companion, his pantomimic roguery is always tinged with a little of the ridiculous, of the pathetic.[37]

In 1762, two events occurred that had great significance for the life of the Foire: the first is that its theater, the Opéra-Comique, was annexed by the Théâtre-Italien; the second is that a great fire completely destroyed the Foire

[37] See, e.g., the pantomime *Le Pédant* (1748), reproduced in Parfaict and Abguerbe, *Dictionnaire des Théâtres*, VII, 641-49.

Saint-Germain. Both debilitated the fairs, the one by removing the Foire theater from the faubourgs to the Rue
Mauconseil, into the Hôtel de Bourgogne; the other by en-
couraging a shift in the locale of the entertainments left behind by the fire and the marauding Italians. Three years
earlier, in 1759, an actor of the Foire, Jean-Baptiste Nicolet,
had opened a small theater on the now-defunct Boulevard
du Temple, where he gave little comedies, *opéra-comiques*,
and acrobatic interludes. With the suppression of the
Théâtre de la Foire and the destruction of the Foire Saint-
Germain, his theater began to attract the fairs' clientele;
and like Bertrand, his spirited predecessor, he was em-
boldened to tread upon the privileges of the French and
Italians. He engaged a certain Robineau de Beaunoir to
compose pantomimes, comedies, *parades,* and farces for his
little troupe; and the success his enterprise enjoyed stimu-
lated others to follow his lead. On the eve of the Revolu-
tion, the Foire Saint-Laurent was all but dead and deserted: the life of its spectacles was trickling out upon the
Boulevard du Temple, and washed along with it was an in-
conspicuous, unprepossessing figure in white.

But before we take up this new stage in Pierrot's development, we must look briefly at the theater of the Hôtel de
Bourgogne, reclaimed home of the new Italian troupe in
1716. When the régent called the Italians back to Paris,
Pierrot did not have a place in their number; in fact, he had
only a shadowy existence among these comedians
throughout the century. Dominique *fils,* who left the Foire
the year after the Italians' return, made his debut in the
company in the white dress of Giaratone's creation; but he
had only a lukewarm reception in the role and immediately
abandoned the costume for that of Trivelin.[38] We are told
that Fabio Sticotti took up the mask shortly afterwards and
acquitted himself well in the part, and that his son,
Antoine-Jean, stepped into the ribboned shoes after his
father's death (1741) to carry on the tradition until his own

[38] Courville, *Luigi Riccoboni*, II, 104.

retirement in 1759.[39] Pierrot was obviously an unimportant personage for this new company, however, judging by the infrequency with which he appears in its plays. Old pieces from Gherardi's repertoire were still produced, of course,[40] and in those Pierrot assumed his familiar role; but in the last (1753) edition of the *Nouveau Théâtre Italien*, a collection of plays first performed between 1720 and 1743, he appears only once—in Delisle de la Drévetière's *La Faucon et les Oyes de Bocace* (1725). And in this play, he is closer to Molière's peasant than to Giaratone's valet. Towards the end of the century, when all the company but its Harlequin had been replaced by French players, the "Italian Comedians" performed several new pieces by Piis and Barré, *"comédie-parades,"* in which Pierrot again appears in his traditional role as valet; yet a play like *Cassandre oculiste* (1780) preserves only "the wraiths of Pantalone in Cassandre himself, of Pierrot and of Colombine."[41]

The most significant developments on this stage for the Pierrot of the next century are not to be uncovered by studying the doltish character of Delisle's shepherd or the wispy vaudevillian of Piis and Barré. We must, in fact, turn away from Pierrot altogether and look at the curious evolution of another of his fellow masks at the new Théâtre-Italien—the evolution of Harlequin. The memorable Harlequins of this stage, particularly Tomaso Vicentini ("Thomassin") and Carlo Bertinazzi ("Carlin"), were generally less coarse and buffoonish than Dominique's perverse creation. Marmontel most accurately describes their masks when he writes of Harlequin himself:

> His character is a mixture of ignorance, simplicity, wit, awkwardness and grace. He is not so much a fully-developed man as a great child with glimmerings of rationality and intelligence, whose mistakes and

[39] Campardon, *Comédiens du roi*, II, 145.
[40] They were added to the repertoire in 1718; see T.-S. Gueullette, *Notes et souvenirs*, pp. 87ff.
[41] Nicoll, *World*, p. 190.

clumsy actions have a certain piquancy. The true
model of his performance is the suppleness, agility,
grace of a kitten, with a rough exterior which adds to
the delight of his action; his role is that of a patient
servant, loyal, credulous, greedy, always amorous,
always getting his master or himself into a scrape,
who weeps and dries his tears with the ease of a child,
whose grief is as amusing as his joy.[42]

When Marivaux and Delisle began writing comedies for
the new troupe, Harlequin proved himself to be quite capable of putting off childish things. In *Arlequin poli par
l'Amour* (1720), he is slowly transformed by the power of
love from a gaping, drooling, squalling infant to a lover of
decision and refinement. And in *Arlequin sauvage* (1721),
Delisle's first essay for the Italians, he is *poli par la Nature*.
But it is not until the end of the century that Harlequin
undergoes his most significant series of transformations, in
the hands of J.-P. Claris de Florian. Between 1779 and
1790, Florian wrote three plays he considered to be "the
novel of [his] Harlequin," showing him "in the three most
interesting states of life, those of the lover, the husband,
and the father."[43] The authority he invoked for his project
was neither Marivaux nor Delisle ("The one has more delicacy, the other more profundity than I"),[44] but rather—La
Chaussée. His intention, as he observes in his preface to
the trilogy, was to unite the comedy of intrigue with the
comedy of sentiment. To effect this union successfully, he
had to ensure that "the spectator was amused and touched
at the same time, that he was as much moved by the interest of the action as delighted by the drollery of the actor, in
a word that the same character drew tears and laughter
both at once. For that, I needed Harlequin."[45]

 That Harlequin was, for Florian, as sentimentally susceptible to tears as he was given to roguish laughter is most

[42] Cited in ibid., pp. 73f.
[43] "Avant-Propos" of Vol. IX of the *Œuvres de Florian* (Paris, 1810), p.
11.
[44] Ibid., IX, 8.   [45] Ibid., IX, 6.

tellingly suggested by his role in *Le Bon Ménage* (1782), the best chapter of Florian's "novel." A doting father and husband, Harlequin is moved first to rage, then to ineffable sadness, when he suspects his wife of infidelity; and in the scene in which he announces his intention to leave her, he rises to heights of lachrymose passion. His *cri de cœur* is worth quoting at length:

> . . . since I've decided to forget you entirely, I've come to give you back everything that could remind me that we ever loved each other. (*He unbuttons his jacket and opens a little bag that hangs about his neck.*) It's all in this little bag. I put it here (*he indicates his heart*) so that everything that we've given each other was together. I'm going to empty the bag in front of you, so that you won't think I'm holding something back. (*He takes out a picture.*) First, here's your portrait: it hasn't changed, as you have; it's still beautiful: just this morning it resembled you, but it doesn't any longer. Here it is, Madam. (*He sets it up on a table and draws out a creased piece of paper.*) Here's the first note that you wrote me, that Scapin stole from me, and that I had the happiness to get back again. There, Madam: I give it back to you: I don't like living with liars. (*He takes out a withered bouquet.*) And here's an old bouquet of violets that I gave you the first day I declared my love for you. After carrying them all day, you threw them away in the evening: I went to pick them up. . . . Here: they still have a sweet smell. . . . I would never have believed these violets would last longer than your love. There they are, Madam. (*He shows her the bag.*) There's nothing else: look. This little bag, that took years to fill, is empty in a moment.[46]

The Harlequin of this play has left far behind him the loutish ways of little Arlecchino: he is, in the words of his creator, "good, gentle, ingenuous, simple without being

[46] Ibid., IX, 102f.

stupid, speaking purely and expressing with näiveté the
sentiments of a very tender heart."[47] He is one of the last
and most curious symbols of the Age of Sensibility. And
with his tears, the *commedia dell'arte* expires in a quiet, un-
resisting sigh.

The comedies of Florian slipped very easily into the repertoire of the Boulevard theaters. As the century came to a
close, his Harlequin freely shared the stage with his much
livelier counterpart of the pantomime.[48] Among all the old
masks, in fact, Harlequin came to reign unchallenged on
the Boulevard, while Pierrot was absorbed and supplanted
by Gilles.[49] Pierrot's character, as we have seen, had lost a
good deal of its cohesion at the fairs, and his subsequent
role in pantomime undoubtedly owed much of its interpretation to the popular but clownish Pierrots of English pantos. Consequently, the line between Pierrot and Gilles, the
gross buffoon of the *parade,* must have become very thin
indeed. Not for many years was Pierrot able to recover
enough wit and verve to allow him to contend with Harlequin for supremacy of the Boulevard stage. He had to wait
for interpreters of the stature of Giaratone and of
Hamoche.

But the Pierrot that eventually appeared not only displaced his black-masked rival but displaced him at Harlequin's own expense; and concealing under his white livery
the heart of Harlequin *larmoyant,*[50] he came to enjoy the

[47] Ibid., IX, 8.
[48] Of the little theaters flourishing at the end of the century for which
L.-Henry Lecomte has provided the repertoire, all list performances of
one or several of Florian's Harlequin plays. In Lecomte's *Histoire des
Théâtres de Paris* series, see, e.g., *Les Variétés Amusants* (Paris, 1908), p. 215;
Le Théâtre de la Cité (Paris, 1910), pp. 157, 286; and *Le Théâtre National / Le
Théâtre de l'Egalité* (Paris, 1907), pp. 26, 143, 145.
[49] See below, Chapter III.
[50] Maurice Willson Disher, in his *Clowns and Pantomimes* (London,

greatest vogue of his career. The character that finally
emerged, however, was not a limpid symbol, like Florian's
zanni, for an Age of Sensibility, but one of more turbid and
tenebrous complexity—more befitting an Age of Spleen.

1925), has been the first to suggest that Florian's Harlequin "reappeared
as Pierrot" in the nineteenth century (p. 135). But as I shall later demonstrate (see Chapter IV), he is wrong in attributing this transformation to
the great mime Deburau.

III

Gilles and Clown

Le plâtre de son front et le fard de sa joue
Font merveille. Il pérore et se tait tout soudain,
Reçoit des coups de pieds au derrière, badin,
Baise au cou sa commère énorme, et fait la roue.
        —Paul Verlaine, "Le Pitre"

Bobèche, adieu! bonsoir, Paillasse! arrière,
  Gille!
Place, bouffons vieillis, au parfait plaisantin,
Place! très grave, très discret et très hautain,
Voici venir le maître à tous, le clown agile.
        —Paul Verlaine, "Le Clown"

The history of Pierrot might be written as a succession of great and small interpreters, from Giuseppe Giaratone among the *Comédiens italiens du Roi* to the finical eccentric in Wallace Stevens' *Harmonium*. But we must guard against an approach to our subject that would reduce it to these simple terms. Pierrot's dimensions at any moment in his long career cannot be taken as we can Hamlet's, for example, by our taking the measure of a Garrick or a Kean or an Olivier. As his friend Guildenstern is quick to discover, Hamlet has a formidable number of stops; but it is, nevertheless, a manageably finite number. The heart of his mystery is hidden in about thirty-nine hundred lines, some twenty scenes, and five acts. And no matter how violently Kean may tremble or grimace, or with how much tight-lipped restraint Olivier may rage, Hamlet still must finger the same noisome skull and ask the same vexing questions.

Pierrot is a different kind of character. Certainly he is
sustained by a notable line of very able interpreters, all of
whom add significant strokes of their own to his delineation. But while Hamlet lives in a comparatively "closed"
world, one that is hedged in by castle walls, where the in-
habitants speak in Elizabethan verse, and where the old
catastrophe occurs and recurs with each appearance of its
hero, Pierrot lives in an "open" one: he thrives as comfort-
ably in Astrakhan as in Paris; he can sing his way through
a scene as easily as talk; and when deprived of song and
speech altogether, he can still manage a successful, though
mute, adjustment. Each of Pierrot's adjustments, however, leaves its mark on his personality. Though he may
preserve a central core of characteristics as he passes from
theater to theater and from genre to genre, he is never
quite the same personage from one to the other. Both
Giaratone and Hamoche were successful in assimilating
and harmonizing the disparate and sometimes contradictory elements of Pierrot's character, but the *zanni* of their
creation are far from identical: the fact that one often sings
his sentiments instead of speaking them, that one serves a
Turkish master with diligence and the other a Frenchman
with reluctance, fosters inevitable differences. Here it is
not so much a matter of shadings of character—shadings
that distinguish, say, a tempestuous Hamlet from a sullen
one—as a matter of full tones and hues of personality.

And when we turn from the greater to the lesser interpreters of the *zanni,* we encounter an even more slippery
figure. We have already noticed that Pierrot sometimes has
a tendency to disintegrate or to contract, to allow all but
one or two traits of character to shrink disproportionately.
That this is the work not only of the writers who give him a
parchment birth, but also of those actors who pull on his
white blouse and breeches, is implied by some of his appearances, as schizophrenic doubles or triples, in pantomime. So, in Les Trois Pierrots (1850),[1] written to show off

[1] Presented at the Théâtre des Funambules with Charles Deburau as

the talents of three nineteenth-century mimes, appear Pierrots who are, severally, clever, naïve, and loyal. And we shall see how far this process of disintegration—and even distortion—can go when we take a look at the moonsmitten children sprung, sometimes piteously imperfect, from the brains of the late Romantics.

But to say that Pierrot's character can be coarsened and distorted is to imply, of course, that he has both a persistent and a continuous identity, despite the ravages of his fortuitous and very uneven existence. The continuity of his identity has never been disputed: Constant Mic, in fact, goes a step further than I would be willing to venture and says that a historical connection between "the celebrated Pierrots of Willette" and the Pedrolino of classical *commedia dell'arte* is "absolutely evident."[2] But the learned critic has some difficulty—one shared by a good many scholars who have touched on this subject—in recognizing common characteristics between the two types and, consequently, any surviving traces of the original personality across the line of succession. I should simply like to suggest at this point that the fortunes of Pierrot in the nineteenth century are often wayward ones, and if we focus on the cartoonings of Willette we must certainly have the same difficulty as Mic, since Willette's delicate *zanni* represent Pierrot near the height of a *crise d'identité*. Let us keep in mind, however, that up to and long past the time when Pierrot becomes literary grist for the Romantics (and we can fix that time very nearly to the day and hour), he is still a figure of public property; and the response of the public consciousness to his personality is an invariably ingenuous one. In the course of a discussion about Harlequin, Georges Doutrepont makes some reflections that apply equally well to Pierrot which may help explain this remark:

Pierrot *le rusé*, Alexandre Guyon as Pierrot *le naïf*, and Paul Legrand as Pierrot *le dévoué*: see Louis Péricaud, *Le Théâtre des Funambules* (Paris, 1897), p. 355.

[2] *La Commedia dell'arte*, p. 211.

But perhaps one will raise the objection: "If Harlequin was so supple and especially if he was successively so many different beings, the essential and fundamental particularities that made up his character . . . must have disappeared just as often in the actor-transformists who played him. . . ." Without a doubt. . . . But the public did not require more. Moreover, it usually recovered [in him] something of the first man. I imagine that its mentality, in this case, resembled that of regular patrons of the movies, who go to see Charlot [Charlie Chaplin]. They await their "man" with the tranquil confidence of people who "know." First, they know (or are persuaded) that the promised role, the announced transformation, will be "funny." Next, or in addition, they know that in the great number of previous films their Charlot has presented a fairly clear aspect, that he has been the *type* of the bullied, of the abused man. They think or hope that, despite everything, something of this type, of this symbolic figure, will appear on the screen. Which, moreover, almost always happens.[3]

That the *individuality*, the *particularities* of Pierrot's original character are often lost upon the stages of the fairgrounds, as well as in all his subsequent transformations, I think no one would deny. But though he does not have the consistently familiar outline of a Hamlet, he does have, at least in the popular consciousness, a central core of persistent characteristics. As we shall see, the Pierrot of nineteenth-century pantomime takes on many of the qualities of Harlequin. But despite his occasional wooing and winning of Columbine and his suppleness of body and mind, he can never be confused with his black-masked companion. The notorious abuse that Pierrot suffers at the hands of some of the Decadents and their heirs may even be considered, from one point of view, as a redefinition of

[3] *Les Types populaires,* II, 40f.

the two *zanni*'s roles, not only by a sharpening of the burlesque sensitivity and ineffectual insularity of Giaratone's
creation, but also by an exaggeration of these qualities almost to the point of tragedy.

The nineteenth century was prodigal with Pierrot: he
was admitted as freely to the circus ring as to the purple-
curtained chambers of Axel's castle. It is precisely his
ubiquity during these years and the facility with which his
multifarious interpreters daubed their own colors upon his
white *casaque*, however, that would lead us to predict a
kind of death by dissipation, to suspect that a search for
figures assuming his original character in the twentieth
century would be fruitless. And so it would, were we to
expect those characters to be identical. But if we allow for
the adjustments that enable the type to acclimate to worlds
radically different in tone, that enable him—more
importantly—to absorb and embody concerns that a less
pliable figure could not, we will find, behind the sophisticated voices and under the shabby dress of a few
twentieth-century "masks," much of the same equivocal
intelligence that glimmered in the brain of Giaratone's ingenious creation.

The reason for this persistence is not, I think, an especially subtle one; but before I proffer it, we may do well to
inspect more narrowly the kind of çreature that Giaratone
and the forains bequeathed to the Boulevard stages, to describe more precisely the comic type that their Pierrots—
either singly or in the composite—preserve. Our flourfaced
friend has spiritual affinities with a fair number of comic
personages, in both popular and literary history. The folk
and court fools are two such familiar types; and the clownish slaves of the ancient Atellan mime have spawned at
least one admirably persuasive attempt[4] to penetrate what
K. M. Lea calls "the silence of the Middle Ages," and to
uncover real historical connections between the Oscan
farce and *commedia dell'arte*. But as Lea herself observes,

---

[4] I refer to Nicoll's *Masks, Mimes and Miracles*.

"the comic possibilities of the caricature of a great nose, a
bald head, a ragged garment, or a protruding stomach
might occur to any buffoon though he never came into contact, consciously or unconsciously, with Maccus, Pappus,
or the *mimus centunculus*";[5] and, similarly, the kind of role
and intelligence created by Giaratone for the *Comédiens italiens du Roi* required no precedent for his *zanni* to succeed
on the stage of the Hôtel de Bourgogne. The Pierrot of
Gherardi's comedies is a character of such obvious appeal
that we may recover his personality, almost wholly intact,
from a Proverb-voiding Swag-belly who has no theatrical
pretensions at all—from the reluctant squire of Don Quixote. In both, there is the same confusion of simplicity and
common sense, the same unflagging and confident sententiousness, the same submissiveness in accepting the uncertain benefits of a master's man. Their shrewdness and
honesty profess a respect for all that is of the senses, their
simplicity being more often born of ignorance and credu-
lity than dullness. Each enjoys—or suffers—a tenuous independence from his fellow fools as well as a certain capacity for self-reflection; and both share a pathetic sensitivity
that elicits tears at the loss of Dapple or cruel Columbine.
They are types of humanity that are ingenuously adaptable
and resourceful. The government of an "island" or the
education of a willful young girl is undertaken with the
same aplomb as the care of the master's robe or Mam-
brino's helmet.

Another trait common to both these characters and of
considerable importance is their general aloofness from
physical activity. Granted, both are prone to lift their
hands only high enough to reach their mouths; and in the
case of Pierrot, we have already noted how his role in
Gherardi's uncomplicated comedies helped encourage this
enviable inactivity. But this trait is not one to be simply accounted for and dismissed without our considering its effect on the symbolic stature of the personality that exhibits

[5] *Italian Popular Comedy,* I, 228.

it; for it is a trait that, significantly, disappears from the
Pierrot of early, nineteenth-century French pantomime. To
suggest what that effect is, I must call up those two characters who have stood at the fringe of our study from its
conception—Pedrolino and Hamlet.

Throughout these few pages, I have deemphasized the
character of Pedrolino in Pierrot's evolutionary history,
preferring to accept the valet of Gherardi's stage as the
proper progenitor of the type. This is not simply because
the historical connection between the two characters cannot be clearly established, but because, like Hamlet and
Harlequin, they "inhabit utterly different worlds." The
"type" as it appeared in classical *commedia dell'arte* and
the "type" as it flourished on the seventeenth- and eighteenth-century French stages have two separate and different identities. It is true that the personalities of Pierrot and
Pedrolino are roughly the same; but the part that the *commedia dell'arte* required Pedrolino to assume as a "first"
zanni imbued him with a symbolic tone that his successor
lacks altogether. We may think of Pierrot as dwelling in a
world midway between Hamlet's Elsinore and Pedrolino's
Rome. And perhaps the best way to illustrate the distance
between the two is to imagine what might happen if we
shrink it to nothing and drop Hamlet, problems and all,
into the middle of a *commedia*-inspired farce. Now adroitly
eluding Polonius-Pantalone, now courting Ophelia-
Columbine with bawdy ardor, Hamlet would move over
the stage in such a play with the rapid and capricious assurance of a principal *zanni*. And like Pedrolino, he would
be happily divested of the pale cast of thought. He would
still soliloquize; but he would brood, like a character in a
melodrama, upon the primacy of Filial Devotion, upon the
necessity of a Just Revenge, upon the nobility of Disinter-
ested Love, upon (in a word) sentiments we might peel
from his skin as neatly as his doublet. With this loss of
"depth," however, he would acquire Pedrolino's near-
inviolable and inexhaustible authority: and, for once, he

would live to see time put back in joint. But then he would no longer be Hamlet.

Our illustration aside, let us now consider Pierrot's place between these two very different personages. Like the melancholy Dane, Pierrot is largely a static figure, one who is even given to occasional fits of morose brooding. Yet he shares with his predecessor of the *commedia dell'arte* a dogged talent for multiplication. While Hamlet lives in a close, solipsistic void and Pedrolino in a rare ether of fantasy, Pierrot plods through a world that is as generous or intractable, however bizarre or familiar the landscape, as the one on which the sun shines. And unlike Pedrolino, who is an irrepressible symbolic type, Pierrot is content to be simply a duplicative one.

Pierrot duplicates himself with prolific ease—and here we arrive at our point—because he parodies a pervasive and surprisingly vulnerable type of humanity: the temperamentally ordinary. A "natural" to his eighteenth-century audiences, Pierrot gave and still gives delight by powdering the skin of the normal, by overlaying his ignorance with eloquence and obscuring his wit with obtuseness, by betraying his propensity for the romantic pose while indulging, at the same time, his weakness for *fricassées de poulets*. He is a character whose essential slackness of personality is given parodic relief by the elasticity of his passions. And when, as in the nineteenth century, his personality is inverted and these passions themselves become the *données* of his character, the inevitability with which they tend towards the prosaic—or invite even more serious frustration—imbues him with comedy's sympathetic tones: the pitiful and tragicomic.

We do not have to look far for the stuff of which inverted Pierrots are made. Those two characters which stand at the limits of *le monde pierrotique*—Pedrolino and Hamlet—are both dangerously susceptible of slipping toward its center. Hamlet, in fact, appears at the end of the nineteenth century as Pierrot's half-brother; and in the early decades of that same century, Pierrot himself is seized with the spirit of his Italian predecessor. It should come as no surprise that a figure possessed of Pedrolino's authority should have had an especial attraction for the Romantics: when such a creature trips over his own feet, his fall has something ludicrously magisterial about it. To understand the reasons for Pierrot's transformation, we should turn away from these abstract speculations, however, and consider a confluence of certain forces. The Pierrot of Romantic notoriety is a figure who was virtually recreated by his great pantomimic interpreters, but he was assisted at birth by the midwifery of several influences. Florian's Harlequin was one; for two others of some importance, we must investigate developments occurring outside the booths of the French fairs and across the English Channel in the eighteenth century, developments that culminated in the theater of Gilles and the theater of Clown.

Not all of the early troupes of Italian comedians that carried the *commedia dell'arte* throughout Russia and western Europe met with the acclaim or patronage of the more celebrated players—of the *Gelosi, Uniti,* or *Confidenti*. Many of the companies were poor and ill-managed; their performances were sometimes pitiably incompetent affairs; and they deserved, probably more often than not, the disapprobation and ridicule they received. These were the troupes that rarely saw the inside of a theater, that depended, very likely for their livelihood, upon the glib talents of the *opérateurs* or charlatans who accompanied them. Curiously, however, it was just these troupes—and those of their emulators—that longest preserved the fitful spirit of the *commedia dell'arte* in France. And while the masks of the Hôtel de Bourgogne were aiming clever gibes at their Parisian hosts and the *zanni forains* were giving their persecutors tit for tat, these players were scrabbling through the eternal fortunes of Isabelle and Léandre out on the Pont-Neuf or outside the theaters of the fairgrounds.

Among these *artistes* of the street and open-air stages we find thriving several of Pierrot's close kin—many of indeterminate birth, most of Italian inspiration, and a few destined for careers in less straitened circumstances. One of these characters, closely associated with Pierrot yet preserving an independent identity of his own, is Gilles. Although it is not until the beginning of the eighteenth century that he clearly comes before us, Gilles (or "Gille") seems to have earlier, albeit obscure, origins. It has been suggested that the type and name both date from the old sixteenth-century expression *faire gille,* meaning "to go bankrupt" or "to run away," on the authority of which hypothesis the dictionaries explain that "the Gilles of the fair is he who runs away when he is called."[6] Others derive his name from that of Saint Gilles, whose flight from his native country for fear of being crowned king might also have given birth to the curious locution.[7] A third and most likely possibility is that the figure was the creation of a French comedian who called himself Gille le Niais (Gille the Simpleton) and who enjoyed a vogue around the middle of the seventeenth century. According to a few remarks in *Les Véritables précieuses* (1660) by Antoine Somaize, the comedian's real name was the Sieur de la Force; and he boasted of having descended from an impressive line of French *farceurs.* Apparently, he was at the head of a small troupe of players who presented farces of his own composition, plays in which popular songs formed an essential part of the entertainment.[8]

But it is quite possible, as Victor Fournel implies, that Gille le Niais was only "a sobriquet of a type, applied to several personages,"[9] a type that may have had its origins

[6] See Doutrepont, *Les Types populaires,* II, 73.
[7] Ibid.
[8] Ibid., pp. 73-74; and Victor Fournel, *Les Spectacles populaires* (Paris, 1863), pp. 265-67.
[9] *Les Spectacles populaires,* p. 266.

as far back as 1531, in the *zanni* Giglio of an early company of Italian players, the academic *Intronati*. [10] Inasmuch as all these explanations are only conjectural, and inconsequential, it is probably reasonable to accept the year 1697 as the birthdate of the French type, when Marc, an actor-tumbler, made his debut at the Foire Saint-Germain in the dress and character of the naïve buffoon. For it was this forain who first undertook the role of Gilles for the amusement of the fairs' patrons[11] and who thereby fathered successive imitators to perpetuate the type.

Gilles is a character who found no scarcity of interpreters at the fairgrounds: the tumblers Benville and Drouin succeeded Marc in the role that very same year. [12] Among the notable Gilles that followed were Crespin (1701), called Gilles le Boiteux, a performer of "grace and lightness" despite the infirmity of his body; Génois (1711), whose grimaces and dances over the rope in wooden shoes earned him a unique reputation; and Maillot (1702), "one of the best Gilles that appeared at the Foire."[13] A note concerning this last actor has been hazarded by a redoubtable student of the popular types, Ludovic Celler, that suggests at least one source of the obscurity through which we see the character of Gilles in the eighteenth century:

> At first [Maillot] played the roles of Pierrot under the pseudonym of Gilles: since he was talented and successful, his *nom de guerre* served to designate the employ. Hence was created the Gilles who took, as a result, a rather important place in the *parades* of the Boulevards and caused the French Pierrot to be almost completely forgotten. [14]

[10] Doutrepont, *Les Types populaires*, II, 74; Mic, *La Commedia dell'arte*, p. 33n.

[11] Campardon, *Spectacles*, II, 108.   [12] Parfaict, *Mémoires*, I, 6.

[13] Campardon, *Spectacles*, I, 218; Parfaict and Abguerbe, *Dictionnaire des Théâtres*, III, 21, 293.

[14] *Les Types populaires au théâtre* (Paris, 1870), pp. 119-20; cited in Doutrepont, *Les Types populaires*, II, 75.

That Gilles was often confused with Pierrot during this century is evident to any admirer of Watteau; for among those titles that identify the early engravings of the *fêtes galantes*, the names of Pierrot and Gilles appear under figures identical in dress and attitude. But though the two types were closely associated, often to the point of being indistinguishable,[15] they seem to have assumed distinctly different roles at the Foire. An appearance as a principal character in one of Lesage and Dorneval's comedies—*La Conquête de la Toison d'or* (1724), for example[16]—was a rare one for Gilles. Usually when he turned up at all, it was in a minor, sometimes transfigured role. His real place at the Foire was in the *parade*, the farcical entertainment staged in front of the theaters to attract the spectators inside. It was on an open-air *tréteau* at the Foire Saint-Laurent that Gilles first caught the attention of the polite world and, as a consequence, gained a kind of dubious immortality.

On a summer night around 1707, the young apprentice barrister T.-S. Gueullette and a few of his friends, capping an evening of pleasure at the fair, stopped before one of the booths to watch a performance of *Le Chapeau de Fortunatus*: Gilles is being sent by his master on one of his countless ill-starred errands, this time to fetch three horses from Holland. Hardly is he out the door before he runs into Sans-Quartier and Divertissant, two lucky rogues who have just discovered (in the middle of the street, presumably) a hat of magical properties, the fabled hat (*"Ah chapeau des chapeaux!"*) of Fortunatus. Gilles has the hat and the rogues have his money in less time than it takes him to say his own name—Gilles Bambinois Cadet

---

[15] Columbine calls Pierrot a "Gille" in Piron's *L'Ane d'Or* (Piron, *Œuvres*, IV, 296), and in the course of a magistrate's report describing the prologue to Lesage's *Arlequin, valet de Merlin*, presented at the Foire Saint-Germain in 1718, the officer refers to Pierrot indiscriminately as "Pierrot" or as "Gilles" (in Campardon, *Spectacles*, II, 367).

[16] Described in Parfaict and Abguerbe, *Dictionnaire des Théâtres*, V, 479ff.

L'Aisné—and he is pulling it over his ears just as his master comes pottering in:

THE MASTER. They told me my valet Gilles hasn't left yet. I'm afraid that rogue's having a good time over the bottle and they've stolen all my money from him.

GILLES. He doesn't see me. Hee, hee, hee . . .

THE MASTER. I believe I see him.

GILLES. Ah: it's because he thinks I haven't put the hat on my head.

THE MASTER. What're you doing there, you knave?

GILLES. I'm invisible.

THE MASTER. What's that supposed to mean, invisible?

GILLES. It means you don't see me. And if you knew what this hat was, you'd know you don't see me.

THE MASTER, *boxing his ears.* What're you talking about, I can't see you, you rogue: take that! and that![17]

Gueullette and his friends were so amused by this little farce that they performed it themselves before their hosts of a subsequent evening. The *parade* was a warmly received success, and other evenings saw other performances—of *parades*, or of scenes from the Théâtre-Italien and Comédie-Française—some played impromptu, others, like Regnard's *Joueur*, from memory. Shortly afterwards, Gueullette formed "an extremely agreeable society" among several stagestruck acquaintances and, having built a theater "*très galant*" at Auteuil, began receiving "an astonishing concourse of spectators of the first rank" to applaud the foolery of Gilles.[18] Other *théâtres de société* were established under Gueullette's quick-witted direction

---

[17] *Le Chapeau de Fortunatus,* in the *Théâtre des Boulevards* (Paris, 1756), III, 333-34.

[18] T.-S. Gueullette, "Préface" to "Parades anciennes," Fonds français MS. 9340, Bibliothèque Nationale, Paris; cited in J.-E. Gueullette, *Un Magistrat du XVIIIᵉ siècle, ami des lettres, du théâtre et des plaisirs: Thomas-Simon Gueullette* (Paris, 1938), pp. 62-63.

at Maisons and Choisy, and the *parade* very soon became *à la mode.*[19]

Its popularity showed no signs of diminishing during the eighteenth century. While the gawkers of the Foire smirked at the perennial *niaiseries* of Gilles and M. Parlaventrebleu, ladies of fashion smiled behind their fans at the productions of Collé, Sallé, Fagan, and, somewhat later, of the author of *Le Mariage de Figaro.* In 1756, a collection of these popular farces appeared anonymously as the *Théâtre des Boulevards;* and the blushful *boulevardiers* were as quick to repudiate these bastard children (*"delicta juventutis meæ,"* in the words of Gueullette)[20] as they were to acknowledge their mutually doubtful authorship.[21] For the life that Gilles enjoys in the pages of these volumes, as no doubt he enjoyed on the stage, is a decidedly indelicate one.

A character of more simplicity than sense and of less decency than either, Gilles inherits the ignoble side of the *commedia*'s comic masks. When his ingenuity is taxed to help out the Lovers, he rarely improves upon the stratagem of *Isabelle, Grosse par vertu,* where the young lady is counseled to hug a tureen under her dress to convince the indefatigably amorous Doctor she is *grosse* by her beau. When Harlequin assumes the role of "first" *zanni,* Gilles limits himself to cleverly obscene asides upon the action, or appeals (*"Sainte Merde!"*) to rather dubious agencies.[22] He is usually the valet of one of the old men—Cassandre or M. Parlaventrebleu—but unlike his quick-witted Italian counterpart, he is more duped than duping. Harlequin, in *Le Marchand de Merde,* for example, convinces him that excrement is selling at a premium; and Gilles piles a wheelbarrow high to peddle it about the streets (*"Qui veut*

---

[19] See J.-E. Gueullette, *Thomas-Simon Gueullette,* pp. 19-21, 62-72.

[20] Cited in ibid., p. 161.

[21] For a full discussion of the history of attributions of authorship for these plays, see ibid., pp. 161-62.

[22] See, e.g., *Léandre Fiacre,* in the *Théâtre des Boulevards,* I.

de ma merde? . . . c'est de la fraîche"). In another play, he is
stripped to the skin by Laisse-Rien and Prens-Tout, who
swear they have spied a tarantula scuttling into his vest:

GILLE. Where is it?
PRENS-TOUT. It's squashed, but that's not going to stop
  either of us from dying of it. (*He pretends to cry.*)
GILLE. O heavens! Does a body have to die so misera-
  bly? Mboo-hoo-hoo . . .
LAISSE-RIEN. It's not a matter of crying, Sir; on the contrary, you have to laugh. See the faces my brother's
  making because he's stopped jumping and dancing?
  So dance if you don't want to be dead in a quarter of
  an hour. You see how my brother's started up
  again. It's the only remedy against the bite of the
  tarantula. Talalerita, lalerita . . .
GILLE. My legs are numb with fright. It doesn't matter:
  we'll dance till the heat's left our bodies, seeing as
  we have to and since that's the only way we can be
  cured.
(*The thieves take him by the hand, sing, make him sing and
dance, take up his clothes, and run off. Meanwhile,* GILLE
keeps dancing.)[23]

Gilles' gullet and belly are prodigiously insatiable. It is
probably because he is a creature of such atavistic wit and
appetites that he seems to thrive, as effortlessly as Pedrolino, in an inexhaustible present. But if that latter *zanni*
often shares the ether with Ariel, Gilles tumbles, with
Puck's witless companions, among the cornflowers.

In 1758, a parody of Anseaume's *Le Peintre amoureux de
son modèle* appeared at the Foire Saint-Germain under the
title of *Gilles garçon peintre z'amoureux-t-et rival.*[24] The *parade*
failed in its first production, but when Anseaume was
commissioned to burlesque his own ariettas, the piece
found a delighted and appreciative audience. In the words

[23] T.-S. Gueullette, *Troisième Parade*, in *Parades inédites* (Paris, 1885), pp.
253-54.
[24] Published in the *Nouveau Théâtre de la Foire* (Paris, 1763), IV.

of its author, Poinsinet: "Then poor Gilles was called back to mind; they wanted to see him again. He reappeared, and the *parade* had a hundred and thirty productions. It was performed in the best houses of Paris and in all our provinces."[25] And when the *zanni* of this play was admitted to the stage of the Comédie-Italienne in 1767, he enjoyed, we are told, just as much success.[26]

It may have been owing to the popularity of this parody that Gilles found, in the last half of the century, such favor among the Boulevard audiences. For even after the sobering grotesqueries of the Terror, when Pierrot had given his name to a *zanni manqué* of the New Republic,[27] it was Gilles who was fetching the crowds into the little theaters and putting his white-frocked twin in the shade.[28] His vogue was undistinguished, however, by comparison with the éclat with which Pierrot reappeared; and to better prepare the stage for that reappearance, we should leave the Boulevard and France to review briefly another important development during these years—the rise of the English pantomime.

The motley entertainment that was born in early eighteenth-century England, catching the public favor about 1723 and reaching, a hundred years later, a peak of popularity and excellence with Joe Grimaldi's great Clown, was probably of more Gallic than Italian inspiration. The pantomime, it is true, was the only long-lasting development of the *commedia dell'arte* in England; but the seeds of its growth there were transplanted via Paris, particularly

[25] Cited in Georges Cucuel, *Les Créateurs de l'Opéra-Comique français* (Paris, 1914), p. 101.

[26] Ibid.

[27] We find in Max Frey's *Les Transformations du Vocabulaire français à l'époque de la Révolution (1789-1800)* (Paris, 1925) the appellation *Robespierrot.*

[28] See Lecomte, *Théâtre de la Cité*, pp. 81, 99, 102, 131, 145, 183, 267; and *Variétés Amusantes*, pp. 22, 25, 46, 57, 95, 211, 234.

via the Théâtre-Italien and Parisian fairs, after the *commedia*
had imbibed a spirit and flavor that were, as we have seen,
characteristically French. It was probably visits by Scaramouche Fiorilli and his
troupe from Paris that sparked the first serious interest in
the Italian masks among native English dramatists and en-
tertainers. The Elizabethan playwrights had, of course,
frequently alluded to Zany, Pantaloon, and Harlakan, as
well as to the Italians' extempore manner of acting. They
had even gone so far as to introduce "panteloun" and
Zany into a few plays, masques, and jigs.[29] But although
"the contact between the English [Elizabethan] stage and
the Commedia dell'arte was considerable, . . . the Italian
influence was mainly sporadic and superficial."[30] After
Fiorilli's performances in London during the summers of
1673 and 1675, however, Drury Lane produced in May
1677 "A Comedy after the Italian Manner" by Edward
Ravenscroft: *Scaramouch a Philosopher, Harlequin a School-
Boy, Bravo, Merchant, and Magician,* a farce that "thoroughly acclimatised" the Italian types.[31] Soon after, other
dramatists began to seize upon the Italian characters to re-
plenish their farces and comedies. The ingenious Mrs.
Behn introduced a Harlequin who spoke Italian—possibly
extempore—into the second part of *The Rover* (1681); and
she adapted Fatouville's *Arlequin, Empereur dans la Lune* to
provide the Duke's Theatre, Dorset Garden, with one of its
successes of 1687, *The Emperor of the Moon.* A year previ-
ously, William Mountfort had seen, on the same stage, his
Life and Death of Doctor Faustus, Made into a Farce embel-
lished with "the Humours of *Harlequin* and *Scaramouche*";
and in Motteux's *The Novelty. Every Act a Play* (1697), Pantalone, Mezzetin, "Pasquarel," and Nicholas, "a Clown,"
all appeared in the last act, "a short Farce, after the *Italian*
manner," entitled "Natural Magic."

[29] See Lea, *Italian Popular Comedy*, II, 388-90.
[30] Ibid., p. 453.
[31] Allardyce Nicoll, *A History of English Drama, 1660-1900,* I (Cambridge, England, 1952), 243.

None of these plays was pantomime. They were, rather, farcical comedies that caught and, in some measure, exploited the then-current taste for novelties upon the stage. The waning of the century saw the appearance of other curiosities, many of foreign importation, to satisfy and sharpen this taste: dancing, singing, instrumental interludes, acrobatic exercises, animal exhibitions, imitations—all of which were offered at the London theaters at the end and between the acts of regular dramas. The year 1718 was the first of the new century to see the arrival of a consolidated troupe of comedians from abroad, the earliest of a series of companies that provided London almost continuously with Continental entertainment up to the closing years of the next decade.[32] Although its members grandly styled themselves as "lately arrived from the Theatre Royal at Paris" and included three of Molière's plays in their repertoire, the first troupe had been formed at the Foire Saint-Germain in 1715 under the direction of Harlequin Francisque. A good many of its offerings betrayed its sawdust origins, with Regnard and Dufresny's *La Foire Saint-Germain* opening the season. Interspersed with plays from Gherardi's *Théâtre* and staples of the Foire repertory were acrobatic exercises and feats of skill; and the Sieur Antoni's Pierrot was not at all loath to join these amusements. On January 6, 1719, he was advertised as performing a somersault through twelve hoops, all standing twelve feet from the ground.[33] On a later occasion Pierrot introduced, to the delight of his English audience, "the Scene of the Monkey never perform'd in England before."[34]

[32] For a full account of these visits, see Emmett L. Avery, "Foreign Performers in the London Theaters in the Early Eighteenth Century," *Philological Quarterly*, XVI (April 1937), 105-23; and Sybil Rosenfeld, *Foreign Theatrical Companies in Great Britain in the 17th and 18th Centuries* (London, 1955).

[33] Avery, "Foreign Performers," p. 107n.

[34] We cannot be certain that this Pierrot was Antoni, however, since another anonymous Pierrot had joined the troupe on January 29, 1719 (Rosenfeld, *Foreign Theatrical Companies*, p. 7).

The Pierrot arriving with the next troupe, in 1720, was
Roger, who seems to have enjoyed even more success than
Antoni. Not only did he return on subsequent visits late in
the same year and again in 1724, but he also joined the
Drury Lane actors in 1725, composed for them a ballet, *La
Follette,* and took the part of Pierrot in several of their pan-
tomimes. In 1728, he was still directing ballets and dancing
for that theater.[35]

The French and Italian troupes that appeared in London
throughout the first half of the eighteenth century obviously appealed to their audiences by the farcical nature of
their comedies, afterpieces, and "night scenes"—and, particularly, by the singing, dancing, and tumbling that accompanied them. For critics of this "Foreign Invasion"—as
one journalist styled the Continental influx[36]—all of this
argued a deplorable debasement of the English stage. As
early as Francisque's first appearance in 1718, John Ozell
had anticipated some of these complaints when, in a prologue to his translation of *La Foire Saint-Germain,* he imagined a few of the *zanni* discoursing upon their probable reception in London. Harlequin's doubts of success are
brushed aside by Pierrot:

> PIER. Pox on ye, you're always prognosticating ill luck.
>   Tho' 'twere only for our Tumbling, 'tis odds but—
> HARL. Devil take you and your Tumbling; 'tis the very
>   Thing that has made us contemptible.
> COL. So here's the Source and Cause of our Grief.
>   Well, I'll take upon me myself to beg the Town to
>   have the Patience to see ye once, and if they are not
>   pleas'd with you, you shall appear no more.[37]

It was not, however, the foreign visitors alone who were
playing to houses of divided loyalties: during this same

[35] Avery, "Foreign Performers," pp. 108, 110, 111n, 113, 117.

[36] Aaron Hill, *The Prompter,* December 24, 1734; cited in Rosenfeld,
Foreign Theatrical Companies, p. 20.

[37] Cited in Avery, "Foreign Performers," p. 106n.

half-century, English pantomime was getting on its feet, and encountering opponents as redoubtable as Henry Fielding, proponents as dubious as Colley Cibber.[38] Probably an outgrowth of those entertainments of dancing, foolery, and scenes "after the Italian manner" which were popular at the turn of the century, the pantomime found an early inventor and apologist in one John Weaver, a Drury Lane dancing-master, whose *History of the Mimes and Pantomimes* (1728) is the only systematic account we have of the development of the form. Though his *History* concedes that the genre is indebted to the early Italian (or rather, Italianate) entertainments, Weaver insists that English pantomimes are distinct from and superior to the former, "since those have been only us'd for the Introducing, or Explanation of some following or foregoing Scene; and *ours* are Representations of entire Stories, carried on by various *Motions, Action,* and *dumb Show.*"[39] The first of these representations to appear on an English stage "was performed in Grotesque Characters, after the manner of the Modern *Italians,* such as *Harlequin, Scaramouch,* &c. and was called *The Tavern Bilkers,* Composed by Mr. *Weaver* and first performed in *Drury-Lane* Theatre, 1702."[40] Weaver divides the form into three types: those in "Grotesque Characters," those in "Serious Characters," and those of a "mixt" type employing both (*Amadis, or The Loves of Harlequin and Columbine* [1718] is an early example). Of the three, the "mixt" entertainment survived longest and became the basis for the stylized, nineteenth-century panto.

Relatively few printed pantomime scripts remain from the eighteenth century, and Weaver's claim of having introduced the genre is still in question: a certain John Rich

[38] See Emmett L. Avery, "The Defense and Criticism of Pantomimic Entertainments in the Early Eighteenth Century," *ELH,* V (June 1938), 127-45; and Charles Washburn Nichols, "Fielding's Satire on Pantomime," *PMLA,* XLVI (1931), 1107-12.
[39] John Weaver, *The History of the Mimes and Pantomimes* (London, 1728), pp. 3-4.
[40] Ibid., p. 45.

(called "Lun") has received as much attention as being the true innovator. This popular Harlequin and composer of pantomimes for Lincoln's Inn Fields offered Drury Lane a formidable competition from the year 1717 in drawing the crowds with elaborately mounted productions.[41] The nature of a typical "mixt" entertainment as staged by Rich is suggested in a passage from the *Memoirs of the Life of David Garrick, Esq.* by Thomas Davies:

> . . . it consisted of two parts, one serious and the other comic. By the help of gay scenes, fine habits grand dances, appropriate musick, and other decorations, he exhibited a story from Ovid's Metamorphoses, or some other fabulous writer: between the pauses or acts of this serious representation, he interwove a comick fable [later known as the "harlequinade"], consisting chiefly of the Courtship of Harlequin and Colombine, with a variety of surprising adventures and tricks which were produced by the magick Wand of Harlequin; such as the sudden transformation of palaces and temples to huts and cottages; of men and women into wheel-barrows and joint stools; of trees turned to houses; colonnades to beds of tulips; and Mechanick's shops [*sic*: read "hops"] into serpents or ostriches.[42]

Pierrot's place in this "fable" was usually secure but never very prominent throughout the century. His adoption by the English apparently had been quiet and unheralded. We know that Fiorilli and his company had first performed the *Aggiunta al Convitato di pietra*, the play in which Pierrot made his debut among the Italians, only months before they visited London in 1673. But since their

[41] See Emmett L. Avery, "Dancing and Pantomime on the English Stage, 1700-1737," *Studies in Philology*, XXXI (July 1934), 417-52.

[42] (Boston, 1818), I, 78; cited in Mitchell P. Wells, "Some Notes on the Early Eighteenth-Century Pantomime," *Studies in Philology*, XXXII (October 1935), 599.

repertory for that visit is unrecorded, we have no idea whether this scenario, as well as any others in which Pierrot might have appeared, was enacted. If Giaratone did accompany the troupe, we must conclude that his impression on the London public was not very great, since Pierrot has no place in the English farces that followed the company's departure. Even in Mrs. Behn's *The Emperor of the Moon*, his role is appropriated by Scaramouch. Neither does his name appear among the dancing-entertainments and "night scenes" of the early 1700's, though both "Punchanello" and "Mezetin" sometimes found their way beside the everpopular Scaramouch and Harlequin. It is possible that the "French Peasant" or "French Clown" who was danced by "Mr. Firbank" (among others) at the Queen's Theatre around 1706 was none other than our whitefaced *naïf*;[43] but about this we can only conjecture.

The *zanni*'s first appearance in an English entertainment for which I have found record was on April 29, 1717, when a certain Mr. Griffin undertook the role for *The Jealous Doctor; or, The Intriguing Dame*, a pantomime by Rich.[44] Two years later, Pierrot was familiar enough to London audiences for Mrs. Aubert to introduce him into a "mock-opera," *Harlequin-Hydaspes: or, The Greshamite*, in which he plays Arbaces, captain of the guard to the king of Persia (the Doctor). In the pantomimes that followed this piece and for which we have printed scripts, Pierrot appears fairly regularly, though usually in a minor, sometimes obscurely defined role. As "Pierot" in John Thurmond's *Harlequin Doctor Faustus: with the Masque of the Deities* (1724), one of several popular pantos on the Faust theme, he accompanies Punch and Scaramouch about London as a companion (valet?) of Harlequin-Faustus. In *The Miser; or, Wagner and Abericock* (1727), also by Thurmond, he is introduced as "the Miser's starv'd Servant." A short passage

[43] Emmett L. Avery, ed., *The London Stage, 1660-1800*, pt. 2, I (Carbondale, Ill., 1960), 123, 126.
[44] Ibid., p. 448.

from this last play may give us some idea of what the "business" of these little farces was like, as well as suggest the difficulties they offer in providing clues to Pierrot's English character:

> *Pierot* enters with a Bag of Money, which he has been to receive for his Master. The Clown enters, drest as a Lady of the Town. A Scene of Courtship passes between 'em; during which, *Harlequin* in the Habit of a Nurse takes an Opportunity of changing the Bag. *Pierot* and the Clown part Amorously. On hearing a Child cry, *Pierot* examines his Bag, and finds an Infant in it, and runs off frightened, &c.[45]

The sketchiness of the scene gives little ground for comment about the manner in which Pierrot was played. Indeed, many of the "mixt" pantomimes that have come down to us only indicate the interludes of comic action rather than describe them.

Several considerations lead us to believe, however, that "Pierot"—as well as his fellow masks—was probably delineated with coarse, crude strokes; that he appeared most often as a somewhat clownish grotesque. We know, for example, from the first edition of *The Miser; or, Wagner and Abericock*, that Roger wore the *zanni's* white blouse in this pantomime; and we are reminded that it was this dancer-acrobat who was familiar to London audiences in the role rather than the more celebrated forain actors Belloni and Hamoche. We have, moreover, Weaver's own admission in his *History* of the genre that, as for the "Grotesque" (i.e., *commedia dell'arte*) characters, "in lieu of regulated Gesture, you meet with distorted and ridiculous *Actions*, and Grin and Grimace take up entirely that Countenance where the *Passions* and *Affections* of the Mind should be expressed."[46] In *The Top of the Tree; or, A Tit Bit for a Nice Palate*, a pantomime produced at Bartholomew Fair in 1739, Pierrot was

---

[45] (London, 1727), p. 8.
[46] Weaver, *History of the Mimes*, p. 56.

played by one Signor Arthurini, "who has a most surpriz-
ing talent at Grimace and will in this Occasion introduce
upwards of 50 Whimsical, Sorrowful, Comical and Diverting Faces."[47] The most notable interpreter of the *zanni* in
England was Carlo Delpini (1740-1828), who "kept strictly
to the idea of a creature so stupid as to think that if he
raised his leg level with his shoulder he could use it as a
gun."[48]

At the end of the century, the personage known simply
as Clown, a lumpish bumpkin, began to claim as great a
part in the pantomime as Pierrot. In several of the entertainments that appeared around 1800, both Clown and
Pierrot (sometimes "Pero") play roles of equal importance.
Before this date, as Richard Findlater tells us, Clown was
cast

> as the stooge in the comic scenes, the "feed" who got
> the rough end of the knockabout, the pre-ordained
> butt, victim and second *zanno* [*sic*]; under the name of
> Dulman, Blunder, Simon, Clodpate or Clodpoll, he
> was usually played by a member of the acting com-
> pany, not by a pantomimist. . . . Clodpoll was usually
> dressed in a plain smock and trousers, in a recogniza-
> bly bucolic *couture,* and the traditional red wig of the
> countryman.[49]

On April 14, 1800, the spectators of the Easter pantomime
at the small, provincial theater of Sadler's Wells were witness to the debut of a great comic actor in the stooge's role,
one who would soon found a new school for clowns. In
that panto, entitled *Peter Wilkins; or, The Flying World,* two
clodpates, Guzzle the Drinking Clown and Gobble the Eating Clown, competed for the audience's applause, the one
swallowing quart after quart of stage beer and the other

[47] Cited in Sybil Rosenfeld, *The Theatre of the London Fairs in the 18th Century* (Cambridge, England, 1960), pp. 45f.

[48] Disher, *Clowns and Pantomimes,* p. 135.

[49] *Grimaldi: King of Clowns* (London, 1955), p. 145.

wolfing down strings of sausages. The first was a certain Jean-Baptiste Dubois, a French tumbler and dancer who had come to the pantomime stage by way of the English circus; the second was Joey Grimaldi.

It was Grimaldi who was probably responsible not only for the gradual effacement of Pierrot from English pantomime but also for the eloquence ultimately attained by that entertainment itself. From his first great success in *Harlequin and Mother Goose; or, The Golden Egg!* in 1806, Grimaldi and English pantomime became almost synonymous; and on the figure that he created began to pivot the maliciously uninhibited grotesqueries of the harlequinade. In the pantomimes the Regency has left us, Clown reigns in a bizarre and fabulous world, the stability of which is never certain. When he sucks on an orange, it is likely to turn into a wasp; when he brings a horn to his lips, it flies down his throat. A coach may suddenly be metamorphosed into a balloon, a brickfield into a garden and villa. Crocodiles slither out of pianos, and huge heads materialize from the flooring to gobble down tables of food. What Harlequin accomplishes with a touch of his magic bat, Clown brings off through deft inadvertence: he joins a sheep's head to its body and sends it gamboling away; he fashions men from a candle, from a keg of rum, from a crate of earthenware—and they all saunter into the wings of this unsettling, unpredictable world. Clown and Harlequin, Pantaloon and Columbine remain, themselves, indestructable, imperishable beings. If Clown shoots Harlequin's flesh from his bones, he can just as easily shoot it on again; if Clown himself is eaten by a giant cat, he can be scraped from her teeth and pasted together with iron glue. Of the illimitable power enjoyed by the characters of English pantomime, Théodore de Banville observed:

> Between the adjective *possible* and the adjective *impossible*, the English mime has made his choice: he has

chosen the adjective *impossible*. It is in the impossible
that he dwells; whatever is impossible is what he
does. He hides where he cannot hide, he passes
through openings smaller than his body, he takes up
residence on props too weak to support his weight; he
executes, under the very eye that watches him, absolutely invisible movements; he balances on an umbrella; he curls up without a cramp in a violincase;
and—above all and always—he runs away, he escapes, he rushes off, he flies away![50]

Though first in prominence, Grimaldi's Joey was not the
only Clown of the Regency to achieve distinction. Banville's remark is actually a tribute, not to the king of
Clowns, but rather to several of Joey's successors who carried their art across the Channel.[51] One of Grimaldi's celebrated contemporaries deserves especial attention here as
the Clown who indirectly influenced the technique and
tone of the French Pierrot's theater: Laurent. An apprentice of the great circus showman Philip Astley, Laurent
was attracted early in his career to the rabble-filled Parisian
boulevards; and when he found an opportunity to escape
his master's eye, he booked passage to his native country,
where Astley found him operating a marionette booth near
the Pont-Neuf. He was, however, persuaded to return to
England and became "the foremost circus clown of his
day."[52] Said to be "ingenious, not humourous," Laurent,
according to Willson Disher, "never adopted the national
[English] type of schoolboy humour"; he seemed "inspired
by mischievous malice," and though "less characteristic"
than Grimaldi, was "more agile" and "well above the
common run in his mastery and finished skill."[53]

In 1820, Laurent's son Clément-Philippe left London for

[50] "Préface" to [Richard Lesclide], *Mémoires et pantomimes des Frères
Hanlon-Lees* (Paris, [1880]), p. 9.
[51] I.e., the Hanlon-Lees. For several specimens of that art, see their
Mémoires et pantomimes, cited above.
[52] Disher, *Clowns and Pantomimes*, p. 137.   [53] Ibid., p. 136.

France, attracted, like his father, by the boulevard theaters of Paris.[54] He took with him an intimate knowledge of English pantomime, its tricks and machinery, as well as a facility for writing his own pantomimic scripts. Not long after the young performer's arrival, he was joined by his brother John for an engagement at an unimposing little theater on the Boulevard du Temple, the Théâtre des Funambules. The engagement must not have seemed a very propitious one: the small, smoky, noisome Funambules was licensed to present only mimed and acrobatic acts, its actors having to make their ignominious entrances turning somersaults or balancing upon a rope. But before the decade was out, Harlequin Philippe was known to *tout Paris*. He had imparted to the French pantomime stage an exhilaratingly bullish verve and ebullience, and both he and his whitefaced confrere, a drolly mute Gilles-Pierrot, were jostling Shakespeare for the attention of men drunk with lyricism and with art.

[54] Tristan Rémy, *Les Clowns* (Paris, 1945), pp. 31f.

IV

Romantic Adolescence:
The Nineteenth Century

Le bon Pierrot, que la foule contemple,
Ayant fini les noces d'Arlequin,
Suit en songeant le boulevard du Temple.
Une fillette au souple casaquin
En vain l'agace avec son œil coquin;
Et cependant mystérieuse et lisse
Faisant de lui sa plus chère délice,
La blanche Lune aux cornes de taureau
Jette un regard de son œil en coulisse
A son ami Jean Gaspard Deburau.
—Théodore de Banville, "Pierrot"

"Ten years ago, in days gone by," wrote Théophile
Gautier in 1842,

it was the fashion, among painters and men of letters,
to frequent a little theater on the Boulevard du Temple
where a celebrated clown attracted the crowd. We
habitually occupied a ground-floor stage-box, somewhat like a drawer of a chest, and Pierrot was so ac-
customed to see us that he never sat down to a single
banquet on the stage without giving us our portion of
it. What slices of bread smeared with grape jam he cut
for us! Those were wonderful times, the times of the
Bœuf enragé . . . and of *Ma Mère l'Oie*, another masterpiece. . . . What plays! But then what a theater—and
above all, what spectators![1]

[1] "Shakspeare aux Funambules," *Revue de Paris*, September 4, 1842;

The little theater was the Théâtre des Funambules, and the Pierrot who so scrupulously shared his bread and jam with the literati was Jean-Gaspard, called Baptiste, Deburau. A mime whom Gautier later praised as "the most perfect actor who ever lived" and whose talents became legendary for several generations of performers, Deburau created a stage Pierrot that eclipsed all previous interpreters of the *zanni* and hung, like a white shade, over most of his pantomimic successors. This actor has often and justly been acknowledged as the godparent of the multifarious, moonstruck Pierrots who gradually found their way into Romantic, Decadent, and Symbolist literature; but Deburau's real role in the transmission of the type from the popular to the literary world—and in its transformation from *naïf* to neurasthenic pariah—has been only imperfectly understood, when it has been understood at all. To chart the development of Pierrot's character in the nineteenth century, we must, therefore, follow the career of this actor quite closely. We must, moreover, distinguish Baptiste from the Pierrot he created and, more importantly, from his heirs to the *casaque* at the Théâtre des Funambules.

Jean-Gaspard Deburau was born in Neukolin, Bohemia, in 1796, the son of a former soldier in the Austrian army, though a native of Amiens, Philippe Deburau.[2] Around the year 1814, M. Philippe appeared in Paris at the head of a troupe of nomadic tumblers and rope-dancers, most of whom were probably his own children; and not long thereafter, the little company began giving presentations in the courtyard of number 100 Rue Saint-Maur Popincourt. Here, in 1816, one of the directors of the Funambules, Nicolas-Michel Bertrand, saw these acrobats perform and engaged them for his theater. In his eagerness to

---

reprinted in Théophile Gautier, *Souvenirs de théâtre, d'art et de critique* (Paris, 1883), p. 55.

[2] My chief source for the details of the mime's life and career is Tristan Rémy, *Jean-Gaspard Deburau* (Paris, 1954).

procure the services of this "foreign" company—an attractive curiosity on the Boulevard—he took Jean-Gaspard, the clumsiest member of the troupe, "into the bargain."

Apparently, the young Deburau served his apprenticeship at the Funambules as a stagehand, not, at any rate, as a mime; his debut as Pierrot came many years later, in 1825. Deburau's son Charles has reported, however, that the character and costume of his father's *zanni* had been established even before the Deburau troupe arrived in Paris. According to a conversation Charles had with one of his own *élèves,* Louis Rouffe, Jean-Gaspard had been the student of an old Italian mime named Jacomo (or "Yacomo"), a Harlequin in Philippe Deburau's company. In one of Yacomo's pantomimes, the apprentice was charged with the role of a revenant; and, in "making himself up,"

> before giving his eyes and cheeks a sunken look, [Deburau] saw that his *facies* had taken on an interesting aspect. Without letting fall a word, one evening, for himself alone, he powdered the shine of his white greasepaint to a perfect whiteness and dullness. Something was lacking in this mask. What? The eyebrows and eyes accentuated with black. That was better already. What more? Some rouge on the lips to offset the white. Better and better, already captivating, and yet it wasn't complete. What had to be added? Ah! the black skullcap of Yacomo's Harlequin. And oh! miracle! Pierrot was born. The spirit of the *mimus albus* of Rome had passed into Deburau.[3]

We have the story at third-hand, recounted in the *Souvenirs* of the mime Séverin. Yet regardless of the truth or falseness of the anecdote, it interestingly suggests what will become obvious to Deburau's admirers at the Funambules: that this Pierrot is a recreator and innovator of his role. In the traditional costume itself, Deburau made significant alterations: he laid aside the *zanni*'s woolen hat and

[3] Séverin, *L'Homme Blanc: Souvenirs d'un Pierrot* (Paris, 1929), pp. 56-57.

exchanged the white skullcap for the black; to free his long and limber neck for comic effects, he dispensed with his predecessors' frilled collarette; and he replaced the close-fitting woolen jacket with a cotton blouse, its sleeves long and wide.

The style of interpreting the *zanni* was also changed. Deburau seemed to unite in himself the intelligence of Pierrot, the malice of Clown, and the gross instincts of Gilles. Théodore de Banville made note of the "absolute indifference" of this new Pierrot;[4] and Louis Péricaud, the chronicler of the Funambules, observed that "the placidity which Baptiste Deburau brought to his roles . . . formed an enormous contrast with the exuberance, the superabundance of gestures, of leaps, that had been displayed by his predecessors."[5] We must not assume from these remarks, however, that the pantomime of Baptiste was in any way comparable to the elegant sketches of a Marceau: Deburau was, despite his studied sang-froid, an exponent of the pantomime *sautante*, a type of entertainment that relied for its success upon frenetic action and movement. The brothers Laurent had been engaged at the Funambules several years before Deburau's debut; and the elder, Philippe—"*l'Homme Truc,*" as he came to be known—soon succeeded in popularizing the *genre anglais* at the little theater. Deburau's first notice of recognition probably came, in fact, as a result of his appearance in a pantomime by Laurent, one of the *chef-d'œuvres* that Gautier recalled with such affection, *Le Bœuf enragé*.

Animated by the infallibly comic machinery of English pantomimes—malignant shop signs and medicinals, unruly animals, drubbings, and malicious magic—this piece is nothing more than the familiar chase of Harlequin and Columbine by Cassandre and his man Pierrot. But though familiar, *Le Bœuf enragé*, like the pantos of its kind that followed, acquired uncustomary brilliance in the hands of its

---

[4] *Mes Souvenirs* (Paris, 1882), p. 218.
[5] *Le Théâtre des Funambules*, p. 28.

performers. On the nineteenth of July, 1828, the year following the highly successful run of this piece, appeared an unsigned article in the *Pandore*—doubtless the work of a regular contributor, the *spirituel* Charles Nodier. In a few eulogistic paragraphs, it offered the ignorant world outside the Boulevard a peep into Bertrand's obscure theater, and an especially tantalizing glimpse at two of the performers: Laurent *aîné* and Deburau. The latter's talents seemed particularly commendable, since Pierrot "is a character whose infinite nuances are difficult to render. Ingenuous like a child, cowardly, crafty, lazy, mischievous by instinct, obliging, jeering, gluttonous, thieving, blustering, greedy, clumsy, ingenious in the arts that tend to the satisfaction of his tastes: he is a naïve and clownish Satan."[6] Nodier's enthusiasm prompted him to devise a piece of his own for these talented mimes, and before the year was out, it was presented on Bertrand's stage as *Le Songe d'or ou Arlequin et l'avare*. He persuaded the members of his *cénacle* at the Bibliothèque de l'Arsenal to accompany him to the theater; and when, in 1830, the Théâtre des Funambules offered its public an adaptation of *Mother Goose*, it found itself entertaining a coterie of artists and poets, their plaudits rivaling those of the paradise for Laurent and Deburau.

That year saw a much more memorable event for this enthusiastic group of admirers, however—an event that influenced, in an oblique way, their reception of the *fourberies* of Pierrot. At two o'clock on February 25, 1830, the doors to the Théâtre-Français were opened. With a negligent, dandiacal air, a crowd of these young men took their seats in the empty hall. There, until ten in the evening, they gabbled out animal noises, joined in singing a few ballads of Hugo, and waited for the curtain to rise on the first performance of *Hernani*. This play marked an apex in the history of French drama, and the fervor with which it was embraced by Hugo's disciples warmed and fermented the heady spirit of the young Romantic movement.

[6] Cited in ibid., p. 78.

It must be difficult [wrote Gautier in his *Histoire du romantisme*] for the present generation to imagine the state of excitement of all minds at that time. A movement analogous to that of the Renaissance was taking place. A sap of new life was running hotly; everything was germinating, budding, blooming at one and the same time; intoxicating scents filled the air, which itself went to the head; men were drunk with lyricism and art.[7]

"At that time," he continued, "it was the fashion, in the Romanticist school, for a man to be wan, livid, greenish, and somewhat cadaverous, if possible, for thus did one attain the fateful, Byronic, Giaour look of one devoured by passion and remorse."[8] But it was not only in the poetry of Byron that the Romantics found a model for their passionate life and work. In 1827, at the Odéon, an English touring company presented *Hamlet* to an audience that included Hugo, Nerval, Alexandre Dumas, Alfred de Vigny, Hector Berlioz, and Eugène Delacroix. Dumas' response may be taken as typical: "This was the first time that I saw in the theatre real passions felt by men and women of real flesh and blood."[9] Hugo's "Préface" to *Cromwell*, completed in the month after this performance, placed Shakespeare at "the poetic summit" of the modern age. "Shakespeare," he wrote, "is the Drama; and the drama, which smelts under the same blast the grotesque and the sublime, the dreadful and the clownish, the tragic and the comic—the drama is the proper form . . . of today's literature."[10]

We seem to have left the pantomime of the Funambules far behind us, since any suggestion of resemblance be-

---

[7] *A History of Romanticism* in *The Complete Works of Théophile Gautier*, trans. and ed. F. C. DeSumichrast (New York, 1910), VIII (pt. 2), 16.

[8] Ibid., VIII (pt. 2), 49f.

[9] Cited in Robert Baldick, *The Life and Times of Frédérick Lemaître* (London, 1959), p. 50.

[10] Victor Hugo, *Œuvres dramatiques complètes / œuvres critiques complètes*, ed. Francis Bouvet (Paris, 1963), p. 143.

tween *Le Bœuf enragé* and *Hamlet,* between Shakespeare and the tumbler Laurent, demands an unconscionable stretch of the imagination. Yet before we dismiss such a suggestion as frivolous, let us realize that the Shakespeare who enthralled Hugo's disciples at the Odéon and of whom the *Maître* himself wrote with such adulation was not the dramatist as we ordinarily think of him. Most of the Romantics knew only the playwright of Letourneur's somewhat revised translations, and when they encountered his characters speaking their native tongue, they were led, as Robert Baldick suggests, "into some curious errors."

> In the first place, they tended to misjudge the players, taking pretty Harriet Smithson for a great actress, when the London public knew her to be merely competent. Similarly, and this was more serious, they misjudged the plays. Ignoring the beauty of the verse, which they could not appreciate, and fastening instead on the more sensational pieces of stage business, such as Miss Smithson's grimaces, Kean's convulsions and Kemble's sardonic laughter, they saw little more in Shakespeare than a combination of picturesque costumes, crude contrasts and violent action.[11]

His remarks are surely exaggerated; but Baldick is probably right in suggesting that the unbridled, grandiloquent gestures of a Romantic *Hamlet*—like those of young Hugo and Byron—struck these spectators with greatest effect. "This was the traditional recipe for melodrama, and if violence was a novelty at the Odéon it was a commonplace on the Boulevard du [Temple]."[12]

The ingenuous heroines, nefarious suitors, intractable guardians, and unscrupulous valets—all the "grotesques" of the harlequinade—had been offering melodramatic excitement to the Boulevard's habitués for over fifty years. To

[11] *Frédérick Lemaître,* p. 50.   [12] Ibid.

the ebullient Romantics, for whom even the puerilities of Harlequin and Columbine could shadow forth both real and eternal passions, these naïve grotesques were as capable as Shakespeare's creations of admitting a peek at the sublime:

> The pantomime [as Banville wrote in his *Souvenirs*] unfolded in the midst of incidents that were clownish, extravagant, and multifarious enough to tear us away from the prosaic miseries that beset us; and, at the same time, what it expressed was truly Life, but simplified, pristine, idealized by an intense and ambulatory fancy, which swept the mind up in a whirlwind of gaiety, of admiration, of madness, of ecstasy, of nimble and potent dream.[13]

Banville's effusion probably says more about the power of his own fancy than of what actually transpired on the stage of the Funambules. Indeed, at this time, during the early years of Deburau's career, the characters of the pantomime were beginning to vibrate slightly beneath their stage masks, to detach themselves subtly from their actor-interpreters and assume imaginative dimensions of which those interpreters themselves were utterly ignorant. In 1832, Jules Janin, the *"prince des critiques,"* published a highly influential account of Deburau's life and career. "Pierrot," he wrote, "exposed as he is to all the malice of Harlequin and Columbine—do you know what Pierrot is? He is the Misanthrope of Molière."

> In the one, man succumbs to the calumny and all the ridicule of the salon; with Deburau, man is exposed to kicks and boxes on the ears. . . . [I]n these two great characters of human life, the Misanthrope and Pierrot, the social distinctions are observed. The Misanthrope flies into passions, he is peevish, he is haughty, he is frank, he is a great lord among beautiful women and

[13] P. 217.

great lords. Pierrot, on the contrary, who is the people among the people, the people with Columbine, the lewd daughter of the people—Pierrot is patient beyond measure; Pierrot is a loafer; Pierrot pokes fun under his breath; Pierrot has the air of knowing everything; Pierrot plays the fool; Pierrot possesses an admirable sang-froid; Pierrot—is the creation of Deburau.[14]

On the occasion of the celebrated mime's first meeting with George Sand, the novelist asked his opinion of Janin's *"opuscule spirituel."* "Its intention is good for me and the effect is of service to my reputation," he replied, "but all that is not the art, it's not the idea I have of it. It is not true, and the Deburau of M. Janin is not me: he has not understood me."[15]

In 1836, Philippe Laurent accepted an engagement at the Cirque Olympique, leaving Deburau to occupy the limelight of the Funambules alone. From that moment, Pierrot began to assume roles of unprecedented character and importance in the pantomime. Only once at the Funambules had the traditional dénouement of the harlequinade been travestied and overturned when, in *La Baleine* (1833), Pierrot had married Columbine at the play's pyrotechnical apotheosis. But soon after the departure of Harlequin Laurent, it was Pierrot who wedded Ninette in *Le Diable boiteux* and won the fortune and hand of the ingénue in *La Sorcière ou le Démon protecteur,* in *Pierrot errant,* and in *Les Recruteurs écossais.*[16] Recalling a pantomime of 1839 in which the conventions were similarly betrayed, Gautier wrote that "Deburau was in *Pierrot partout* a triumpher, never a Pierrot."[17]

With him [he noted elsewhere of the famous mime], the role of Pierrot was widened, enlarged. It ended by

[14] *Deburau, Histoire du Théâtre à quatre sous* (Paris, 1881), pp. 155-57.
[15] Cited in George Sand, *Histoire de ma vie* (Paris, 1856), VIII, 248.
[16] Rémy, *Deburau,* pp. 166f.   [17] Cited in ibid., p. 167.

occupying the entire piece, and, be it said with all the respect due to the memory of the most perfect actor who ever lived, by departing entirely from its origin and being denaturalized. Pierrot, under the flour and blouse of the illustrious Bohemian, assumed the airs of a master and an aplomb unsuited to his character: he gave kicks and no longer received them; Harlequin now scarcely dared touch his shoulders with his bat; Cassandre would think twice before boxing his ears. He would kiss Columbine and pass an arm around her waist like a seducer of comic opera; he made the action revolve around himself alone, and he attained such a degree of insolence and effrontery that he even beat his own good genius. . . . But the old Pierrot, the Pierrot so timid and cowardly, had been quite fearful of such audacities.[18]

The old Pierrot, yes. But not Pedrolino. In violating the traditions of his role, Deburau seems to have assumed inadvertently the mask of the old Italian *zanni*. There were, of course, important differences between the two figures: Deburau's Pierrot, unlike many of the characters of the pantomime, was virtually mute,[19] thereby observing a convention completely foreign to Pellesini's improvised art. Moreover, that art itself, during its two centuries of foreign accommodation, had evolved in the direction of the farcical harlequinade, leaving behind it all vestiges of the tautness and comic integrity of the classical *commedia.* Despite these differences, however, we can detect in the two *zanni* an almost identical spirit of impudence and authority; and for Pierrot, the absorption of this spirit created an unprecedented perversion of temperament. "Yes, Pierrot," wrote Gautier, "drunk with glory, applause, and

[18] Théophile Gautier, *Histoire de l'art dramatique en France depuis vingt-cinq ans*, V (Paris, 1859), 25.
[19] Deburau reportedly spoke no more than two words on stage: "*Achetez salade!*" in *Le Marchand de salade,* a pantomime produced at the Funambules in 1829 (Péricaud, *Le Théâtre des Funambules,* p. 92).

triumphs, boxed Ahriman with his feet and fists and gave bruises to Ormazd, without respect for the blue glow of his diadem; he treated, as one treats silly street-boys, the symbols of Zoroaster's cosmogony and the myths of the Zend-Avesta."[20] Symbols with which Pierrot had yet to reckon were biding a revenge, however; for in 1842, a play was produced at the Funambules that deflated the *zanni*'s Harlequinesque hubris and gave him, by consequence, new and sobering dimensions.

Le Marrrchand d'habits: pantomime en 4 tableaux was an experiment for Bertrand and his associates, and a rather unprofitable one. Written by the theater's administrator, Cot d'Ordan, this little piece enjoyed a run of only seven performances—a stint hardly comparable to the phenomenal success of *Le Bœuf enragé*. The nature of the play itself, and particularly its macabre ending, did not sit well with the Funambules' public; and it is possible that the actor who assumed Baptiste's *casaque* for the production—a Pierrot who at several points broke the silence of his performance with strangely high-pitched cries—disappointed the admirers of Deburau's mute and unperturbable aplomb. Whatever the reasons for their dislike, *le peuple* would have none of this disturbing little piece—not until, several years later, its final scene was revised along more conventional lines.

There was one spectator, however, who had sat rapt before the play. On the night of its opening or the evening following, Théophile Gautier had ventured hesitantly into Bertrand's *"bouge dramatique,"* jealous of his memories of the theater and a bit suspicious of the nauseous "perfume" of vaudeville that hung in the air. He had just started to leave, routed by "vague apprehensions of comic opera," when the rising of the curtain constrained him to sit and watch the performance. The drama he saw unfold was one worthy, as he declared in his wonderful review, of "Shakspeare," of the author of *Macbeth*. For *Le Marrrchand*

[20] *Histoire de l'art dramatique*, V, 25.

d'habits is the tragedy of a Faustian Pierrot's passion, crime, remorse—and death. Enamored of a duchess but too poor to pay her court, Pierrot murders an old clothes merchant and robs him of his garments—garments that gain him immediate access to the lady's society and affections. At the wedding of Pierrot and the duchess, the ghost of the peddlar rises up through the floor; he dances an infernal waltz with the groom and impales him on the very sword that the *zanni* had thrust through his back. The final curtain falls upon the clamor of the horrified wedding guests and upon the shocking death of Pierrot.

An element of the macabre had never been entirely absent from the pantomime. In England, the Signor Grimaldi, Joe's father, had played Pierrot and Pantaloon with strong overtones of melancholy and cruelty. An eccentric tomb-haunter in real life, he also is said to have invented the pantomimic "skeleton scene," a dark interlude in which the terrified Clown sometimes died of fright.[21] For Auguste Vacquerie, the very nature of pantomime seemed to invite such humorless experiments: "Pantomimes have always moved more than cheered me," the critic once told Champfleury; "I have never looked upon these mutes that come and go, speaking in gestures, without an involuntary apprehension. This silence ultimately disquiets me, like the night, which is the silence of sleep."[22]

To Charles Baudelaire, the slow grace and emaciated pallor of Baptiste invested Pierrot with slightly ominous qualities, making of him a figure as "pale as the moon, mysterious as silence, supple and mute as the serpent, thin and long as a gibbet."[23] Certainly the violent and some-

[21] Richard Findlater, ed., *Memoirs of Joseph Grimaldi* (New York, 1968), pp. 295, 82; see also Findlater, *Grimaldi: King of Clowns*, p. 37. An *Arlequin squelette* appeared in Deburau's repertoire, according to Rémy, *Clowns*, p. 55.

[22] Cited in Champfleury, *Souvenirs des Funambules* (Paris, 1859), p. 269.

[23] "De l'Essence du rire et généralement du comique dans les arts plastiques," *Le Portefeuille*, July 8, 1855; reprinted in Charles Baudelaire, *Œuvres complètes* (Paris, 1968), p. 376.

times sinister cruelty that Deburau brought to his role had
at least part of its source in the brooding rancor of his own
temperament. On a spring day in 1836, he had shown to
what lengths this rancor could carry him, when, while
strolling with his young wife and children, he had warmed
to anger under a street-boy's taunts and brought his heavy
cane down on the young man's skull, killing him with a
single blow. The court had acquitted the fashionable
mime, but his act seemed to darken the already deepening
shadows of Pierrot's billowy tunic. Although his biog-
rapher protests that, on stage, Deburau was "neither gay
nor sinister," he concedes that

> the face and gestures of Jean-Gaspard showed, each
> time a scene gave him occasion, that he was reckoning
> with a world that he made laugh at will, he whom the
> world had never made laugh. His liberated rancor
> burst out on stage especially when, under his floured
> mask, he expressed his whole personality. Only in
> this way could he reveal those parts of himself that he
> kept contained. The bottle whose label "Laudanum"
> he smilingly revealed after Cassandre had drained it,
> the back of the razor he passed over the old man's
> neck, were toys which he could not be allowed to take
> seriously and thus put to the test his patience, his re-
> serve, his sang-froid.

"When he powdered his face," Rémy concludes, "his nature, in fact, took the upper hand. He stood then at the
measure of his life—bitter, vindictive, and unhappy."[24]

Though *Marrrchand d'habits* has often been associated
with Deburau,[25] it is unlikely that the mime ever appeared
in the piece. As "deplorable" as the "commercial spirit" of
Cot d'Ordan and Bertrand was, neither man "could have
suggested that Deburau play a character who embodied an

[24] *Deburau,* pp. 143, 144.
[25] Both Marcel Carné's film *Les Enfants du Paradis* (1945) and Sacha
Guitry's play *Deburau* (1918) suggest that *Marrrchand d'habits* was characteristic of Deburau's art.

all too personal truth."[26] For several years, the mime's health had been failing; in 1840, the managers of the Funambules contracted with a young actor, Charles-Dominique Legrand, to double Baptiste in the roles of Pierrot. Legrand, called Paul Legrand, had been engaged at the theater in 1839 to play the part of Léandre; and when the mime pulled on Pierrot's blouse, he seemed to bring to the mask the sensitivity of an *amoureux*. An actor whose talents were dramatic rather than acrobatic, Legrand in fact resuscitated the spirit of Harlequin *larmoyant* under the white flour and vestments. And it was this mime, insists Rémy, who played the Pierrot of *Marrrchand d'habits*.

The dramatic pathos of Legrand's *jeu*, the undispelled shadows of Baptiste's cruelty and daring, the mélange of macabre and melodramatic knockabout—all these elements needed only the fine, ironic intelligence of Gautier to be drawn into a coherent and arresting synthesis. And the poet accomplished this synthesis in the last paragraph of his review:

> This *parade* conceals a myth that is very profound, perfectly whole, and highly moral, a myth that need only be formulated in Sanskrit to give rise to a swarm of commentaries. Pierrot, walking the street in his white blouse, his white trousers, his floured face, preoccupied with vague desires—is he not the symbol of the human heart still white and innocent, tormented by infinite aspirations toward the higher spheres? The hilt of the saber that seems to offer itself to Pierrot's hand, beckoning him by the perfidious twinkling of its yellow blade—is it not a striking emblem of the power of opportunity on already tempted and vacillating minds? The ease with which the blade enters the body of its victim shows how effortless it is to commit a crime, and how a single action can cost us our immortal soul. When Pierrot took the sword, he had no other

[26] Rémy, *Deburau*, p. 174.

idea than of pulling a little prank! The specter of the
old clothes man rising from the cellar shows that crime
cannot be hidden; and when Pierrot knocks the ghost
of the plaintive victim back into the hole with blows
from his club—is not the author most ingeniously
suggesting that, although precautions can sometimes
delay a crime's discovery, the day of vengeance always arrives? The specter himself symbolizes remorse
in the most dramatic and terrible fashion. That simple
phrase—Ol' clo's!—which throws such a profound
terror into Pierrot's heart, is a true stroke of genius
and is worth, at least, the famous "He had so much
blood!" of Macbeth. . . . Pierrot, like Don Juan, pro-
vokes Heaven's wrath; he has reached the highest
stage of callousness; so, when he is about to marry the
princess, the avenging specter reappears, and this
time Pierrot cannot force him back into the trap that
has vomited him up. . . . That hellish waltz, when the
point of the saber sticking through the peddlar's body
enters Pierrot's chest, piercing him through and
through, signifies that men are punished by the very
crime they commit, and that the point of the knife
with which the murderer stabs his victim penetrates
still more deeply into his own heart. The surprise of
the parents at the sight of this marvel clearly shows
the danger for duchesses to marry pierrots without
finding out anything about them, and this calls upon
the spectators to be more circumspect in their social re-
lations. Do you know many tragedies that could
undergo a like analysis?[27]

These playful questions mark an important point of
transition in the history of Pierrot's theater, the point at
which the pantomime and its masks clearly become the
symbolic properties of the Romantic imagination. The earlier remarks of Nodier and Janin are suggestive but some-

[27] *Souvenirs de théâtre*, pp. 65-67.

what fuzzy; those of Gautier, on the other hand, ingeniously give form and metaphorical significance to the whole
pantomimic world. And it is apparent that Gautier wrote
his review with this end in mind. Though the article
nowhere betrays him, Gautier in fact missed the first scene
of the performance. The sketchy résumé of this scene in
the original script probably gives a more accurate index to
the playwright's "intention" than the poet's Olympian
prose:

> Cassandre is served luncheon by Pierrot, who tricks
> him out of several morsels from time to time, much to
> the annoyance of the avaricious old man. Cassandre
> leaves after having locked up the remnants of his
> meal.
>
> The Duchess enters, followed by her groom: she
> asks to speak to Cassandre.
>
> Pierrot tries to pay court to her because he finds her
> very pretty. She makes fun of him.
>
> Cassandre returns. The Duchess gives him a gar-
> ment to mend and then leaves.
>
> Pierrot complains of the manner in which he is
> treated by his master, who feeds him very badly and
> never pays him.
>
> Cassandre answers his protests by a kick in the rear
> which sends him out the door. A comic scuffle.[28]

So skillfully did Gautier transmute such worn puerilities
that, several years later, Champfleury described the review
as if it had preceded and inspired the pantomime.[29] And
when, in 1896, the play was revived by Catulle Mendès for
the mime Séverin, the theater programs announced that
the piece was "*d'après un feuilleton de Théophile Gautier.*"[30]

The more subtle implications of Gautier's little analysis
were not to be uncovered until the 1880's. But there was

[28] Cited in Péricaud, *Le Théâtre des Funambules*, p. 251.
[29] Champfleury, *Souvenirs*, p. 9.
[30] Cited in Séverin, *L'Homme Blanc*, p. 193n.

one aspect of its subject that seemed to be thrown into immediate relief, an aspect not so much discovered as finally given clear articulation: the implicit, ironic sympathy of the literary public with Pierrot. Of course not all of the public (and here we are speaking only of *les romantiques*) shared this sympathy. Hugo, for example, is reported to have been altogether unmoved by Pierrot's dumb tribulations. After once spending an evening at the Funambules, the poet was asked his opinion of the entertainment by the enthusiastic Banville, to whom the *Maître* replied: "In hearing the orchestra, I would like to have been deaf; in watching the play, I would like to have been blind."[31] But for Banville himself, as well as for quite a few others of his circle, the clown's white figure seemed to describe gestures of a touching intimacy. To the spectators of the eighteenth century, Pierrot had been, indeed, a figure inspiring as much admiration as derision. But the admiration had been respect for his sporadic wit; his romantic *malheur* was, at least to the cultivated public, the mark of a common and clownish naïveté. It was ridiculous, and Pierrot himself was a fool, an *original*. Among the literati of post-Revolutionary France, however, it was commonly *les classiques* alone who entertained such prejudices; the Romantics' sympathies, either real or affected, were with the naïvely passionate People. And *le peuple*, as Janin had insisted early in the century, was Pierrot.

Gautier himself suggested the direction in which these sympathies were tending when he wrote, in 1847, that Pierrot is "the ancient slave, the modern proletarian, the pariah, the passive and disinherited being. . . ."[32] That the Romantics, suffering from a Byronic *mal du siècle*, could see themselves as much disinherited as Pierrot or *le peuple* is not at all surprising; and for Banville and Charles Baudelaire, the life of the *saltimbanques*—the Gilles and Pierrots of the streets—soon became a symbol for that of

[31] Cited in Péricaud, *Le Théâtre des Funambules*, p. 314.
[32] *Histoire de l'art dramatique*, V, 24.

the artist. Banville chose not to inspect too narrowly the vulgar glamor of these scruffy showmen,[33] but Baudelaire saw clearly the squalid and ironic pathos of their lonely existence. The figure of a decrepit performer disappearing into his tent became that of "the old poet without friends, without family, without children, degraded by his misery and the ingratitude of the public, into whose booth the forgetful world no longer wants to enter."[34]

Images of a similar, if not more graphic, poignancy were given relief in the canvases of Daumier, Baudelaire's friend of twenty years. A Pierrot sitting hunched with fatigue in the wings of a showman's tent, or hurrying through a narrow street with unsmiling deliberation, or standing before the bored specimens of a sideshow, his emaciated face contorted by a shout at the crowd—these figures mirrored the democratic passion of a self-dramatizing artist, one who possessed "the heart of Don Quixote in the body of Sancho."[35]

Neither Banville nor Baudelaire nor Daumier, however, was intent upon discovering any impressions of the artist's face in the performer's mask itself.[36] Like Gavarni, whose satirical *Ecole des Pierrots* (1851) presents a gallery of Parisian fools in the *zanni*'s vestments, they were concerned with the life beneath the mask, with the passions of the *saltimbanques* or the vacuity of the maskers. And the little *pierrotades* that Banville and Gautier—and Flaubert—composed around the middle of the century had no less modest pretentions. Banville wrote his *Folies-Nouvelles* (1854) to

[33] See, e.g., Théodore de Banville, *Les Pauvres Saltimbanques* (Paris, 1853), p. 13.

[34] Charles Baudelaire, "Le Vieux Saltimbanque," in *Revue Fantaisiste*, November 1, 1861; reprinted in *Petits Poëmes en prose*, ed. Robert Kopp (Paris, 1969), p. 40.

[35] Jean Adhémar, *Honoré Daumier* (Paris, 1954), p. 64.

[36] Yet Banville writes of Deburau in his *Souvenirs* as if the mime's Pierrot, "strolling through the universe with a detachment of the artist and poet" (p. 218), has strong affinities with the naïve, insouciant artist of the Romantic ideal. Cf. also "Ancien Pierrot" (1857) in the *Œuvres de Théodore de Banville* (Paris, [1889-1892?]), III, 136.

commemorate Paul Legrand's debut at that theater, the re-
furbished and rechristened Folies-Concertantes; and the
Pierrot of this playlet, like Legrand's most typical inspira-
tions, is simply the mischievous, good-hearted child of the
People. Gautier's *Pierrot posthume* (1847), commissioned by
the director of the Vaudeville, has the same unpretentious
appeal: its Pierrot is a creature of traditional *bêtise* and
naïveté. As for Flaubert's youthful *Pierrot au Sérail* (*c*. 1840),
there the *zanni* is a gourmand of prodigious and fatal appetites. Having attained to a sultanate during a sojourn in
Arabia, Pierrot is quickly jaded by the extra-gustative
pleasures of his seraglio. He turns a cold shoulder to the
fervid overtures of the Sultana and his Columbine, and sits
down to the board to eat and drink *"sans discernement."*
When his belly bursts under the strain, he ascends to a
Mohammedan paradise, where the trees are festooned
with sausages and capons, and where young ladies in red
tights sit at small tables with circus strongmen, drinking
Strasbourgian bocks.

The Pierrots of these little productions are convenient
masks beneath which their creators indulge in an occasional carnival gesture, in a *"je m'en moque."* The clown's
naïveté and insouciance permit each of these artists the
cartoonish expression of his democratic fervor, his artistic
innocence, his unregulated impudence. Here, in other
words, Pierrot's traditional traits of personality offer a
casual vehicle for high spirits. The performer himself does
not stare out through the flour—but neither does he sub-
due the *zanni*'s character to his artist's will.

In a curious novella by Henri Rivière, however, we see
the performer and the mask, a willful artist and his
whitefaced creation, dissolving at last into a single figure,
one that has already, in 1860, an odor of decadence hanging about the folds of its blouse. Obviously influenced by
Gautier's account of *Marrrchand d'habits* and by memories
of Deburau's misanthropic *jeu*, Rivière's story describes the
career of a young mime, Charles Servieux, who conceives

of Pierrot as the "fallen angel." Having accompanied the narrator of his history to the Funambules one evening, Servieux is struck by the audacity and sinister gaiety of Baptiste's performance; and, as he later explains to his friend, "there began to take shape slowly in my brain a genius of evil, grandiose and melancholic, of an irresistible seductiveness, cynical one instant and clownish the next—in order to raise himself up still higher after having fallen."[37] Servieux picks out his Columbine from a company of traveling *saltimbanques* and takes her to Paris, where they are soon performing before an enthralled public at the Funambules. The young soubrette plays more true to type than Servieux would have wished, however, for she abandons her pallid lover—now importunate both on and off the stage—for the company's Harlequin. When the jealous Pierrot can no longer brook her unfaithfulness, he decapitates his rival in full view of his audience during one of his own little macabre productions.

Despite the influence that the white mask seems to exercise over the hero of this novella, Pierrot has yet to achieve symbolic autonomy; it is largely the personality of the hero himself that imbues the *zanni* with his disturbingly psychopathic character. Before Servieux sees Deburau perform at the Funambules, it is revealed that he has spent several years at sea, where the despair of a near-drowning has deranged his senses. A second incident, in which he helped apprehend and denounce a would-be murderer, has compounded derangement with guilt; and when he at last appears before his public in the dress of Pierrot, he brings to the role, as he admits in a moment of lucidity, "the genius of madness."[38]

At the time of the publication of this tale, Deburau was no longer familiar nor the macabre welcome to the popular audiences of pantomime. The great mime had died in 1846, leaving behind him two students of his art at the Funam-

[37] Henri Rivière, *Pierrot,* in *Pierrot / Caïn* (Paris, 1860), p. 27.
[38] Ibid., p. 69.

bules, his own son, Jean-Charles, and Paul Legrand. The young Charles (1829-1873) made his debut as Pierrot the year after his father's death in *Les Trois Planètes, ou la Vie d'une rose, grande pantomime arlequinade, féerie, dialoguée dans le genre anglais*. His performance in this piece immediately recalled the agility and suppleness of his father's *zanni*, and it was as a Pierrot in the naïve tradition of Jean-Gaspard that Charles enjoyed eight years of success at the Funambules.

Legrand, as we have already noted, took the pantomime in an altogether different direction.[39] The remarks of his contemporaries and his published repertory of plays both suggest his talent for shading the farcical with the dramatic. Although he was the actor who, almost alone, sustained the Parisian pantomimic tradition until the close of the century (and whose "uneasy gaiety" animated more than one Decadent Pierrot), he was sometimes accused by his critics of straining the popular conventions of his role. Gautier deplored his occasional abandonment of the white smock and trousers to dress his *zanni* in costumes of character—a practice that owed more to *le grand Deburau* than the poet suspected.[40] Banville, though he praised *"la finesse du jeu et la pensée"* of the mime,[41] seemed not altogether pleased with Legrand's easy susceptibility to tears.[42] But it was probably Legrand's pathetic sensitivity that had encouraged Gautier to analyze the subtle strain of malaise underlying Pierrot's Romantic character; and it was certainly as a result of that analysis that the Funambules soon found itself entertaining its first experiments in the "literary" and self-consciously macabre.

[39] Félix Larcher, in his "Préface" to the *Pantomimes de Paul Legrand* (Paris, 1887), published in collaboration with his brother Eugène, observed that "Gaspard Deburau left two heirs: his son, Charles, who conserved his agility, and Paul Legrand, who pushed the pantomime towards drama and sentiment" (p. xvi).

[40] See Gautier, *Histoire de l'art dramatique*, IV, 318; cf. Péricaud, *Le Théâtre des Funambules*, pp. 490ff.

[41] "Commentaire" to *Les Folies-Nouvelles*, in *Œuvres*, II, 326.

[42] See Larcher, *Pantomimes de Paul Legrand*, p. xvi.

Champfleury, under the influence of Gautier's "Shakspeare aux Funambules" and the Swedenborgian exhortations of an obscure Christian pamphlet, composed *Pierrot, valet de la Mort* for Legrand in 1846. Here Pierrot, symbolizing *"l'homme spirituel,"* dies after receiving a wound from Harlequin and descends, in the third scene of the panto, to the "cabinet" of Death. Having had a rather unprosperous day, Death allows Pierrot back into the land of the living on condition that he send Harlequin and Polichinelle to take his place. But after a few pierrotish attempts to make good his bargain, the *zanni* is smitten by conscience. He breaks his contract, thereby disembarrassing himself of mortality and attaining (as the little pamphlet behind the play had predicted) "his higher destinies": a place among the witnesses at the nuptials of Harlequin and Columbine. One month later, Champfleury followed this piece with *Pierrot pendu*, in which Pierrot is pursued to the gallows, just as the murderer of *Marrrchand d'habits* is pursued to the netherworld, by the voice of a man he has robbed, crying, "Pierrot, you shall hang!" Champfleury's third production for the Funambules was, inevitably, a pantomime *réaliste*—but even in this latter playlet he was loath to relinquish the macabre. In *Pierrot Marquis* (1847), Pierrot is a miller and Polichinelle a miser whose humps conceal his fortune (plausibility is thus conferred upon the pallor of the one and the misshapenness of the other), and in a grisly *scène de la vie populaire*, Pierrot assists an unscrupulous doctor in removing the hunchback's assets. These last two pantomimes found great favor with what Gautier called *"les notabilités de l'art."*[43] But there is little reason to think that the People themselves shared the *littérateurs'* enthusiasm. The evidence suggests, in fact, that until the last two decades of the century, all attempts to sustain a "philosophical" or graveyard tone in the pantomimes of the popular theater met with a lukewarm reception at best. Péricaud observes that *Marrrchand d'habits* was later re-

[43] *Histoire de l'art dramatique*, V, 34.

vived by Legrand as *Mort et Remords* "with great success" at the Folies-Nouvelles;[44] but he neglects to mention that the revisions made by the mime and Charles Bridault included a final scene of atonement, in which Pierrot brings the peddlar back to life by pulling the sword from his chest, then is forgiven by the "genius of Pardon" and united with the duchess.[45] It was not until 1896 that the original ending of this play elicited the applause of *le peuple.*[46]

Legrand left the Funambules in 1853, and two years later Charles Deburau joined the company of the Délassements-Comiques. With the loss of these two mimes, the Théâtre des Funambules lapsed into a jejune mediocrity. An actor called Kalpestri was hired to replace Legrand soon after his departure; but this mime, according to Péricaud, was "the beginning of the end of Pierrots."[47] Lumpish, gross, and lewd (he is said to have once licked his fingers with relish after dibbling them in the watery chocolate in a chamberpot), Kalpestri apparently interpreted the *zanni* as a simpleminded Gilles. In 1855, the engagement of the Englishman Forrest, a Pierrot-Clown, took the Funambules' public back to the unillustrious days before Baptiste, when they had applauded "the superabundance of gestures, of leaps," of his predecessors.

Not only did the center of French pantomime shift from the Funambules in the second half of the century, but it also shifted from Paris itself.[48] Charles Deburau, who often performed outside the capital after 1860, was engaged at the Alcazar in Marseille about the year 1867; and there a young spectator and aspirant to the white *casaque* was immediately enamored of his elegant art. Four or five years

[44] *Le Théâtre des Funambules,* p. 257.
[45] See L.-Henry Lecomte, *Les Folies-Nouvelles* (Paris, 1909), pp. 65ff.
[46] See Séverin, *L'Homme Blanc,* pp. 196ff.
[47] *Le Théâtre des Funambules,* p. 399.
[48] For the development of the pantomime outside Paris, see the section devoted to Charles Deburau in Paul Hugounet, *Mimes et Pierrots* (Paris, 1889), and also Séverin, *L'Homme Blanc,* pp. 36ff.

later, the admirer became the student of the mime when
Charles accepted the directorship of a theater at Bordeaux.
This student, Louis Rouffe, later founded the Marseille
"school" of pantomime.

Rouffe (1849-1885) seems to have broken even more
dramatically than his predecessors with the traditions of
the harlequinade, for one of his own *élèves* reports that he

> transported Pierrot . . . into all worlds, into all times.
> He permitted him to escape more often [than before]
> the fictive realm whose sole inhabitants were Harle-
> quin, Léandre, Columbine, Pulcinello [*sic*], Cas-
> sandre, and their kind. He made him live in all
> milieus, from the top to the bottom of the lad-
> der. . . . [H]e could change his vestments, just as a
> red-, yellow-, or black-skinned person can dress as a
> European. . . .
> My master lent such humanity to this character that,
> from his time, the artists and public of Marseille no
> longer called him Pierrot but *l'Homme Blanc*. [49]

The author of these remarks, Séverin (1863-1930), was one
of the last great Pierrots of the century. After playing many
years in the south of France, he was drawn to Paris by the
rumored popularity of *L'Enfant prodigue* (1890), a pantomime by Michel Carré *fils* in which both M. and Mme.
Pierrot weep over their wayward son. There he presented,
at the Eldorado, a piece of his own composition called
Pauvre Pierrot, ou Après le bal (1891), the tragic, flourfaced
hero of which was among the first of the luckless *zanni* to
enjoy a popular success.

Behind the reception of these plays was a "movement"
begun in the 1880's that was to see an important revival of
literary interest in Parisian pantomime. The movement (if
such it can be called) had its "modest precursor" in a
young man barely twenty-one years old, a stagestruck
Romantic, intoxicated by the "unbridled passions" of

[49] Séverin, *L'Homme Blanc*, p. 47.

Musset and Byron: Paul Margueritte. In the summer of 1881, Paul and his brother Victor transformed an atelier at Valvins into a little theater. This first of their *tréteaux* was little more than a few crude boards supported by trestles; its curtain was a bedsheet; its scenery, a few folding-screens. But for producer and occasional poet, the Théâtre de Valvins had Margueritte's uncle, Stéphane Mallarmé; for its Columbine, Mallarmé's daughter Geneviève; and for Pierrot, the young Paul himself. In the preface to his slim volume of pantomimes, the future novelist describes how he came to be enamored of the white flour and blouse and to write the curious piece that carried Pierrot into his next pantomimic avatar:

> Why and how did it come to me, this idea [of being a mime]? In playing the *Pierrot héritier* of [Paul] Arène[50] and the *Pierrot posthume* of Gautier. The indulgent wonder of Mallarmé before the pallid personage did the rest. He had seen Deburau *fils,* Paul Legrand. His recollections excited my emulation. Pierrot, henceforth, inhabited me.
>
> . . . .
>
> The reading of a tragic story by Commandant [Henri] Rivière, as well as two lines by Gautier—
>
> *L'histoire du Pierrot qui chatouilla sa femme*
> *Et lui fit de la sorte, en riant, rendre l'âme.*[51]
> [The tale of Pierrot, who tickled his wife
> And thus made her, with laughter, give up her life.]
>
> —induced my satanic, ultra-Romantic, and yet very modern conception: a subtle, neurotic, cruel, and ingenuous Pierrot, uniting in himself all contrasts, a ver-

[50] First produced at the Odéon, October 2, 1865. In this *"première œuvre d'un jeune homme,"* Pierrot, after being momentarily intoxicated by inherited wealth, is restored to his old role of *"le doux rêveur, le maigre artiste"* with the disappearance of the fortune—and is awarded the hand of his beloved, Columbine, with its recovery.

[51] *Pierrot posthume,* scene 14, in Théophile Gautier, *Théâtre: Mystère, comédies et ballets* (Paris, 1872), p. 202 (slightly misquoted).

itable psychical Proteus, a bit sadistic, willingly
drunken and perfectly villainous.

It is thus with *Pierrot assassin de sa femme*—a tragic
nightmare in the manner of Hoffmann or Edgar [Al-
lan] Poe, in which Pierrot makes his wife die from
laughter by tickling the soles of her feet—that I was
one of the precursors of the pantomime's revival, and
in the year 1881, I could almost say: the precursor.[52]

Pierrot assassin de sa femme won the teasingly oblique
praises of Mallarmé;[53] and although the Théâtre de Valvins
was to last only one summer more, Margueritte followed
this play with still other pantomimes for his protean *zanni*.
At the time of these "timid essays" (as Margueritte called
his pantomimic productions) Pierrots began to multiply in
legion upon the Parisian stages. And the *zanni* proved to be
not only protean but androgynous as well. In 1883, at the
Trocadéro, Sarah Bernhardt pulled on the white vestments
for the *Pierrot assassin* of Jean Richepin, and ten years later,
at the Menus-Plaisirs, Mlle. Peppa Invernizzi created *Le
Docteur blanc* of Catulle Mendès. Félicia Mallet had brought
yet another woman's sensitivity to the role as the Pierrot
fils of *L'Enfant prodigue,* though her tearful hero had little
else in common with the murderous *zanni* of Mendès and
the *César des gueux.*

It was also during these years that Pierrots of a disturbing *nervosisme* began to invade the salons, the music-halls,
and circus. Edmond de Goncourt, in a journal entry for
1887, records an evening spent at Alphonse Daudet's,
where Margueritte animated his sadistic clown to a disquieting musical accompaniment by Paul Vidal.[54] In one of

[52] Preface to Paul Margueritte, ed., *Nos Tréteaux: Charades de Victor Margueritte; Pantomimes de Paul Margueritte* (Paris, 1910), pp. 15f. My translation of *Pierrot assassin de sa femme* appears in the Fall 1978 number of
the *Denver Quarterly.*
[53] See Paul Margueritte, *Le Printemps tourmenté* (Paris, 1925), pp. 26f,
and Stéphane Mallarmé, *Œuvres complètes* (Paris, 1945), p. 310.
[54] Edmond and Jules de Goncourt, *Journal,* ed. Robert Ricatte, XIV
(Monaco, 1956), 195.

his *Croquis parisiens*, J.-K. Huysmans describes the "lugubrious farce" and "sinister buffoonery" of a troupe of gymnastic Pierrots from the *"pays du spleen"*: the Hanlon-Lees.[55] From an evening spent at the Folies-Bergère, where these black-frocked Pierrots were performing in 1879, Huysmans and his friend Léon Hennique took away an enthusiastic admiration for their art, "so genuine in its dispassionate madness, so ferociously comic in its excess."[56] Two years later, the literary fruit of these two friends' evening appeared as *Pierrot sceptique*, a pantomimic scenario illustrated by another *ami de* Pierrot, Jules Chéret. The apotheosis of Decadent Pierrots, their black-suited *zanni* (in mourning for his wife) murders his tailor, assaults a beautiful display-window mannequin, and burns down his rooms in a fit of pique. As the supernumeraries perish in the apocalyptic flames, Pierrot makes off to a dressmaker's shop, from which he abducts its dummy. He tucks his cardboard lady under one arm and, ignoring the obstreperous clanging of a firebell, disappears at a brisk trot up the street.

It may appear from our discussion up to this point that as Pierrot approached the *fin du siècle* he was ineluctably infected with its malaise. But even several years after the publication of *Pierrot sceptique*, Banville could introduce an engagingly sensitive *zanni* into a little comedy in verse, *Le Baiser* (1887). Indeed, the aging poet was somewhat disturbed by the turn that Pierrot had taken in these waning years of the century: "If Pierrot is tragic," he asked Paul Margueritte, "what advantage has he over Thyestes?"[57] Legrand himself, whose performance in *Marrrchand d'habits* had been more than a little responsible for this turn, was nonplussed by the sadistic hero of *Pierrot assassin de sa femme*. "The macabre, the terrible," wrote Margueritte after interviewing the mime, "Paul Legrand only tolerated

[55] In *Œuvres complètes de J.-K. Huysmans*, VIII (Paris, 1929), 21ff.
[56] Ibid., VIII, 23.
[57] Cited in Margueritte, *Printemps tourmenté*, p. 40.

it as accidental, quickly borne away by fantasy and dream."[58]

Owing perhaps in part to the realization that Pierrot was beginning to lose all traces of his old identity—that his character was starting to dissipate, as it had done in the previous century—the Cercle Funambulesque was founded in 1888 by Margueritte, Félix Larcher, and Raoul de Najac.[59] The published aims of the society were to revive the classical pantomime *sautante;* to restore to the stage the farces of the Foire, the comedies of the Théâtre-Italien, and the *parades* of the Boulevard; to encourage the writing of plays in the manner of *commedia dell'arte;* and to provide the composers and musicians of the modern pantomime with a theater, an orchestra, and an audience for their work. At the Cercle's inaugural evening, Legrand performed in a prologue in the dress of Pierrot, after which two modern pantomimes alternated with a scene from Regnard's *Théâtre Italien* and a *parade* entitled *Léandre Ambassadeur.* The Cercle Funambulesque enjoyed only a brief existence, however. As Rémy points out, "each of the promoters . . . had personal projects, projects that were disparate, that were even opposed to one another"; and "even though they were to succeed in gathering together about a hundred and fifty enthusiasts of a forsaken art for fourteen presentations, in the course of which sixty-five unpublished playlets of thirty-nine authors were performed, three of the first founders withdrew because of divergence of opinion and never was the pantomime [*sautante*] closer to disappearing."[60]

From the pantomime, Pierrot passed into the graphic arts at the end of the century, but his image on the *affiches* of Jules Chéret and in the illustrations of Adolphe Willette

[58] Ibid., p. 36.
[59] See Raoul de Najac, *Souvenirs d'un Mime* (Paris, 1909), pp. 17-20. For a detailed account of the activities of the Cercle Funambulesque, see also Hugounet, *Mimes et Pierrots,* pp. 237ff, and especially Félix Larcher and Paul Hugounet, *Les Soirées Funambulesques* (Paris, [1890-1892]).
[60] *Deburau,* p. 212.

evinced a deliberate vagueness and tenuity of outline. No longer reserving his inky habit for funereal occasions, he appeared as often in black trousers and tails as in his traditional white blouse. According to Chéret, neither color, neither black nor white, was inherently appropriate to the *zanni*, since "Pierrot is for me," he explained, "a ONE, and you know all that can be classified behind that indefinite pronoun":

ONE: It is YOU, it is WE, it is THEY.

The famishing and gormandizing Pierrot has had his day: for a new age, a new avatar. His incarnation in the nineteenth century must be modernistic and must leave to the Italian tradition and to the Funambules the puppet-Pierrot that amused the contemporaries of Deburau.

. . . .

This modern type, thrown into a life too great for his atavistically contracted brain, a little brat lost in the immensity of an enormous pair of breeches: Pierrot must represent him for me. He will add to this figure the mysteriousness of his character, which disquiets the spectator with its expressionless white face (*sa seule face blanche*). The make-up that covers him will be the hermetic curtain behind which one will try to see the man. On his familiar face of wrinkles, themselves distracting the scrutinizer, only the black features of his eyebrows, fluttering over the sockets of the piercing eyes, and the mouth, a blood-red line like the edge of a Moroccan executioner's yataghan, will twitch in a grimace.[61]

The effeminately sensitive Pierrot of Willette's *histoires sans paroles* is more sympathetic than Chéret's anemic creation, but he is often as bloodless a figure. Now courting his muse (and a *cocotte*) by candlelight, now dancing drunkenly before three indulgent and weakly smiling

[61] Cited in Hugounet, *Mimes et Pierrots*, pp. 222-23.

moons, the *zanni* of Willette "is no longer the jocular
scoundrel of the funambulesque tradition: he has become a
poet, an artist; but precisely because of his two talents,
which never lend themselves to serious professions, the
unfortunate Pierrot remains and will remain a malingerer,
a whitefaced simpleton, a simple whiteface."[62] In the car-
toons and drawings that appeared in Willette's review *Le
Pierrot* (1888-1889, 1891), as well as in his other productions, the *zanni* "is not of Italian origin . . . he does not
have all the vices . . . he has only those of his race . . . he
is French."[63] But his character is notably lacking in French
clarté. "It was, above all, Pierrot's costume that seduced
me," Willette once told Adolphe Brisson; "I needed a character vague enough to construe, by the play of his figure,
all of the human passions . . .; the white blouse, the black
skullcap, and the foamy collarette of Pierrot place him outside the common man and yet close to him: they are the
vestments of dream."[64]

Pierrot's unblemished figure invited seduction by most
of his nineteenth-century interpreters. "Because Pierrot is
white . . . like the melancholy wanness of the moon," observed Catulle Mendès, "we have, little by little, made of
him an elegiac guitarist who gives aubades to the closed
windows of a beloved, a poet in love with dreams. . . . We
are mistaken; deceived by the same lunar snow, we have
transformed the popular Pierrot, the true Pierrot, into the
poetic, subtle, and even perverse Gilles of Wateau [*sic*]."[65]
After being rediscovered in the first half of the century,
Watteau's *fêtes galantes* offered thresholds of imaginative
escape to poets condemned, like Gautier, to live in an "atmosphere of hydrogen gas and the treacle of modern
civilization."[66] The radiant landscapes of these paintings,

[62] Adolphe Willette, *Feu Pierrot, 1857-19?* (Paris, 1919), p. 128.
[63] Ibid.
[64] In Adolphe Brisson, *Nos Humoristes* (Paris, 1900), pp. 152-54.
[65] *L'Art au théâtre*, II (Paris, 1897), 240.
[66] Cited in Jacques-Henry Bornecque, *Lumières sur les* Fêtes Galantes *de
Paul Verlaine* (Paris, 1959), p. 26.

washed by a paradisiacal luminescence, seemed imbued
with the *"luxe, calme et volupté"* of Baudelaire's ideal domain; and the Gilles-Pierrot loitering in their verdant gar-
dens endowed the *zanni* of pantomime and farce with a
hauntingly poignant *mystère*. Standing with his arms
naïvely at his sides, his mouth trembling in a vague,
slightly guarded, yet innocent smile, the Gilles of Watteau's portrait was, in some measure, artlessly responsible
for the sensitivity of Banville's, the delicate melancholy of
Willette's Pierrots.

But if the heart of a sensitive singer of aubades lies hidden beneath the blouse of Watteau's creation, the heart of
darker passions—of, say, *Pierrot assassin*—certainly does
not. Yet the white frock of Margueritte's hero and of
Richepin's *zanni* appears to have been no less appropriate
a costume for their psychopathic *jeu*. To Margueritte, it
seemed perplexing that Pierrot's snowy *casaque* should
have been for so long a symbol of comic innocence:

> My Pierrot is tragic [he once told Paul Hugounet].
> Tragic because he is afraid: he is fright [itself], crime,
> anguish. . . . And indeed, why has this idea not oc-
> curred to anyone else? Why has no one been struck by
> the enigmatic movement of Pierrot, gliding without a
> sound in the fullness of his vestments, which assume
> in moments of stillness the rigidity of stone; and espe-
> cially by that which is the most disquieting of all—his
> head of a plaster statue? Willette, Huysmans favor the
> black dress, but no, no, it must be the white.[67]

The attraction that Pierrot had for Margueritte, as well as
for the Romantic *pierrotistes* who preceded and followed
him, lay not, however, in the magic whiteness of his
clothes alone. Nor did it lie wholly in the purity, complexity, or intensity of emotion embodied by his popular
pantomimic predecessors: by Pierrot-Baptiste, Pierrot-
Legrand, Pierrot-Hanlon-Lees. Certainly, the passions

[67] Cited in Hugounet, *Mimes et Pierrots*, p. 228.

that now belonged to the mask could offer an exhilarating
sense of liberation or indulgence to whoever might pull on
his blouse; and writers of as different a temperament as
Banville and Huysmans could thereby escape their "prosaic miseries" by a flight into ecstatic dream or a debauch
in sadistic excess. But it is obvious that, as a character of
passion, Pierrot is hardly the compeer of a Manfred or a
Faust or an Axel. Granted, not many of the *zanni*'s admirers could essay the grandeur of these creations; but once
we have conceded this, we are no closer to understanding
the power that put *pauvre* Pierrot in their company. His votaries themselves seemed ignorant of the source of this
power, yet a casual remark by Paul Margueritte hints of at
least one explanation for the *zanni*'s allure. "It is a curious
thing," he wrote of *Pierrot assassin de sa femme*, "that the
spectators who, with a religious silence, welcomed the
sadistic cruelty of Pierrot, thought that *Hernani* was a farce.
The grandiloquence of the verse, the exaggeration of the
sentiments, the bombast of certain scenes inspired them
with an irresistible gaiety."[68] Margueritte was writing of an
audience in the 1880's, more than fifty years after the first
performance of Hugo's masterpiece; and we may justifi-
ably suspect that this public, entranced by the sadism, at
once ludicrous and disturbing, of Pierrot's thinly moti-
vated cruelty, had begun to feel the Nordic breath of Kier-
kegaard and Schopenhauer—that it was beginning to succumb at last to the pervasive *mal du siècle*. But its reception
of *Hernani* suggests even more; what it suggests most
graphically is the embarrassing vulnerability of the Romantic imagination. A temperament that sent Hugo "flying,
flying over abysses, flying up into the eternal gases" (as
T. E. Hulme later complains) often warmed the wax on his
wings to a dangerously high degree; and for the spectators
at Valvins, his enthusiasm seemed stridently immature.
There is, of course, an obvious and genuine measure of

[68] Margueritte, *Printemps tourmenté*, pp. 50-51.

adolescent bravura in the Romantic pose, and usually it is .
only by a voluntary relaxation of our tight grip on the prosaic that we can empathize with Manfred, Harold, or Cain.
But Pierrot demands no such relaxation. He is, by long
history, a fool—a fool, moreover, of adolescent *bêtise*. And
when he is shaken by "Shakspearean" transports, he
trembles less nakedly behind his flour than we might suppose. He is, in other words, a creature who provides his
own irony of manner, who can admit of the most unlikely
excesses of passion because his transports are an occasion
for laughter. For a young Romantic such as Margueritte,
who "wanted too much to live a magnificent novel to be
able to write it,"[69] he is an ideal mask, revealing emotion
that would seem unconscionably extravagant were it not
for the white flour on his cheek and the billowy blouse on
his back. And the ironic duplicity of the figure suggests yet
another source of the clown's fascination: the ambiguity of
his Romantic identity. Unlike Harlequin, whose impassive
black *demi-loup* seems to conceal the unfathomable motives
of his caprice, or Polichinelle, whose hooked nose and chin
perpetually stretch his lips into a disingenuous smile, Pierrot seems to present a guileless and candid face to the
world, a face only faintly obscured by its thin layer of
powder. But from the first performance of *Marrrchand
d'habits*, the candor of his white mask became as questionable as the purity of his conscience. Jules Chéret could
speak with perfect justice of the clown's mysterious inscrutability.
   The allure of his white vestments, the expanse and extravagance of his passions, the ironic duplicity of his
mask—all of these attractions had been in the Pierrots
funambulesques of Baptiste and Legrand quite early in the
century. Yet it is important for us to realize that, for some
of his interpreters, the pantomimic world of the clown had
changed considerably by 1880. It is important because the

[69] Ibid., p. 19.

aspect that this world assumed greatly influenced the
course of the *zanni*'s development in the next century. Already we have noted the taste for violence and cruelty in
the *fin-de-siècle* Pierrot, a taste that awaits further discussion to be fully accounted for. But behind the ferocity of
the clown's demeanor, we can detect a certain sense of ir-
resolution: we suspect a *crise d'identité* under the inscrutable flour. To confirm these suspicions, as well as to suggest
what manner of crisis Pierrot is suffering, we have only to
look in detail at several little pieces that appeared around
the close of the century. The first is the sequence of *"rondels bergamasques"* published in 1884 by Albert Giraud, the
poet *"hors du siècle."* The second is a pantomime by Margueritte; and the third, a sonnet by Paul Verlaine.

On first reading the fifty little rondels in Giraud's *Pierrot
lunaire,* we may be hard pressed to discover their fascination for a composer like Schoenberg. The exquisite
Willette-Pierrot of these verses—a poet who offers up his
heart as a host for the *"cruelle Eucharistie"*; an artist for
whom "Beautiful verses are great crosses / On which red
Poets bleed"—seems hardly worth the intellectual expend-
iture of the notoriously revolutionary song cycle. Yet a
closer look at the landscape of these poems does much to
explain the almost mystical attraction that Giraud's texts
had for the composer. Like all the worlds inhabited by the
commedia masks, that of *Pierrot lunaire* is a teasingly fanciful
one; but the bizarreness of Giraud's fancy has few prece-
dents in pantomime. Here a wine that only the eyes can
drink spills out of the moon to submerge silent horizons;
great black butterflies swarm in the skies, their wings blot-
ting out the sun's disk; the sun itself oozes red blood, and
the phthisic moon oozes white. With profound abstraction, Pierrot drags a cello's bow across Cassandre's belly
and bores a smoking-hole into his bald pate; he makes up
his face with moonlight, then vainly, furiously, brushes its
spots from his jacket. The *zanni* is suffering from a malady
familiar to Pierrots of his age:

Pierrot de Bergame s'ennuie:
Il renonce aux charmes du vol;
Son étrange gaîté de fol
Comme un oiseau blanc s'est enfuie.[70]

What is unique about the splenetic *ennui* of Pierrot *lunaire* is that it manifests itself all about him. In these little poems we have passed into an interior world. The columbine that the clown seeks to gather *"le long du Léthé"* radiates a tremulously mystical light because it is more than woman or flower: it is an incandescent spunk of vague desire glowing feebly in Pierrot's brain. At times, this world can take on a frightening complexion: the moon, "a white saber / On a somber cushion of watered silk," threatens to come whistling down on the sinful *zanni*'s neck; the amorous allure of the gallows, Pierrot's destined mistress, "is like a nail / That drunkenness drives into his head." But the fright that sends the *zanni* quaking to his knees is as ephemeral as the moonlight over his pallid face. The edges of this landscape have been magically softened and blurred. In the manner of Verlaine's *Fêtes Galantes*, the tints have been applied by Shakespeare (a Gallic Shakespeare) and Watteau (a Romantic Watteau).

But to turn from these poems to Margueritte's *La Peur* is to lay down our Claude Glass. In this little pantomime (on which Paul's brother Victor collaborated), the confused color and atmospheric richness of Giraud's poems have disappeared. And neither the *"très mince"* Harlequin, the *"Crispins laids,"* nor the gormandizing Gilles disfigures the landscape of Pierrot's crepuscular *cerveau*. He appears alone, a single resident of an ordinary room. But not quite ordinary. It is a room filled with vague and invisible presences, presences none the less palpable for their invisibility. Pierrot moves about in it, drawing a taper from corner to corner, much as a sleeper stumbles through his dream.

[70] "Pierrot of Bergamo is bored: / He renounces the pleasures of thievery; / His strange, mad gaiety / Has flown away like a white bird": "Spleen," in Albert Giraud, *Pierrot lunaire* (Paris, 1884), p. 29.

He is groping among the white bones of his own skull, and finding little in the shadows to allay an unsettling and fearful sense of strangeness. Let us follow him into this tenebrous domain.

FEAR

Pierrot pushes open the door, so prudently, slowly, that it appears to open by itself; but from behind it, the uneasy and fearful powdered face steals forth and investigates.

—There's no one lying in ambush behind the doorleaf?

—No one.

And Pierrot, as flat as a flounder, slips into the room and very quickly shuts the door, so that no one—or nothing—can enter.

—A turn of the key!

—Crick-crack!

—Now throw the bolt: clack!

—Ha ha!

He rubs his hands, winks one eye, then becomes motionless, like a long, mocking ray of moonlight in the half-shadows.

—Quick! light the candles!

Gropingly, and seized again by a groundless dread, which sends him colliding in fright against a piece of furniture, he walks with stumbling and shuddering step to the mantelpiece. A spectral shape, he steps back, pointing at an intruder, his pale counterpart: a vague reflection in the mirror.

—Imbecile! Afraid of your own image!

He lights two tapers, sees himself more clearly.

—But . . . yes. It's me . . . Me? . . . Me . . .

Strangeness and mystery.

—Me! Pierrot? . . . Me! my hands, my body, my face, my mouth, my eyes. Quite pale, quite gaunt, a funereal face: the cavities of the eyesockets, the strained laugh: rigid, immobile, dead. Mbrr.

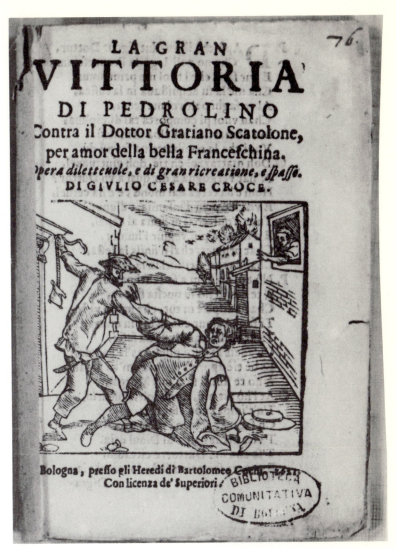

1. Pedrolino Scuffles with the Doctor. Woodcut on title-page of Giulio Cesare Croce, *La Gran Vittoria di Pedrolino* (Bologna, 1621).

2. Pierrot. Illustration #17 in Luigi Riccoboni, *Histoire du théâtre italien*, II (Paris, 1731).

3. Antoine Watteau. *Italian Comedians* (c. 1719). Oil on canvas, 63.8 × 76.2 cm. National Gallery of Art, Washington, D.C. Samuel H. Kress Collection.

4. Cupids Disguised as Characters of the Italian Comedy. Frontispiece to Vol. VI of Evaristo Gherardi, *Le Théâtre Italien* (Paris, 1741).

5. Harlequin and Pierrot among the Amazons. Frontispiece to *L'Isle des Amazones* in Lesage and Dorneval, *Le Théâtre de la Foire*, III (Paris, 1737).

Le Rémouleur d'Amour.

6. Pierrot, Cupid's Tool-sharpener. Frontispiece to *Le Rémouleur d'Amour* in Lesage and Dorneval, *Le Théâtre de la Foire*, V (Paris, 1724).

Ah! papa, papa, c'est pour nous?

7. Harlequin *Larmoyant* Comes Home to His Children. Illustration for *Le Bon Ménage* in J.-P. Claris de Florian, *Œuvres complètes* (Paris, 1803), III.

GILLE LE NIAIS

8. Gille le Niais. Seventeenth-century engraving in the Cabinet des Estampes, Bibliothèque Nationale, Paris.

9. Antoine Watteau. *Gilles and Four Other Characters of the Commedia dell'Arte* (*c.* 1717). Oil on canvas, 184 × 149 cm. Museum of the Louvre, Paris.

10. Clowns (figures in upper row and single figure at left of bottom row are Grimaldi; two remaining figures in lower row are James Kirby). Illustration in a toy theater sheet published by I. K. Green, London, 1812.

11. Baptiste Deburau. Painting by Pezous (collection, Georges Wague), originally in the Café des Pierrots, Place du Châtelet (today, Dréher), Paris.

12. Charles Deburau. Photograph reproduced in Séverin, *L'Homme Blanc* (Paris, 1929), p. 64.

PAUL LEGRAND
dans Pierrot quaker

13. Paul Legrand. Lithograph in Charles Geoffroy, *Nouvelle Galerie des artistes dramatiques vivants* (Paris, 1855), II.

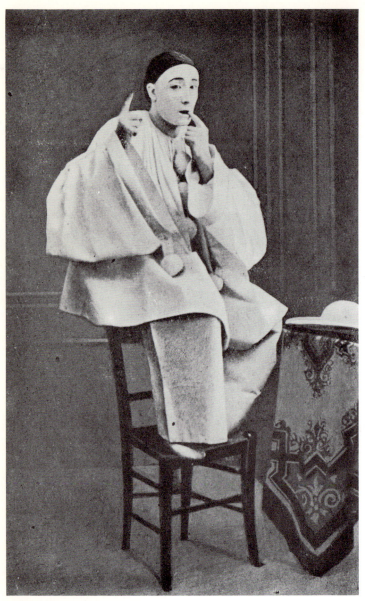

14. Louis Rouffe. Photograph reproduced in Séverin, *L'Homme Blanc* (Paris, 1929), p. 65.

15. Séverin. Photograph reproduced in Séverin, *L'Homme Blanc* (Paris, 1929), p. 176.

16. Jean-Louis Barrault as Deburau in *Marrrchand d'Habits*. Frame from Marcel Carné's film *Children of Paradise* (1945).

17. Honoré Daumier. *The Strong Man* (c. 1865). Oil on wood panel, 26.7 × 34.9 cm. The Phillips Collection, Washington, D.C.

18. Jules Chéret. Pierrot Abducts a Mannequin (1881). Illustration for J.-K. Huysmans and Léon Hennique, *Pierrot sceptique* (Paris, 1881).

19. Jules Chéret. Pierrot in the Hands of the Law (1886). Dust jacket design for Jules Moinaux, *Le Bureau du Commissaire* (Paris, 1886).

20. Willette as Pierrot. Photograph by Carpin for *La Revue illustrée*, June 15, 1898.

21. Adolphe Willette. *Au Clair de la Lune* (*c.* 1882). Cartoon-sketch for *Le Chat noir*, reproduced in Adolphe Willette, *Pauvre Pierrot* (Paris, [1885]).

22. Adolphe Willette. *Pierrot's Widow* (1886). After a reproduction in Adolphe Willette, *Feu Pierrot* (Paris, 1919).

23. Henri Rousseau. *A Carnival Night* (1886). Oil on canvas, 116 × 89 cm. Philadelphia Museum of Art, Philadelphia. Collection, Louis E. Stern.

24. James Ensor. *Pierrot and Skeleton in Yellow Robe.* 1893. Oil on panel, 38 × 48 cm. Collection, Mr. and Mrs. Jeff de Lange.

25. Aubrey Beardsley. *The Death of Pierrot* (1896). Sketch for *The Savoy*, No. 6.

26. Aubrey Beardsley. *The Pierrot of the Minute* (1897). Frontispiece to Ernest Dowson, *The Pierrot of the Minute* (London, 1897).

27. Pablo Picasso. *Pierrot*. 1918. Oil on canvas, 92.7 × 73 cm. Collection, The Museum of Modern Art, New York. Sam A. Lewisohn Bequest.

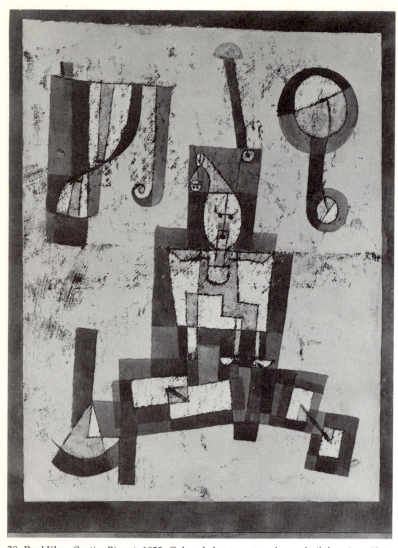

28. Paul Klee. *Captive Pierrot*. 1923. Colored sheet, watercolor and oil drawing, 40 × 30 cm. Detroit Institute of Arts, Detroit. Robert H. Tannahill Bequest.

29. Juan Gris. *Pierrot with Book*. 1924. Oil on canvas, 65 × 50 cm. Private Collection, England.

30. Georges Rouault. *Pierrot* (1926). Oil on cardboard, 100 × 72.5 cm. Stedelijk Museum, Amsterdam.

31. Jacques Lipchitz. *Pierrot Escapes* (1927). Bronze, 49 × 31 × 16 cm. Kunsthaus Zürich, Switzerland.

32. Pablo Picasso. *Pierrot and Harlequin*. 1970. Pencil on paper, 65 × 50 cm. Galerie Louise Leiris, Paris.

He looks at the candles. They flicker strangely.
Why? A puff of air. Where is it coming from? With his
mouth, he imitates the mysterious wind skimming
over the ground, crying under doors, the wind that
comes in invisible but alive. A being, a presence: it is
here, and the flames waver, disquietingly.

—Ah yes, disquietingly. What an odd and unfamil-
iar aspect one's rooms take on. What's hiding under
the veil of this coat-stand? Nothing. Over there, that
hanging shape, in the little nook of shadow: what is it?
Ah! what is it? A body, you might say.

—Arm yourself with the tongs—no! with the club. If
it's a trick, some robber or killer on the lookout? Knock
him on the head!

Some old clothes fall down: an empty rag.

—Nothing, obviously, but who knows whether
someone's not behind the door there, spying on me,
waiting for me to go to sleep to break the lock and
then . . . Sssh! Go up to it, on your tiptoes. Now your
ear, close up to the wood. Yes . . . yes . . . someone's
there, behind the door. And if I open it: ah! two
crooked hands seize me around the throat! . . . He's
breathing, yes, breathing there behind the door
. . . No, it's me, it's the rattling in my throat, it's my
heart I hear . . .

He goes back to the middle of the room and slowly
turns about, his index finger below his eye and a
shriveled smile on his face.

—Through the keyhole, an eye gazes into the room
and you suddenly feel yourself run through with an
inexplicable anguish. It's the gaze that has so
treacherously affected you. Stop it up! Shut it out!
Don't let its evil spell in!

With trembling hands, flat against the door, then
with a twisted piece of paper stuffed into the keyhole,
Pierrot closes up the chink as one would put out an
eye.

—Is that enough? No, barricade it with this chest, this table, the chair! There. But then there's the window. He could put up a ladder. Rung by rung, in his bare feet, *he* is coming up! *He* mounts! His face appears at the windowpane, his fist knocks it out, the latch gives way, *he* throws himself . . .

—On my knees! don't kill me! mercy! have pity!

His eyes bulging with horror, his mouth gaping, Pierrot stands up:

—But since there's nothing, no one . . . Nothing but me, me and my shivers. Doesn't matter: make sure the window's tightly closed; shut the curtains. It's reassuring not to see anything.

No sooner said than done. He notices that the hearth's fireplate is raised. A grimace of suspicion distorts his features.

—I don't like that. He could come down through this flue, tumble down like a big spider crouched on the ground—(he imitates him)—then his body straightens, his arms shoot out, his head pokes up, his legs stretch out—(he swells and grows accordingly)—and then he . . .

Pierrot catches sight of himself with terrifying swiftness in the mirror.

—Ah! that's how he would be! wild-looking, horrible! What a sight! Hide this image! I don't want anymore . . . I don't want to see myself anymore. I frighten myself.

He tears down one of the bedcurtains, veils the mirror, lowers the fireplate, then slowly wipes away the sweat that trickles from his moist forehead.

—What's that noise? Zzz! zzz! A strange vibration. Ah! that big fly: it's repulsive, not like other flies. Hear how it buzzes: zzz, zzz.

He gives chase to it; with the cunning of an apache, he ends up by trapping it. It gets away from him, he knocks it down with a blow from a duster; and with a great, horrified gesture, his arms raised, with a foot that shrinks back, scraping the floor, he crushes it.

A profound silence; a long moment of uneasiness.

—That odor? Is it an odor? Yes, something smells of death, of decay. Is it this piece of furniture? (He sniffs at it.) My hands? No. Rather these flowers, these flowers in the vase. Yes, that's what it is: these dead flowers in stagnant water. Throw them out: it's as simple as that. But wouldn't you have to open the door?

He does not dare.

—Open the window?

He does not dare.

—Throw them in the hearth and raise up the fire-plate?

He does not dare.

—Oh well, go to sleep. Sleep is calming, refreshing. You don't think then. But yes! you do! You think, dream, start, fret: you have nightmare crouching on your chest. Doesn't matter: there are gentle, angelic kinds of sleep, the sleep of a child. Try to sleep.

He moves near the bed.

—Oh! oh! what a suspicion: first it was very small, then large, then a man, this apprehension. At the moment when you have one knee on the bed and your other foot leaves the ground—what if you feel a hand, ah! a hand stealing out from under the bed to seize this foot, ah! and drag it down? Foolishness! There's no one under the bed. There's never anyone under the bed. Anyway, you can see for yourself, with the candle. And to be more careful, arm yourself.

He takes up a kitchenknife, tests its point on his finger and the edge on the sole of his foot. A good knife.

Go to it!

On his knees, then flat on his belly, he investigates carefully with his eyes, sculls his arms beneath the

bed, turns the light here and there, and probes with
his knife.
   —I knew it: nobody. Get to bed.
He leans his knee on the bed but is hesitant about
raising his foot from the floor:
   —Hup!
He does not dare.
   —What are you afraid of? Hup!
He does not dare.
   —Count to three. One, two . . .
He hesitates to say *three*.
   —Look, this is getting ridiculous!
   —Three! Get up there now.
He raises his foot; an invisible hand seizes it in
mid-air and holds it. Pierrot, in the imaginary grip,
shaking his leg imprisoned by terror, turns up a
paralyzed face, the mask of counterfeit death. He
kicks desperately, tears at the hand that deludes him,
and, with the convulsive quaking of a cornered animal, takes refuge in a corner of the room. Curled up
there by a spasm and a hoarse sob, he rolls himself
into a ball, retracting his limbs and head like a turtle.
   —These horrors are truly unbearable. Some way to
escape them, oh! some way!
And his hands implore a celestial clemency.
   —Sleep: he knows quite well he won't sleep. To escape, to escape from himself at all cost! In drunkenness then?
   To open a cupboard with a mad gesture, to break
the neck of a bottle on the table and drink, to drink it
down in one breath: there! the work of a minute. Yes:
better. He catches his breath. He shakes the wrinkles
of the clutching anguish out of his ample vestments.
He discharges the hostile appearances. He chases
away the black shapes. He sniggers, he triumphs, he
spits upon fear.

But *She* or *It* is there.
—Someone's spoken!
Pierrot's lips move slightly.
—It's heard!
A puff of wind has passed by:
—The mystery!
Someone has entered on tiptoes:
—*It* is walking, *It* is looking, *It* is passing!
It is the specter of Fear, livid Fear, its eyes wild, its arms trembling, its knees knocking.
—Ah! ah! She's there! She rises up, she opens her arms, she seizes me!
Pierrot utters a piercing cry of hysteria; the spirit (*aura*) passes over him like the wind of a hurricane: he beats the air with his white wings and falls, overwhelmed by the Invisible One.[71]

In this play, Pierrot has become more than a charismatic personage among the pantomimic types or—as in Rivière's *nouvelle*—a mask giving resonance to the personality beneath it. He has become pure symbolic projection ("[Pierrot] is fright, crime, anguish," Margueritte had remarked to Hugounet). The catalyst for this transformation, as for most of Pierrot's Romantic metamorphoses, was Gautier's little *feuilleton* in the *Revue de Paris*. By interpreting *Marrrchand d'habits* as allegory, the poet had been the first to perceive the internal landscape of Pierrot's heart and conscience, the first, indeed, to suggest that the grimaces of his insouciant mask limned deeper, more susceptible passions. Gautier had described the pantomimic world as a clear bubble of consciousness, through which we see the *zanni*'s desire and remorse assume shape all around him. In *La Peur*, such a world is consciously recreated, one in which Pierrot's dark passions turn in upon themselves.

We are now in a position to understand Verlaine's "Pier-

71 In *Nos Tréteaux*, pp. 151ff (undated).

rot" (1868, published 1882), of whose disturbing portrait it
has been said, quite erroneously, that "neither precedent
can be found nor sequel imagined."[72]

> Ce n'est plus le rêveur lunaire du vieil air
> Qui riait aux aïeux dans les dessus de porte;
> Sa gaîté, comme sa chandelle, hélas! est morte,
> Et son spectre aujourd'hui nous hante, mince et clair.
>
> Et voici que parmi l'effroi d'un long éclair
> Sa pâle blouse a l'air, au vent froid qui l'emporte,
> D'un linceul, et sa bouche est béante, de sorte
> Qu'il semble hurler sous les morsures du ver.
>
> Avec le bruit d'un vol d'oiseaux de nuit qui passe,
> Ses manches blanches font vaguement par l'espace
> Des signes fous auxquels personne ne répond.
>
> Ses yeux sont deux grands trous où rampe du phosphore
> Et la farine rend plus effroyable encore
> Sa face exsangue au nez pointu de moribond.[73]

The insidious picture of Dorian Gray seems hardly more
eloquent. The gay Pierrot of "Pantomime," the Pierrot
vaguely glimpsed among the *Fêtes Galantes* (1869), who
*"Vide un flacon sans plus attendre, / Et, pratique, entame un
pâté,"*[74] has been denuded of his gentle mystery; "what

---

[72] A. G. Lehmann, "Pierrot and *fin de siècle*," in Ian Fletcher, ed., *Romantic Mythologies* (London, 1967), p. 216.

[73] "This is no longer the lunar dreamer of the old song / Who laughed at his ancestors at the top of the door; / His gaiety, like his candle, alas! is dead, / And his specter haunts us today, thin and luminous. // And so it is that amidst the terror of a long flash of lightning, / His pale blouse has the aspect, in the cold wind that carries it away, / Of a windingsheet, and his mouth is gaping, so / That he seems to scream under the gnawings of the worm. // With the sound of a passing flock of night birds, / His white sleeves make vaguely through space / Mad signs to which no one responds. // His eyes are two great holes where phosphorus creeps, / And his flour renders more frightful still / His bloodless face with its pinched nose of one near death."

[74] "Empties a bottle without hesitation / And (an experienced gourmand) cuts into a meat pie."

remains in a timeless, meaningless jumble of fears and re-
grets is the . . . terror of the poet's sense of drift."[75] There
is no denying the candor, the nakedness of the pose:
seared by the cold brilliance of a lightning bolt, the spe-
cious insouciance of both clown and poet has fallen away
with the mask. What has been revealed is an image of the
cringing soul behind it—an image at once pitiful in its
helplessness, frightening in its livid reproach.

Agenbite of inwit. Conscience. Yet here's a spot.

The Pierrot of Verlaine, of Margueritte, of Giraud,
shares the malaise of *Ulysses'* jejune Jesuit. The symptoms
are much the same. But the worm that worries its way
through the shroud of Verlaine's *moribond* is like the one
that feeds upon Blake's crimson Rose: invisible. Unlike the
lucid young Stephen, Pierrot can offer no cause for his
malady. His vague "jumble of fears and regrets" is as
amorphous as his protean character, as the undistinguished whiteness of his blouse. What Pierrot seems to be
suffering most acutely in these little pieces is the anguish-
ing presence of the worm itself. It is interesting to compare, in this connection, the haunted creature of Verlaine's
early sonnet with the Pierrot he describes in "Motif de pantomime":

Pierrot is their friend [i.e., the friend of Harlequin and
Columbine] in a vaguely subservient capacity. He,
too, is happy, without envy, eating everything, drinking everything, cowardly but prudent, libidinous but
outwardly continent. Ah! the pleasures that are his:
the farces that he sometimes makes them endure,
amended by a kick of a pointed toe or a slap in the face
with beringed fingers. It makes no difference: he has

[75] Lehmann, "Pierrot and *fin de siècle*," p. 222.

had his fun, laughed, smiled. And then he has not a
care. At times the others must still use guile to win a
victory over existence. He lives in their wake like a fish
in water. No remorse, no regret for anything, for anything.[76]

The poet's last remark takes on especial poignancy appear-
ing, as it does, in the *Mémoires d'un veuf* (1886). It is the
same poignancy that will suffuse the landscape of *Le Grand
Meaulnes* (1913), a book through which Pierrot stumbles
with frenzied abstraction, trembling before his expulsion
from a charmed domain. The wistful tone of "Motif de
pantomime" announces that imminent expulsion; the pallid wraith of "Pierrot" betokens the outcast's image.

How and why an outcast? The invisible worm that
gnaws at Pierrot's white breast is consciousness being conscious of itself. The hero of Rivière's macabre novella pres-
ages the whole course of Pierrot's Romantic career when
he calls the *zanni* an *"ange déchu."* From the Pedrolino-like
creation of Baptiste, exhausting (like Gilles) the possibilities of the moment, courting (like Clown) the favors of
the impossible, and living "in the wake" of his pantomimic
amis: from this Ariel of the harlequinade to the chastened
zanni of *La Peur* is a plummet indeed. In the terms of our
earlier analogy, Pierrot has journeyed from Rome to Elsinore; but he is finding the rarefied air of the castle disturbingly unsalubrious. Only rarely, as in the *Pierrot Narcisse*
(1887) of Giraud, can he endure stoically the privations of
the Hamletic mind:

> *Ecoute* [he tells the love-struck Eliane]: *il
>   est deux races
> Vieilles comme l'azur et comme la clarté:
> L'une éprise de force et de réalité,
> Belle, luxuriante, héroïque, ravie*

[76] Paul Verlaine, *Œuvres en prose complètes* (Paris, 1972), p. 124. For a full
discussion of Verlaine's use of the figure, see my article, "Verlaine's Pierrots," to appear in Vol. XX (1979-1980) of *Romance Notes*.

> *Par la banalité splendide de la vie.*
> *Et cette race-là c'est celle des heureux!*
> *L'autre est la race des rêveurs, des songe-creux,*
> *Et de ceux qui, nés sous le signe de Saturne,*
> *Ont un lever d'étoile en leur cœur taciturne!*
> *C'est la race farouche et douce des railleurs*
> *Qui traînent par le monde un désir d'être ailleurs,*
> *Et que tue à jamais la chimérique envie*
> *De vivre à pleine bouche et d'observer la vie.*
> *C'est la race de ceux dont les rêves blasés*
> *Se meurent du regret d'être réalisés!*
> *L'une est pleine de joie, et l'autre de rancune,*
> *L'une vient du soleil, et l'autre de la lune;*
> *Et l'on fait mieux d'unir l'antilope au requin*
> *Que les fils de Pierrot aux filles d'Arlequin!*[77]

Aside from a few delusive years of Harlequinesque spontaneity, Pierrot has always been, as Gautier observed, *"profondément égoïste."*[78] Hardly had he taken his first bow at the Ancien Théâtre-Italien, we may recall, before he was mooning over blasted hopes and trembling (fumbling) on the brink of suicide. But his enviable good sense of those years, his sense of *"la banalité splendide de la vie,"* always brought him around to the solidness of things (*"donnons-nous un coup de couteau dans le ventre. Quelque niais! je per-*

---

[77] "Listen: there are two races, / As old as the azure and limpidity [of the sky]: / The one enamored of activity and reality, / Handsome, lusty, heroic, entranced / By the splendid banality of life. / And this race is that of the happy ones. / The other is the race of dreamers, of visionaries, / And of those who, born under Saturn's sign, / Have a rising star [of fate] in their taciturn hearts. / That is the sullen and mild race of jokers / Who trail through the world a longing to be elsewhere / And who are forever being killed by the chimerical desire / Of living greedily and of observing life. / It is the race of those whose wearied dreams / Die of regret once they are realized. / The one is full of joy, the other of rancor; / The one comes from the sun, the other from the moon; / And you would be doing better to unite the antelope with the shark / Than the sons of Pierrot with the daughters of Harlequin": in Albert Giraud, *Héros et Pierrots* (Paris, 1898), p. 223.

[78] *Histoire de l'art dramatique*, IV, 320.

drois tout mon sang"). Now, at the dawn of *la Belle Epoque,*
he seems to have lost that comic judgment. And in abandoning his prudence and clear-headedness for the sub-
limer passions of the mind, he has opened dark portals for
both himself and his maskers: *"Sa gaîté, comme sa chandelle,
hélas! est morte."* He will not recover that gaiety until he
discovers the splendid banality of the world once again
and, having "conceived his voyaging to be / An up and
down between two elements, / A fluctuating between sun
and moon," is reborn in the imagination of Wallace Stevens.

But before we can assist at the labors of that birth, we
must try to understand why a Hamletic self-consciousness
discomfits Pierrot and why such a self-consciousness discomfits his maskers. The amorphous shapes that move
through his skull need, for us, clearer definition—
definition that they rarely assume under the flour of occasional interpreters. Neither Margueritte, for whom Pierrot
effected a *"dédoublement de personnalité,"* [79] nor Giraud, who
wrote *"en Pierrot costumé,"* [80] describes more than vaguely
discernible shadows passing behind the eyes of the mask.
Only a *zanni vivant,* a poet who in fact thought he *lived* the
life of the clown, [81] might admit a clear glimpse of his
saturnine mind; and only one poet of the *fin du siècle* per-
mits us a prolonged and illuminating scrutiny. So with the
opening of the *Complaintes* of Jules Laforgue, we invade
Pierrot's often-protracted silence to hear the guarded, anguished mutterings of his brain.

[79] *Printemps tourmenté,* p. 24.
[80] "Cristal de Bohême," in *Pierrot lunaire,* p. 99.
[81] "Laforgue, almost as much as Adolphe Willette, considered that he
lived the part of Pierrot": Lehmann, "Pierrot and *fin de siècle*," p. 216.

V

Pierrot *Fumiste:*
Jules Laforgue

Quand me rendras-tu, porte-lyre,
Guérisseur de l'esprit blessé,
Neige adorable du passé,
Face de Lune, blanc messire,
O Pierrot! le ressort du rire?
 —Albert Giraud,
 "Supplique"

The appearance of Laforgue's *Complaintes* in 1885 announced a dramatic new role for both its poet and Pierrot.
In this volume the clown discovered his first "modern"
voice and Laforgue an attitude that nearly a whole generation of writers adopted as their own. In all important re-
spects, the voice and the attitude are one—and so aptly
and inextricably one that they seem to create, throughout
the subsequent work of the poet, a manner that is pecul-
iarly "Laforguean."
 Yet the author of the *Complaintes* had undergone no radi-
cal conversion of temperament or philosophy before setting to work on this eccentric little volume. If anything,
these verses simply play variations upon the themes that
had occupied Laforgue since he had earnestly devoted
himself to poetry. Throughout the collection, we find the
same splenetic pessimism and cosmic *ennui* that had been
expressed in much of his earlier verse—in the poem un-
happily entitled "Médiocrité," for example:

Dans l'Infini criblé d'éternelles splendeurs,
Perdu comme un atome, inconnu, solitaire,
Pour quelque jours comptés, un bloc appelé Terre
Vole avec sa vermine aux vastes profondeurs.

Ses fils, blêmes, fiévreux, sous le fouet des labeurs,
Marchent, insoucieux de l'immense mystère,
Et quand ils voient passer un des leurs qu'on enterre,
Saluent, et ne sont pas hérissés de stupeurs.

La plupart vit et meurt sans soupçonner l'histoire
Du globe, sa misère en l'éternelle gloire,
Sa future agonie au soleil moribond.

Vertiges d'univers, cieux à jamais en fête!
Rien, ils n'auront rien su. Combien même s'en vont
Sans avoir seulement visité leur planète. [1]

This adolescent despair was apparently characteristic of the novelistic hero to whom Laforgue was struggling to give voice during his early years; indeed, the notes that survive from the latter project suggest that there was more than authorial kinship between the young Romantic writer and his fictive, cerebral celibate:

It is an autobiography of my organism, of my thought [Laforgue wrote of his novel, *Un Raté*], transferred to . . . a painter-thinker, a pessimistic and macabre Chenavard. A failure of genius. And a virgin, who dreams of four great frescoes: the epic of humanity,

[1] "In the Infinite riddled with eternal splendors, / Lost like an atom, unknown, solitary, / For a number of given days, a block called Earth / Plunges with its vermin into the vast depths. // Its children, wan, feverish, under the whip of labors, / March on, heedless of the immense mystery; / And when they see one of their own passing on to the grave, / They salute him, not at all abashed. // The greater part of them live and die without suspicion of the history / Of the globe, its misery in the eternal glory, / Its final agony in the moribund sun. // Inebriates of the universe, those forever at play! / Nothing: they will have known nothing. How many, indeed, are leaving / Without even having visited their planet?"

the macabre dance of the last days of the planet, *the three stages of Illusion.* An unhappy life, poor, loveless, splenetic; an incurable sadness in the face of life and its nastiness; analyzes himself in order to find symptoms of madness and finally commits suicide.[2]

The reference to *"the three stages of Illusion"* is an echo from the philosophical reading that was absorbing Laforgue during the formative years of his aesthetic, namely, Eduard von Hartmann's *Die Philosophie des Unbewussten.* Itself concerned with a cosmos laid bare by the intellect of Schopenhauer (whose subjective idealism had early stained the young poet's imagination) *The Philosophy of the Unconscious* had nevertheless been written to elevate Reason from the "false and subordinate" position that the pessimist of Frankfurt had accorded it. By the *Unbewussten* or "Unconscious" of his treatise's title, Hartmann was referring not exclusively to the hitherto unexplored substratum of the human mind, but more generally to "a divine understanding, a primordial being," what may be called in Hegelian terms a universal Absolute. This Absolute, according to Hartmann, "works its way toward consciousness in the minds of individuals"; and "the blessed state—wholeness of the Unconscious as both Will and Reason—is reserved for a time before the Fall and after a final Revelation." Warren Ramsey, from whose discussion of Hartmann I have been quoting, describes the nature of this apocalyptic Revelation in the following terms:

> At the Fall the two elements of the Unconscious became separated, Reason was cut off from Will. The latter rules the world as we know it. In order to encourage men to perpetuate themselves, to obstruct progress toward nirvana, Will fosters three illusions: (a) that happiness is actually attainable at a given stage

---

[2] Jules Laforgue, *Mélanges posthumes* (Paris, 1919), p. 9. This collection will be cited hereafter as *Mp* in the text.

of the world's development, is within the grasp of the individual during his earthly life; (b) that men will be happy in a hereafter; (c) that the race will some day be happy in this world. The first of these illusions was cherished by the ancients and is entertained by every man during his childhood; the second was characteristic of the Middle Ages and is typical of the young man; the third is peculiar to modern times and the individual grown old. And the world will die just as the individual dies. Reason, gradually dispelling the three illusions one after another, will so far enlighten mankind, bring it to such a degree of consciousness, that all men will simultaneously thwart the activity of Will, deny the will to live, and attain nirvana by a kind of race suicide.[3]

It is with thoughts such as these that the twenty-year-old Laforgue sketched out his first book of poetry, *Le Sanglot de la terre*, "*un volume de vers que j'appelle philosophiques*":

. . . five parts—*Lamma Sabachtani, Moments of Anguish, Poems of Death, Poems of Spleen, Moments of Resignation*: the story, the journal of a Parisian of 1880, who suffers, doubts, and comes to face nothingness; and all this in a Parisian setting and . . . in an artistic, probing, modern language. . . .

This book will be entitled: The Sobbing of the Earth. Part one: the sobbing of thought, of the brain, of the consciousness of the earth. A second volume in which I shall concentrate all the misery, all the filth of the planet in the innocence of the heavens, the Bacchanalia of history, the splendors of Asia, the barrel organs of Paris, the carnival of the Olympians, the Morgue, the Dupuytren Museum, the hospital, love, alcohol, spleen, massacres, the Thebaïds, madness, the Salpêtrière Asylum. (*Mp*, 8)

[3] *Jules Laforgue and the Ironic Inheritance* (New York, 1953), pp. 83-84.

Much as Baudelaire before him, the young poet was intent upon discovering correspondences between the spleen of his soul and the world passing outside the window of a tiny room on the Rue Berthollet. But if it is a Baudelairean Paris that we are prepared to find crowding the pages of this posthumously published volume, we have been deceived. Most of the poems that survive from *Le Sanglot de la terre* seem mere echoes of voices breaking the austere silence in which they were composed: "Two years of solitude in the libraries," as Laforgue wrote, "without love, without friends, in fear of death. Nights in meditation in an atmosphere of Sinai" (*Mp*, 7). They are the exhalations of a "tragic Buddhist" who watches a "chlorotic" moon ascend, night after night, over a world hurtling towards *Néant*.

Laforgue had begun composing *Le Sanglot de la terre* in 1880, and both this volume and his novel were still occupying him when he accepted a position as reader for the Empress Augusta of Germany late in 1881. Visions of moribund suns smoldering fitfully in the blackness of empty space, of the dead poet's nerves and marrow scattered throughout the illimitable expanse of the universe, of "the last days, when Illusion will be dead, the cities deserted, when man, head shaved, covered with ashes, will await the void"[4]—such visions must have seemed as uncharacteristic of the shy, self-effacing young reader from Paris as lapses in his impeccable tact and courtesy. But at least one observer, a French journalist who made Laforgue's acquaintance during his early weeks in Berlin, guessed that the visitor's unperturbable demeanor masked a self-conscious, introspective, and almost painfully anguished personality. The journalist, Théodore Lindenlaub, later wrote that he had "never met a being more completely lost than Laforgue during his first days in Germany, or one filled with a more intense phobia for creatures and for things."

[4] Jules Laforgue, *Lettres à un ami, 1880-1886* (Paris, 1941), p. 23.

That impenetrable mask, that calm and level voice, hid
an almost morbid state of timidity and uncertainty. . . . I wonder by what extraordinary effort of will
he managed, from one day to another, to go about his
duties, to keep up the appearances of court life, to get
dressed, remember his hours of work, make an en-
trance, utter a greeting, to speak—answer, that is to
say—without anyone noticing in the least his palpitat-
ing distress.[5]

It was to his worksheets, in which the *vers philosophiques*
and novel were taking shape, that Laforgue confided his
distress during these first weeks in Berlin. But even then,
despite its salutary effect on his social anxiety, his writing
was beginning to disgust him by its childishly naked sentiment and strident tone. In early February of 1882, he
wrote to Charles Ephrussi, a friend with whom he had
worked in Paris: "I have realized that my volume of verse
was a heap of nasty little banalities, and I am doing it over
in a rage."[6] Yet the dissatisfaction that eventually led the
poet to abandon *Le Sanglot de la terre* was very nearly coeval
with the work itself. As a young man in Paris, looking for a
spirit kindred to his own, Laforgue had introduced himself
to Paul Bourget; and thus had begun a friendship that was
to have a marked, if belated, influence upon Laforgue's
development as a writer. Then known as *l'aîné des jeunes* by
his admirers, Bourget was a model of dandiacal elegance in
both his person and limpid verse.[7] "It is necessary to see
him at this time," writes Pierre Reboul, "as the most talented of all the young writers. A convinced and militant
'modern,' he is soon going to invent the notion of 'decadence.' Utterly irreligious, he prays to 'Our Father who

[5] Théodore Lindenlaub to G. Jean-Aubry, June 26, 1921, quoted in the
Introduction to Jules Laforgue, *Berlin, la cour et la ville* (Paris, 1922), p. 35;
cited in Ramsey, *Ironic Inheritance*, p. 71.
[6] *Œuvres complètes de Jules Laforgue*, IV (Paris, 1925), 112. This edition
will be cited hereafter as *Œc* in the text.
[7] According to Ramsey, *Ironic Inheritance*, p. 59.

wast in Heaven' and blows the smoke of his cigar in the faces of the fallen gods."[8] As a critic of Laforgue's youthful effusions, Bourget was as merciless as he was clearsighted: "I remember the times," wrote Jules from Germany to his brother Emile, "when I brought Bourget plays, chapters of novels, and piles of verses, thinking: Now with this blow he's going to be knocked silly! And the following Sunday he would say, 'You still do not know the French language, nor do you know the poet's craft, and you are still not thinking for yourself' " (*Œc*, V, 146).

The provocative impudence of Bourget, of "Lord Buddha" (as he appeared to the admiring Jules), undoubtedly came to the poet's mind when he read, in Germany, in 1881, that *jeu d'esprit* of clownesque decadence, *Pierrot sceptique*.[9] The little scenario was not Laforgue's first acquaintance with clowns. On a spring day in 1880, he had, in a way, confessed an affection for Pierrot and his fellow masks by showing his new friend Gustave Kahn "a little lyrical study of Watteau."[10] But it was not the gentle Gilles who amused Laforgue in *Pierrot sceptique*; rather it was the audacious Pierrot of the cabaret and circus ring whom he recognized in the pages of this newly published *saynète*— the whitefaced clown who had in fact delighted him as a young boy at Tarbes. In an early story entitled *Stéphane Vassiliew*, clearly reminiscent of schooldays at the Collège Impérial, Jules' autobiographical hero had been entertained by the clowns of an English circus. Later, in Germany, Laforgue himself once wrote to an acquaintance that he had "just spent five consecutive evenings" applauding the Reinz Pierrots: "Clowns seem to me to have arrived at true wisdom. I should be a clown; I have missed my calling . . ." (*Œc*, IV, 123). Several months after

[8] *Laforgue* (Paris, 1960), p. 35.

[9] In a letter of December 1881, Laforgue inquired of his friend Charles Henry: "Have you read . . . *Pierrot sceptique* of Huysmans and Hennique?" (*Œc*, IV, 67).

[10] Gustave Kahn, *Symbolistes et Décadents* (Paris, 1902); cited by Ramsey, *Ironic Inheritance*, p. 33.

he had read *Pierrot sceptique*, Laforgue announced in August of 1882 a play *pierrotique* of his own, one "that throws
me into convulsions," as he candidly admitted (Œc, IV,
189)—*Pierrot fumiste*. And it was largely owing to his work
on this piece that the young poet at last discovered his
"calling"—as ironist, *fumiste*, and Pierrot.

In May, 1883, Laforgue described a new book to his sister:

> They will perhaps appear bizarre to you. But I have
> abandoned my ideal of the Rue Berthollet, my philo-
> sophical poems.
>   I find it stupid to intone in an oracular voice and to
> posture eloquently. These days, being on the one
> hand more skeptical, less easily carried away, and on
> the other hand possessing my language in a more
> minute, clownesque fashion, I write whimsical little
> poems, having only one aim: to be original at any
> price. (Œc, V, 20)

But this change in aesthetic did not mean a change in philosophy or feeling. In a letter of 1882, he had admitted to a
confidant that "I still suffer sometimes. Only the desire to
utter sublime cries in the ears of my contemporaries on the
boulevards and around the Stock Exchange has passed,
and I limit myself to wringing my heart so that it drips out
curiously shaped pearls" (Œc, IV, 128). These *"perles
curieusement taillées"* took the form of ballad-like popular
songs—*complaintes*—that had caught the poet's fancy as
early as 1880. The collection entertains a motley host of
grievants: there is the complaint of the barrel organ, of the
poet's foetus, of the King of Thulé, of the voices under the
Buddhistic figtree. As bizarre and variegated as this company is, however, the *Complaintes,* as William Jay Smith
suggests, "is the record of many voices seeking to become
one."[11] And the voice that lends its "clownesque" accents

[11] Introduction to *Selected Writings of Jules Laforgue* (New York, 1956), p.
21.

to the many and that will later express their most characteristic sentiments is that of incorrigible Lord Pierrot.

In the "Autre Complainte de Lord Pierrot," the dandy is
confronted with the pander and slave of Maya, of the Illusion against which Reason contends in its struggle to liber-
ate the Unconscious from Will's domination. Pierrot, in
other words, confronts Woman:

> *Celle qui doit me mettre au courant de la Femme!*
> *Nous lui dirons d'abord, de mon air le moins froid:*
> *"La somme des angles d'un triangle, chère âme,*
>   *"Est égale à deux droits."*
>
> *Et si ce cri lui part: "Dieu de Dieu! que je t'aime!"*
> *—"Dieu reconnaîtra les siens." Ou piquée au vif:*
> *—"Mes claviers ont du cœur, tu seras mon seul thème."*
>   *Moi: "Tout est relatif."*
>
> *De tous ses yeux, alors! se sentant trop banale:*
> *"Ah! tu ne m'aimes pas; tant d'autres sont jaloux!"*
> *Et moi, d'un œil qui vers l'Inconscient s'emballe:*
>   *"Merci, pas mal; et vous?"*
>
> *—"Jouons au plus fidèle!"—"A quoi bon, ô Nature!"*
> *"Autant à qui perd gagne!" Alors, autre couplet:*
> *—"Ah! tu te lasseras le premier, j'en suis sûre . . ."*
>   *—"Après vous, s'il vous plaît."*
>
> *Enfin, si, par un soir, elle meurt dans mes livres,*
> *Douce; feignant de n'en pas croire encor mes yeux,*
> *J'aurai un: "Ah çà, mais, nous avions De Quoi vivre!*
>   *"C'était donc sérieux?"*[12]

---

[12] "She who will put me in touch with Woman! / Let's say to her first,
with the mildest of stares, / 'The sum of a triangle's angles, dear soul, / Is
equal to two squares.' // And if she should cry out, 'Oh God! I love you
so!' / 'God will look after his own.' Or, pierced to the bone: / 'My
keyboard has feelings; for you alone I live!' / I: 'Everything is relative.' //
Then, with blazing eyes! renouncing banality: / 'Ah, you don't really love
me; and so many envy you.' / And, with my eyes bolting toward the
Unconscious: / 'Thanks, not so bad, and you?' // 'Let's play Fidelity!' 'O
Nature, what's the use?' / 'But what can you lose, after all!' And then,

The speaker of the "Autre Complainte" is resolutely rein-
ing in his mercurial proclivities the better to deal with a
perversely willful Columbine. The "absolute indifference"
of Gaspard Deburau, the mad aloofness of Pierrot *sceptique,* is given in this poem its definitive philosophical jus-
tification. Woman, the irrational agent and prey of her instincts, the brainless instrument by which the *Wille* enjoys
its blind, prolific life—woman must be resisted at all costs.
Pierrot parries and thrusts as well as he can, fending off
her mechanically passionate appeals with the cool non-
sense of a *zanni.* He is "Lord Pierrot" not only in his regal
blasement but also in his refusal to succumb to the vagaries
of emotion. "Here and in the *Complainte des Noces de Pierrot,*" Lehmann observes, "it is possible to sense the presence of the Observer of the dialogue, the Pierrot-voyeur
whose aim, *en définitive,* is not dupery but dilettantism, the
artistic control of senseless Maya; and in the *Imitation de
Notre Dame la Lune,* where a whole series of Pierrot poems
is really the centre-piece, Pierrot—dandy, dilettante,
artist—proceeds to develop his Schopenhauer pessimism,
unobtrusively, into a veritable aesthetic."[13]

L'Imitation de Notre-Dame la Lune selon Jules Laforgue, to
give this volume its full title, was announced in a letter of
April, 1885, several months before the appearance of the
Complaintes. Describing his plan for the book to Gustave
Kahn, Laforgue promised:

> I'll bring you this bouquet and inscribe a lapidary and
> lunar dedication to you on the first page. I've recap-
> tured this enthusiasm from an old piece of rediscov-
> ered wastepaper on which I had recorded a very
> heartfelt tête-à-tête with the White Lady in question

---

reprise: / 'Ah, you'll get tired of it first, I'm sure . . .' / 'After you, if you
please.' // And at last, if, some evening, she dies in my books, / Pretend-
ing not to believe my eyes, invoke / Sweetly: 'Oh dear! but we had Something to live for! / Was it, then—no joke?' ": Patricia Terry, trans., *Poems
of Jules Laforgue* (Berkeley, Calif., 1958), p. 45.
[13] "Pierrot and *fin de siècle,*" p. 218.

one night last July, from my window, on the Isle de la
Mainau on Lake Constance (still a fondly remembered
time).[14]

The almost flawlessly sustained tête-à-tête of the *Imitation*
is between the "White Lady in question" and her *"blancs
enfants de chœur,"* her Pierrots. Creatures who abhor the
warmth and heat of passion, these choirboys of Selene spit
invectives at her plethoric, solar companion—at the "Fop,
Pimp, Ruffian, Showy Trafficker / In trinkets of golden
eggs"—and they tattoo upon their white hearts *"sentences
lunaires."*

Since the beginning of the century, Pierrot had been carrying on an intermittent flirtation with Our Lady the
Moon, but Laforgue was the first major poet to explore the
subtle metaphoric possibilities of that liaison. His Moon,
like solitary Pierrot, is a "Fossil star / Exiled by all": she
is, in her chaste and flawless innocence, a *"Lune
d'Immaculée-Conception."* Yet her purity is that of stone, of
marble; she brings forth no redeemer; she is barren, not
virgin. *"La Lune,"* as a title in the *Imitation* baldly announces, *"est stérile."* Since "her true worship is Art" and,
as we know from Schopenhauer, "the worship of Art is a
liberation from the Will, a voluntary sterility,"[15] it is only
fitting that her votaries should exalt her at the expense of
the fecund sun. Against the indiscriminate creativity of
Phoebus, these artist-lunologists set a deliberate art of
their own. Their forte is the metaphor, the boundless and
sterile proliferation of resemblances. In the "Litanies des
derniers quartiers de la Lune," for example, they laud the
Eucharist of Arcady, the last pyx of History, the Mirror and
Bible of the Undisturbed, the Sphinx and Gioconda of
worlds extinct (thus do they the hornèd moon present). It
is not, in short, the irreducible essence of their subject that
these artists seek: as mock-scientists of Selene, they ac-

[14] *Lettres à un ami,* p. 100.
[15] Lehmann, "Pierrot and *fin de siècle*," p. 219.

tually uncover none of her attributes but, "knowing only
how to invent, for the sake of tendering [her their] *ennuis*,"
imagine a world undiscovered and undiscoverable:

> *. . . mandragores à visages,*
> *Cactus obéliscals aux fruits en sarcophages,*
> *Forêts de cierges massifs, parcs de polypiers,*
> *Palmiers de corail blanc aux résines d'acier!*[16]
> ("Climat, faune et flore de la Lune")

A "dead mirror" reflecting the eccentric and inexhaustible
fancies of her Pierrots, the moon as poetic subject offers the
psychological solace of escape into an onanistically creat-
ing mind.

The "Navel-Vortex / Of All-Extinction," she is also in
philosophical terms "escape into nirvana, aspiration to
death in nothingness."[17] And those Pierrots who would,
in her cold light, "wash [their] hands of life" have discovered in their traditional attitudes of estrangement and insularity a *raison d'être*. Of thoroughly modern temperament
("School of cromlechs / And factory smokestacks"), they
invite the flirtations of Columbine only to flee, laughing, at
her approach. They are, in their deliberate abstention from
passion, the parodic symbols of man after the Revelation,
of enlightened humanity thirsting for obliteration in the
blind eye of the Unconscious. Just as they bathe their
skulls in the antiseptic light of the moon—the "pill of final
lethargies"—so they purge their bodies with the most in-
substantial and whitest of fare: they seek the bliss of vegetable insentience or, preferably, the pure effacement of Nil:

> *Ils vont, se sustenant d'azur,*
> *Et parfois aussi de légumes,*

[16] ". . . mandrakes with faces, / Obelisk-cacti with sarcophagied
fruit, / Forests of massive candles, parks of polyps, / Palms of white coral
with resins of steel!"
[17] Marc Eigeldinger, *L'Evolution dynamique de l'image dans la poésie française du Romantisme à nos jours* (Paris, 1943), p. 168; cited in Ramsey, *Ironic
Inheritance*, p. 140.

> *De riz plus blanc que leur costume,*
> *De mandarines et d'œufs durs.* [18]
>
> ("Pierrots," I)

Throughout this collection, Pierrot is what Lehmann calls "the complete philosopher of Intuition": "his stylized rôle in the *commedia* is quite dissolved away and in its place Laforgue has set a stylized pose of total, deathlike, amused passivity."[19] It is important for us to realize, however, that Pierrot is more than philosopher and his presence more than pose. Of the poem entitled "Pierrots (*Scène courte mais typique*)," for example, Patricia Terry suggests that the scene is " 'typical,' but of Laforgue himself";[20] and in a note on the sixteen short pieces that make up the *Locutions des Pierrots,* she remarks upon the reversal of roles of poet and hero: "Pierrot is now concealed behind Laforgue's façade."[21] Indeed, in these latter pieces, more quietly introspective than any of the others in the book, Pierrot flits like a moth in and out of the circle of his lady's cool light; teased out of his role by her insensitivity and inscrutability, he at times puts by all but a few shreds of his blouse and exposes his soul to her eyes and the moon.

All these observations should remind us that we are dealing with an artist of masks, yet with a poet, as we are often told, whose subject is always himself. With this in mind, we can begin to understand what may seem otherwise cryptic or gratuitous in his verse—and especially in his poetic gallery of Pierrots. For the shy young Romantic who was fascinated by the profound, tomblike silence of the submarine world, who once wrote a fragment upon "the immutably unique happiness of inorganic aggregates" and still another in which he imagined the ideal

---

[18] "They subsist on the pale sky, / And sometimes also on vegetables, / On rice whiter than their costume, / On mandarins, and hard-boiled eggs."
[19] "Pierrot and *fin de siècle*," p. 219.
[20] *Poems of Jules Laforgue,* p. 197.   [21] Ibid., p. 198.

state to be that of unconscious, vegetable life;[22] for this
writer who often expressed the wish to "revert to the veg-
etative state of coral," to reverse evolution and "go back to
being the madrepore,"[23] it must have seemed only natural
to give his Pierrots *"Un air d'hydrocéphale asperge."* Indeed,
as children of the Unconscious, they all have a singularly
vegetable allure:

> Les yeux sont noyés de l'opium
> De l'indulgence universelle,
> La bouche clownesque ensorcèle
> Comme un singulier géranium. [24]

("Pierrots," I)

Obviously, the successful assumption of these clownish,
cold-creamed masks (his Pierrots are seldom pathetically
alone) allowed Laforgue to practice his temperamental and
philosophical asceticism without baring his heart to the
daws. And yet his poses *pierrotiques* seem to have affected
profoundly, and disturbingly, what we can only call his
consciousness of self. A young man whose reserve and
timidity Lindenlaub found almost morbid, and in whom a
prolonged adolescence never completely abated, Laforgue
as a social and sexual figure has always been a somewhat
furtive topic of interest for both critics and biographers. In
one of the most recent studies of the poet, Reboul writes
that "sexuality in Laforgue seems, indeed, to have been
abnormal (as one says)—rather weak, irritated by an over-
subtle intellect, complicated by a deliberately unchecked
imagination, satisfied especially by sight and thought,
dulled—notwithstanding its very real presence—by the
notion of imperfection and sin."[25] To adopt the libidinous

[22] Both appeared in the *Revue Blanche* in October 1894; cited by François
Ruchon, *Jules Laforgue (1860–1887): sa vie, son œuvre* (Geneva, 1924), p.
48n.
[23] Cited by Reboul, *Laforgue*, pp. 73-74.
[24] "The eyes are drowned in the opium / Of cosmic indulgence, / The
clownesque mouth bewitches / Like an odd geranium."
[25] *Laforgue*, p. 67.

manner of Pierrot *sceptique* would seem to have offered a
release from these inhibitions; but the poet's stronger
temperament overbore the personality of the type. And
Pierrot's plastic character simply bent with the strain.
As a result, the Pierrot of *L'Imitation de Notre-Dame la
Lune* is very often a carnival reflection of his creator. He is a
creature in whom impulse is frustrated and instinct aggra-
vated by analysis, a figure who has reasoned himself into
an attitude of sometimes anguished, sometimes supercili-
ous passivity. But he is also, we should not forget, the
clown. And if Laforgue has deprived him of his intrepid-
ity, he has by no means robbed him of his mockery.
Pierrot-Laforgue is, consequently, at a double remove
from the poet's emotions; he is a wry commentary upon
analytical detachment, a burlesque of the ironic manner. A
Yorick of the *fin du siècle,* he is half-brother to the Hamlet of
the *Moralités*—"Laforgue as Hamlet seeing himself as
Hamlet."[26] As such, he not only encourages in the poet a
maniacally deliberate self-inspection but also, perhaps
paradoxically, dissipates any sense of identity arising from
his direct apprehension of emotional life. As one of Laforgue's earliest and most perceptive critics, François
Ruchon, observed: "Laforgue is the victim of a painful disturbance produced by the torment of meditation, by the in-
trusion of analysis into the smallest act of his life; and this
intellect, fatigued by its eternal analysis and dissociation
from itself, has only one desire: to get outside itself, to repudiate itself, to be absorbed in a kind of Nirvana."[27]
When Pierrot adds his clownish voice to those of the poet's
brain, the disturbance becomes even more acute. "*Comment lui dire,*" asks Pierrot-Laforgue of a young lady in *Des
Fleurs de bonne volonté,*

---

[26] Smith, *Selected Writings,* p. 102. Terry points out that both the Pierrots of the *Imitation* and Laforgue's Hamlet wear an Egyptian scarab, and
that "other details reinforce this concrete indication of relationship"
(*Poems of Jules Laforgue,* p. 196).
[27] *Jules Laforgue,* p. 137.

(Comment lui dire: "Je vous aime"?
Je me connais si peu moi-même.) [28]
(XVIII: "Dimanches")

At times, as we have seen, the mask lets fall some of its
flour, and this voice takes on familiarly melancholy accents. Then we detect, as of old, the sobbing of the brain
through the clown's *maquillage*. When Pierrot-Laforgue
avoids this note, avoids the thinly disguised expression of
what the poet had called in his early verse *"l'angoisse sin-
cère,"* he often assumes "a kind of cruel manner [as it was
once observed of Jean Giraudoux] that would lead one to
believe the author has a tender heart."[29]

For Laforgue, the cruelty is symptomatic of one or two
other things as well. Obviously, it recalls the conventional
névrose of the fashionable Decadent hero, a character
whom Laforgue had met and admired in the works of
Huysmans and Richepin. But much more importantly, it
seems to express that desire of his intellect to "get outside
itself, to repudiate itself" in an act of perversely irrational
impulse. Pierrot is often no less cruel a creature than the
jaded Hamlet of the *Moralités*: as the young bridegroom of
Pierrot fumiste, for example, he has neither scruples nor
conscience. He calls for the *Pornographe illustré* at his wedding and makes his Columbinette pay for it; after long
nights of tender but impotent solicitude, he finally does in
his bride by a bout of beefish lovemaking; "then, in the
morning, whistling, whistling, as if nothing had happened, he packs his bags and departs for Cairo . . ." (*Mp*,
107). The outrageous and sadistic cruelty of the clown
helps to relieve his vacant *ennui*; and by thus diverting his
inward gaze, it enables the poet to ignore for a time the
vexatious gusts of the brain. What Hugh Kenner calls the
"debonair panic"[30] of Laforgue is evident here—as it is in

[28] "(How can I tell her, 'I love you'? / I know so little of myself.)"
[29] The remark was made by P.-J. Toulet of *L'Ecole des indifférents*: cited
by Léon Guichard, *Jules Laforgue et ses poésies* (Paris, 1950), p. 89.
[30] *The Invisible Poet: T. S. Eliot* (New York, 1959), p. 21.

his postures *pierrotiques* throughout both poetry and prose that follow. Lehmann surprisingly concludes that "the epigraphs from Hamlet sprinkled through the *Imitation* and the *Derniers Vers* remind us insistently that behind the mask the comedian has ceased to suffer."[31] But it seems rather likelier that there he is suffering an even more insular misery.

In the end, Laforgue's *zanni* (we might even say the "Laforguean voice") confronts the basic question facing Pierrot and his interpreters at the close of the nineteenth century: how to escape the Hamletic prison of the skull, to recover an equilibrium between the self and the world. Laforgue died at twenty-seven before this problem could be solved; but his verse bequeathed it, as well as the mask, to a whole new generation of poets. The response of two of those poets to their clownesque inheritance is the subject of the concluding chapter of this history.

[31] "Pierrot and *fin de siècle*," p. 219.

VI

Pierrot *Ephèbe:*
T. S. Eliot and
Wallace Stevens

How little it would take to turn the poets
into the only true comedians!
—Wallace Stevens,
Bowl, Cat and Broomstick

In a famous passage from his introduction to the *Selected
Poems* (1928) of Ezra Pound, T. S. Eliot acknowledged an
explicit indebtedness to his French predecessor and *pierrotiste*: "The form in which I began to write, in 1908 or 1909,
was directly drawn from the study of Laforgue together
with the later Elizabethan drama; and I do not know anyone who started from exactly that point."[1] Many years
later, in a lecture at the Italian Institute in London in 1950,
he explained that Laforgue "was the first to teach me how
to speak, to teach me the poetic possibilities of my own
idiom of speech," and continued:

> Such early influences, the influences which, so to
> speak, first introduce one to oneself, are, I think, due
> to an impression which is in one aspect, the recogni-
> tion of a temperament akin to one's own, and in
> another aspect the discovery of a form of expression
> which gives a clue to the discovery of one's own form.

[1] Cited in Edward J. H. Greene, *T. S. Eliot et la France* (Paris, 1951), p.
17.

These are not two things, but two aspects of the same thing.[2]

Eliot had been introduced to Laforgue, as a frequently quoted passage in his writings bears witness,[3] through Arthur Symons' *Symbolist Movement in Literature* (1899); and it may be instructive to recall the "temperament" that he met within the pages of its brief chapter on the influential French poet. "[Laforgue's] portraits," writes Symons early in the essay, "show us a clean-shaved, reticent face, betraying little":

He has invented a new manner of being René or Werther: an inflexible politeness towards man, woman, and destiny. He composes love-poems hat in hand, and smiles with an exasperating tolerance before all the transformations of the eternal feminine. He is very conscious of death, but his *blague* of death is, above all things, gentlemanly. He will not permit himself, at any moment, the luxury of dropping the mask: not at any moment.[4]

It was not, of course, the author of *Le Sanglot de la terre* that Eliot encountered in these lines. It was, rather, the dilettante Buddhist and Lord Pierrot that smiled with "exasperating tolerance" at the young undergraduate—that smiled from possum to possum. "There was an element of this Laforgue already in [Eliot]," writes Herbert Howarth; "it was easy to progress to the pose from the urbane dandyism, the perfection of dress, manners, and accomplishments, which was the Harvard style in his time and in which he excelled."[5]

This last remark, however, suggests that the "poses" of

[2] Cited in Herbert Howarth, *Notes on Some Figures behind T. S. Eliot* (London, 1965), pp. 104-105.
[3] Review of P. Quennell's *Baudelaire and the Symbolists*, in *The Criterion*, January 1930; cited in Greene, *Eliot et la France*, p. 19n.
[4] (New York, 1958), pp. 56, 60-61.   [5] *Notes*, p. 105.

the two poets had quite different origins, were different in
kind. A young man of Laforgue's extreme timidity would
have died a thousand deaths in that triangular London flat
into which Eliot was ushered in late 1914. Yet we have
Wyndham Lewis' word for it that, on the occasion of
Eliot's "review," during his *rite du passage* with "ole uncle
Ezz," the initiate's "ears did not grow red, or I am sure I
should have noticed it."[6] In Laforgue, a temperamental ret-
icence and cautious reserve ("the ultimate cause of his de-
fensive irony,"[7] according to Ramsey) arose from his dis-
tressing sense of social unease—from an "intense phobia,"
as Lindenlaub had put it, "for creatures and for things."
And we have evidence from the letters, if not from the *joie*
that had delighted Huysmans in his poetry, that when the
defenses were down, Laforgue could often be as engagingly candid as he had been embarrassingly so in his *vers
philosophiques.*

Few of the guises under which Eliot is known to have
revealed himself could be called naïve, however, and none
of them seems ever to have seriously belied his self-
possession. He could—and did—give "consummate imitations of the Archdeacon, the Publisher, the Clubman, the
Man of Letters in Europe, the Aged Eagle, the Wag, and
the Public-Spirited Citizen," always refusing to play but
one role only—"the Poet."[8] His own "Lines for Cuscus-
caraway and Mirza Murad Ali Beg" candidly acknowledge
his uncooperativeness in the whole affair:

> How unpleasant to meet Mr. Eliot!
> With his features of clerical cut,
> And his brow so grim
> And his mouth so prim
> And his conversation, so nicely
> Restricted to What Precisely

---

[6] "Early London Environment," in Richard March and Tambimuttu,
eds., *T. S. Eliot: A Symposium* (London, 1948), p. 26.
[7] *Ironic Inheritance*, p. 24.   [8] Kenner, *Invisible Poet*, p. x.

> And If and Perhaps and But. . . .
> How unpleasant to meet Mr. Eliot!
> (Whether his mouth be open or shut).
>   (From "Five-Finger Exercises," V)

All of this suggests that when Eliot made these rather more sober speculations in *A Garland for John Donne* (1931), he was touching upon a point quite salient to the understanding of his early poetic posture:

> . . . at any particular moment, it may happen that the poets who are beginning to write find a particular poet, or a particular type or school of poetry, such as Donne and the school of Donne—and for our time Laforgue and some other French poets as well—with whom or which they have close sympathy, and through whom or which they elicit their talents. . . . [But] it is impossible for us or for anyone else ever to disentangle how much was genuine affinity, genuine appreciation, and how much was just a *reading into* poets like Donne our own sensibility, how much was "subjective."[9]

The temperament that had attracted the young Harvard poet to Jules Laforgue was in good part, I think, invented by Eliot's "reading into" Symons' semifictitious figure a sensibility uniquely his own. The clownish self-possession of Lord Pierrot had been, for Laforgue, a blind. His dandyism had been a self-mocking pose, self-consciously assumed: a technical bridge (in Joyce's famous metaphor) over which the Unconscious could march his troops. But for Eliot, pose and temperament were so nearly one that Laforgue's voice, once discovered, must have seemed (indeed, seems to many readers) more properly his own than Laforgue's. It was partly, I am suggesting, the "exasperating" self-sufficiency of the manner *pierrotique* that attracted Eliot to the earlier French poet; that he felt most sensibly a

[9] Cited in Greene, *Eliot et la France*, p. 21.

part of his own temperament. And in those poems in which he was to "work out the implications of La-forgue,"[10] Eliot explored the manner as both technique and theme through the "velleities and carefully caught re-grets" of his own species of Pierrot.

"Conversation Galante" was the first of four poems written from 1909 to 1911 that were ranged by the poet "under the sign of Laforgue."[11] As almost all of its critics have suggested, it seems to have been inspired by the "Autre Complainte de Lord Pierrot," which Eliot had seen quoted in full in *The Symbolist Movement in Literature*.

> I observe: "Our sentimental friend the moon!
> Or possibly (fantastic, I confess)
> It may be Prester John's balloon
> Or an old battered lantern hung aloft
> To light poor travellers to their distress."
>   She then: "How you digress!"
>
> And I then: "Someone frames upon the keys
> That exquisite nocturne, with which we explain
> The night and moonshine; music which we seize
> To body forth our own vacuity."
>   She then: "Does this refer to me?"
>   "Oh no, it is I who am inane."
>
> "You, madam, are the eternal humorist,
> The eternal enemy of the absolute,
> Giving our vagrant moods the slightest twist!
> With your air indifferent and imperious
> At a stroke our mad poetics to confute—"
>   And—"Are we then so serious?"

[10] Eliot, "On a Recent Piece of Criticism," *Purpose*, April-June 1938, pp. 91-92; cited in Ramsey, *Ironic Inheritance*, p. 199.

[11] "According to the order established by E. J. H. Greene and corrobo-rated by Eliot, 'Jules Laforgue et T. S. Eliot,' *Revue de Littérature Comparée*, July-September 1948, p. 369": Ramsey, *Ironic Inheritance*, p. 261n. For Eliot's earliest Laforguean experiments, see his *Poems Written in Early Youth* (New York, 1967), particularly "Humouresque."

Here, as in the "Autre Complainte," Pierrot is holding at
bay "the eternal humorist, / The eternal enemy of the absolute"; but whether he feels himself a match for his gravely
laconic opponent is questionable. Lacking the blasé
aplomb of Laforgue's insensitive *zanni,* he proceeds from
rumination to reproach rather cautiously, as if stepping
gingerly from stone to stone in treacherous conversational
waters. Beneath him, below his faceless self-possession,
the question evaded by all Eliotic Pierrots flutters, fishlike,
in the subverbal depths. It is for fear of catching the glint
from its back, of becoming "serious," that he keeps his eye
affixed to his sentimental friend the moon. "Conversation
Galante" is not, in other words, a poem to be dismissed as
"too evidently from Laforgue to claim our attention":[12] the
speakers of this little piece suffer a metaphysical estrangement only insofar as metaphysics is the pretext for Pierrot's
insularity. The real motivation behind the *zanni*'s aloofness
seems to elude even his own subtle brain. Consequently,
his tone is less assured, his ripostes less acerbic than those
of unflappable Lord Pierrot.

"Portrait of a Lady," the second of the poems composed
"sous le signe de Laforgue," explores the theme of the "Conversation" with greater subtlety and greater intensity. "I
am always sure that you understand," avers a superan-
nuated Columbine, a *"précieuse ridicule* . . . serving tea
. . . among her bric-à-brac":[13]

> "I am always sure that you understand
> My feelings, always sure that you feel,
> Sure that across the gulf you reach your hand. . . ."

But Pierrot sits punctiliously unperturbed, as he had sat
through confessions of an earlier tête-à-tête. Like the

[12] René Taupin, *L'Influence du symbolisme français sur la poésie américaine
(de 1910 à 1920)* (Paris, 1929), pp. 228-29.
[13] So Conrad Aiken described the Cambridge hostess who was a model
for the Lady: "King Bolo and Others," in March and Tambimuttu, *Symposium,* p. 21.

world through which he moves with immaculate self-sufficiency, the Lady's words "arrange" themselves around her bland, unruffled guest. Invulnerable ("you have no Achilles' heel," she complains), he maintains an assiduously attentive silence and smiles and sips his tea.

The Pierrot of the "Portrait" is a creature in whom deliberation has become essence; one who passes, with easy assurance, unsinged, through the flames of small passions. He sees the flames and feels their heat, but as if at two or three removes—often, in fact, at a discreet, journalistic distance:

> You will see me any morning in the park
> Reading the comics and the sporting page.
> Particularly I remark
> An English countess goes upon the stage.
> A Greek was murdered at a Polish dance,
> Another bank defaulter has confessed.
> I keep my countenance,
> I remain self-possessed . . .

When the Lady threatens that self-possession ("I have been wondering frequently of late / . . . / Why we have not developed into friends"), the flames lick uncomfortably about his mask; and he "must borrow every changing shape / To find expression." For behind the impervious façade, ·Pierrot is by no means as invulnerable as he appears. "Well!" he reflects with Laforguean offhandedness, "and what if she should die some afternoon"—then modulates into a muted, minor key:

> Afternoon grey and smoky, evening yellow and rose;
> Should die and leave me sitting pen in hand
> With the smoke coming down above the housetops;
> Doubtful, for a while
> Not knowing what to feel or if I understand
> Or whether wise or foolish, tardy or too soon . . .
> Would she not have the advantage, after all?

> This music is successful with a "dying fall"
> Now that we talk of dying—
> And should I have the right to smile?

"Behind the décor of self-sufficiency—the ready smile, the poised teacup, lies the Self; a mystery, sometimes an illusion," writes Kenner.[14] The Self of the Eliotic Pierrot is accessible to no one in his world but to all in this who attend carefully to his voice. And to attend is to perceive beneath the full, clicking rhymes the music of a temperament suffering the brain's "monotone," suffering from its being attuned too exquisitely to itself. The steady beat of his mind does not have the same consequences for Eliot's *zanni*, however, as it does for Laforgue's, nor does it have the same cause. The Pierrot of the *Complaintes* replies with nice cruelty to the hungry assaults of Woman. His self-sufficiency is the foil of the philosopher—and of the socially and sexually *maladroit*. For the speaker of the "Portrait," the assaults are repulsed because they infringe what Kenner calls the "mystery"—that mystery about which Pierrot's thought flutters, protectively, in fascination, and with terrible, debilitating insistence. The separation that he enforces between himself and the Lady represents, in short, a greed of soul. It should not be surprising, then, that the result of this estrangement is mute guilt and anguish, suffusing the consciousness of the speaker much as they suffuse the moribund figure of Verlaine's "Pierrot." And in the last of Eliot's experiments with the persona *pierrotique*, both anguish and guilt take on such an intensity that they completely efface the mask's comic pose.

As we turn to "The Love Song of J. Alfred Prufrock," a question clamors to be answered. If, in "Prufrock," the gaiety of the clown is quite dissolved away and he is anchored, with a name, firmly in the quotidian; if he is conscious of losing hair from a traditionally bald pate and sporting, as a novelty, the trousers he has always worn; if,

---

[14] *Invisible Poet,* p. 31.

finally, his mind "teems" (as Kenner observes) with a myriad of learned, Eliotic allusions—if all these things are true, can we indeed say that Prufrock "is" Pierrot? We may do well to consider, first, Kenner's full description of the famous persona:

> He isn't a "character" cut out of the rest of the universe and equipped with a history and a little necessary context, like the speaker of a Browning monologue. We have no information about him whatever; even his age is ambiguous (the poet once referred casually to Prufrock in a lecture as a *young* man). Nor is he an Everyman, surrounded by poetic effects: the range of "treatment" is excessive. Everyman's mind doesn't teem with allusions to Hesiod, Hamlet, Lazarus, Falstaff, entomology, eschatology, John the Baptist, mermaids. What "Prufrock" is, is the name of a possible zone of consciousness where these materials can maintain a vague congruity; no more than that; certainly not a person. [15]

And yet these remarks need a bit of qualification. For Prufrock is neither a person nor merely what Dr. Johnson would have called an "idea'd" soliloquist. He is a consciousness submerged in and colored by a temperament. But, as Kenner implies, those readers who are eager to make of him a stable "character"—a Polonius, for example [16]—err almost as grievously as that early critic who was offended by "the poet's desire to become a crab." [17] Polonius' mind is a tight box; Prufrock's is a pool, it overflows. We could never imagine these lines from "Prufrock" in either the mouth or mind of Shakespeare's pedant:

> And the afternoon, the evening, sleeps so peacefully!
> Smoothed by long fingers,

[15] Ibid., p. 40.

[16] See, e.g., Greene, *Eliot et la France*, p. 45.

[17] Cited in the Introduction to Hugh Kenner, ed., *T. S. Eliot: A Collection of Critical Essays* (Englewood Cliffs, N.J., 1962), p. 1.

> Asleep . . . tired . . . or it malingers,
> Stretched on the floor, here beside you and me.

This is an unmistakably "Prufrockean" utterance—the
voice of a consciousness that spills around and engulfs
disparate images, lapping them in its fluid contours. Only
in one kind of mind can images sink and appear with such
subtle "logic" and fluidity, and that is in Hamlet's:

POLONIUS. . . . How does my good Lord Hamlet?
HAMLET. Well, God-a-mercy.
POL. Do you know me, my lord?
HAM. Excellent well; you are a fishmonger.
POL. Not I, my lord.
HAM. Then I would you were so honest a man.
POL. Honest, my lord!
HAM. Ay, sir; to be honest, as this world goes, is to be
   one man pick'd out of ten thousand.
POL. That's very true, my lord.
HAM. For if the sun breed maggots in a dead dog,
   being a good kissing carrion—Have you a daughter?
POL. I have, my lord.
HAM. Let her not walk i' th' sun. Conception is a bless-
   ing. But as your daughter may conceive—friend,
   look to't.
POL. How say you by that? . . . What do you read, my
   lord?
HAM. Words, words, words.
POL. What is the matter, my lord?
HAM. Between who?
POL. I mean, the matter that you read, my lord.
HAM. Slanders, sir; for the satirical rogue says here
   that old men have grey beards; that their faces are
   wrinkled; their eyes purging thick amber and
   plum-tree gum; and that they have a plentiful lack
   of wit, together with most weak hams—all which,
   sir, though I most powerfully and potently believe,
   yet I hold it not honesty to have it thus set down; for

you yourself, sir, shall grow old as I am, if, like a
crab, you could go backward.

(II.ii.170-203)

But despite the preoccupation that both share for ragged, scuttling things, Prufrock is "not Prince Hamlet, nor
was meant to be." He is hardly a Hamlet *manqué*. Laforgue's Prince is "Hamlet seeing himself as Hamlet";
Eliot's persona is Prufrock seeing himself as Hamlet and
curtly dismissing the resemblance (he has the consciousness but not the temperament). He is

> Politic, cautious, and meticulous;
> Full of high sentence, but a bit obtuse;
> At times, indeed, almost ridiculous—
> Almost, at times, the Fool.

He is "almost" the Fool (he has the temperament—a finical
pomposity *pierrotique*—but not the Fool's insouciant consciousness).

It is possible that the Pierrot-speaker was abandoned by
Eliot after "Prufrock" because of the insoluble, solipsistic
dilemma that he seemed to pose. The incorrigible child of
the Laforguean *zanni* was a no less exasperating father of
the man. As a figure with which to sustain a poetic career,
he could lead nowhere but—narcissistically, disparag-
ingly, yet inevitably—back to himself. In the cryptic utterance of an Eastern thunderclap, and ultimately, at the still
point of the turning world Eliot discovered the truths that
allowed him to escape his own prison of the Self—by pros-
trating its mystery before a higher one. But such truths
have no potency for the cynical and faithless Pierrot: as a
comic creature of the secular imagination, he has to seek an
escape from his private world by unpretentiously worldly
means. And what he must do, at this point in his career, is
dispel the *mal du siècle* that has been his inheritance and recover his confidence in an external world.

He must, in other words, confront the ordinary green of experience and of himself.

In "Imagination as Value," a lecture presented by Wallace Stevens at Columbia University in 1948, the poet suggested that "the chief problems of any artist, as of any man, are the problems of the normal and . . . he needs, in order to solve them, everything that the imagination has to give."[18] Both parts of this statement are important for any approach to Stevens' own art, however oblique or inapropos the first may seem. For this poetry of an exuberant Banjo Boomer, erupting with "verbal pyrotechnics, a shower of exotic colors, wondrous sound-effects, inkhorn words, hoo-hoos and rum-tum-tums, euphonious geography, exquisite insults"[19]—the poetry of Stevens is, for all its verbal glitter, a poetry of and paean to the normal. In a letter of 1935, four years after the first reissue of *Harmonium*, Stevens admitted to a correspondent that "how to write of the normal in a normal way is a problem which I have long since given up trying to solve, because I never feel that I am in the area of poetry until I am a little off the normal. The worst part of this aberration," he continued, "is that I am convinced that it is not an aberration."[20]

To be "a little off the normal" was, for Stevens, to use "a hierophantic phrase" if a poem seemed to call for it; it was to write abstract, meditative poetry when both creative and critical fashions were against it; and it was to express, in 1942, the perverse wish of "do[ing] something for the Ivory Tower." ("There are a lot of exceedingly stupid people saying things about the Ivory Tower who ought to

---

[18] Wallace Stevens, *The Necessary Angel* (New York, 1951), p. 156.
[19] Daniel Fuchs, *The Comic Spirit of Wallace Stevens* (Durham, N.C., 1963), p. 3.
[20] *Letters of Wallace Stevens*, ed. Holly Stevens (New York, 1966), p. 287. The *Letters* will be cited hereafter in the text as *L*.

be made to regret it" [*L*, 403].) It was, also, in 1921-1922, with the writing of "The Comedian as the Letter C" ("this anecdote / Invented for its pith, not doctrinal / In form though in design") to attempt, in raiment *pierrotique*, a metaphorical and uncompromising rapprochement with the normal stuff of the world.

At the end of the first decade of this century, Stevens was far from any such rapprochement, however; he was far, in fact, from any attempt at one. The epistolary confidences he shared with his future wife during these years reveal a temperament that is still unformed, immature. He is enraptured by the natural world outside himself, but prone in his verse to regard that world as mere metaphor for *états d'âme*. He is remarkably self-assured but, at the same time, sentimental in a coyly ironic way. He is impatient with pretentions in art and life, but respectful of the Ideal in both. His temperament, in short, is little different from that of any young man of "artistic inclinations" who happened to be in love but alone in turn-of-the-century New York. It is not surprising that Stevens should have sometimes expressed himself in both his poetry and his letters of this period under the sympathetic guise of Pierrot. A letter to Elsie Moll from the years 1907-1908, for example, includes this mawkishly confessional little sketch:

> And so when summer came, they went in a boat to [a] quiet island, and on the way, Pierrot .pulled out a newspaper and read to Columbine a little news of the stupid world from which he was taking her. But Columbine didn't think it stupid. So Pierrot turned the boat around, and they drifted back to town. Yet even while they were drifting, Columbine thought of the quiet island and she knew that Pierrot was thinking of it too. (*L*, 106)

In the 1908 "Book of Verses" and 1909 "Little June Book" (manuscript sheaves of his early verse that he presented to his affianced Columbine), Stevens penned out several little pieces that are obviously spoken by a moonstruck *naïf*. The themes that obsess him are the transitoriness of life, the *ennui* of earthly existence, and, as in the sketch above, the allure of an ideal world. The last poem of the Little June Book bears the title "Pierrot":

> I lie dreaming 'neath the moon,
> You lie dreaming under ground;
> I lie singing as I dream,
> You lie dreaming of the sound.
>
> Soon I shall lie dreaming too,
> Close beside you where you are—
> Moon: Behold me while I sing,
> Then, behold our empty star.[21]

The murmurous plaint of this lunar *zanni* becomes a torpid cry of *désespoir* in another poem of the period, later published as part of "Carnet de Voyage" in 1914. Its speaker, "evidently a disenchanted Pierrot, limply expresses a *fin de siècle* world-weariness":[22]

> I am weary of the plum and of the cherry,
> And that buff moon in evening's aquarelle;
> I have no heart within to make me merry,
> I read of Heaven and, sometimes, fancy Hell.
>
> All things are old: the new-born swallows fare
> Through the Spring twilight on dead September's wing.
> The dust of Babylon is in the air,
> And settles on my lips the while I sing.
>
> (*S&P*, 223)

Behind both of these lyrics is the attenuated voice of Verlaine, just one of whose "musical" phrases (as Stevens was wont to exclaim) "was exalting enough for the whole

[21] In Holly Stevens, *Souvenirs and Prophecies: The Young Wallace Stevens* (New York, 1977), p. 234. Miss Stevens' study will be cited hereafter as *S&P* in the text.

[22] Robert Buttel, *Wallace Stevens: The Making of* Harmonium (Princeton, N.J., 1967), p. 63.

day!"[23] In none of Verlaine's experiments with Pierrot, however, do we find the Pierrot of these little poems. Even the *zanni* of the *Fêtes Galantes*—whom Stevens' *zanni* most closely resembles—has a lambent gaiety that these speakers obviously lack. The sensibility of Stevens' persona appears to have been stained with Aesthetic tints.

> Music, more music, far away and faint:
> It is an echo of mine heart's complaint.
> Why should I be so musical and sad?
> I wonder why I used to be so glad?
> In single glee I chased blue butterflies,
> Half butterfly myself, but not so wise,
> For they were twain, and I was only one.
> Ah me! how pitiful to be alone.[24]

The speaker of these pathetic lines is also a Pierrot, of Ernest Dowson's *The Pierrot of the Minute*. It is quite possible that Stevens read this little playlet in Arthur Symons' edition of the *Poems of Ernest Dowson* (1905) and, from it, appropriated its plaintive Pierrot. But it seems no less likely that the young American simply read Verlaine with Dowsonian receptivity. The English poet's affinity with the lyricist of *Romances sans paroles*, whose Gallic *tristesse* he often tried to emulate, was undoubtedly shared by Stevens—by the same poet whose undergraduate verse betrays the pervasive influence of the Rhymers. And that the speaker of "Pierrot" in the Little June Book is invested with the qualities that animate—or enervate—the Pierrot of the Minute is probably no more than an indication of the strength of that affinity.

But not all of the *zanni* of Stevens' early manuscript poems suffer the disenchantment of the century's twilight. The speaker of a poem from 1909, "presumably another

[23] Charles Henri Ford, "Verlaine in Hartford," *View*, I (September 1940), 1; cited in Buttel, *Making of* Harmonium, p. 56.

[24] Ernest Dowson, *The Pierrot of the Minute* (1897), in *The Poems of Ernest Dowson*, ed. Mark Longaker (Philadelphia, 1962), p. 154.

Pierrot with his stringed instrument," as Robert Buttel observes, "desires a rich aesthetic and sensuous atmosphere favorable to art and the imagination":[25]

> An odorous bush I seek,
> With lighted clouds hung round,
> To make my golden instrument's
> Wild, golden strings resound,
>
> Resound in quiet night,
> With an Arab moon above,
> Easing the dark sense[']s need,
> Once more, in songs of love.
>
> (*S&P*, 233-34)

So, in a poem of 1908, embodying the sentiments of a like-minded Pierrot, we begin to catch the inflections of a more familiar Stevens and his more familiar clown:

> Hang up brave tapestries:
> Huntsman and warrior there—
> Shut out these mad, white walls.
> I hate a room so bare.
>
> .   .   .   .   .
>
> Then fetch me candles tall.
> Stand them in bright array,
> And go—I need such lights
> And shadows when I pray.
>
> (*S&P*, 191)

The bold and finical assurance of its speaker makes this poem a precursor to the later verse of *Harmonium*, just as his candle-lit genuflections suggest those of that more exquisite Aesthete in *Carlos Among the Candles.* A robustly ironic mockery, apparent for all the preciousness of his pose, has begun to curl the lip of Stevens' Pierrot; and in the verse that follows that of the manuscript books, com-

---

[25] *Making of* Harmonium, p. 61.

posed as experiments toward a personal style, Stevens will sharpen and refine this mockery by way of fashioning his own pierrotish voice.

On September 21, 1909, young Wallace married Elsie Moll, and after a brief honeymoon in Massachusetts, they moved into their New York apartment on West Twenty-first Street. The cuisine bourgeoise of Stevens' new life seems to have sated neither the poet nor Pierrot in him, however, as evidenced by an effusion explicitly *pierrotique* of February 1910:

> Willow soon, and vine;
> But now Saint Valentine,
> To whom I pray: "Speed two
> Their happy winter through:
> Her that I love—and then
> Her Pierrot . . . Amen."

(S&P, 248)

But it was not until the years 1912-1914 that Stevens began to take a professional interest in his verse. These were the years that saw the founding of *Poetry* magazine, the appearance of the first Imagist anthology, the Armory Show of 1913: they were also the years in which Stevens fell in with a number of *littérateurs*, many of them former Harvard classmates, whose enthusiasm for the new and experimental, as Samuel French Morse avers, "must have proved infectious."[26] One of the interests of the presiding spirit of the group, Walter Conrad Arensberg, was the translation of French poetry; in 1914, he published an English version of the "Autre Complainte de Lord Pierrot," the earliest translation of Laforgue to appear in America. Many years later, in recalling the activities of the Arensberg circle, however, Stevens wrote to Hi Simons that "I don't remember any discussion of French poets," and added: "at the time when Walter Arensberg was doing his translation of L'APRÈS MIDI D'UN FAUNE I knew that he was doing it,

[26] *Wallace Stevens: Poetry as Life* (New York, 1970), p. 69.

and that is about all" (*L*, 391). The poetry of the Symbolists and of their early precursors was merely "a good deal in the air" at this time (as Stevens wrote specifically of Mallarmé [*L*, 636]), as was the Laforguean *dandysme*—"*le ton 'pierrot' "*—that critics have made so much of in *Harmonium*. [27] What all of this suggests, of course, is that Stevens' much-discussed assimilation of Laforgue and of his attitude *pierrotique* was by no means as deliberate or original as, say, Eliot's. During the prewar years, Stevens was undoubtedly absorbing Laforgue, much as he had, earlier, absorbed Verlaine; but if he was proceeding upon any course with Eliot-like deliberation, it was the fabrication of a unique voice, purged of accents and affectations that were not wholly his own. As the voice emerges in *Harmonium*, the mannered accents are certainly there, as clearly as the "influence"; but the originality and control of the poet have transformed them into an intractable, Stevensian rhetoric.

So the Pierrot of the manuscript books, the Aesthetic Pierrot, undergoes an imaginative transformation—we might even say resuscitation—during the making of *Harmonium*. His name disappears (a name too evidently redolent of musk-scented slivers of moon) and he begins to cultivate that healthy self-mockery that we find in "Hang up brave tapestries." We first suspect his presence behind the pseudonym that Stevens wished to adopt for his initial appearance in *Poetry*—"Peter Parasol," also the title of a 1919 lyric:

> *Aux taureaux Dieu cornes donne*
> *Et sabots durs aux chevaux . . .*
>
> Why are not women fair,
> All, as Andromache,
> Having, each one, most praisable
> Ears, eyes, souls, skins, hair?

[27] See, e.g., Taupin, *L'Influence du symbolisme*, p. 277.

Ah, good God! That all beasts should have
The tusks of the elephant,
Or be beautiful
As large ferocious tigers are.

It is not so with women.
I wish they were all fair
And walked in fine clothes,
With parasols, in the afternoon air.

But here, obviously, is a regression rather than a recovery:
indeed, Stevens' own "objections" to this little poem, according to Samuel French Morse, "persisted for years."[28]
After having submitted it to *Poetry* among other
"Pecksniffiana," Stevens wrote to Harriet Monroe in the
summer of 1919 requesting that "The Weeping Burgher"
be published in its place: "Not to provoke, but to stifle,
discussion, my reasons are that the element of pastiche
present in Aux Taureaux will not be apparent and [that]
the poem will go off on its substance and not on its
style . . ." (*L*, 214). Morse suggests that the piece was
meant "to be an imitation of the ironic sentimentalities that
Apollinaire handles with such skill in *Le Bestaire* . . . and
Alcools, but it does not quite come off."[29] Its irony seems to
depend too heavily upon the exquisiteness of the speaker's
name itself; the mockery is somewhat rarefied, the burlesque of Aesthetic pretensions too tenuously subtle.

Stevens could perceive these weaknesses in 1919 not
only because he had, behind him, more successful experiments with fastidious Pierrots, but also because he had
changed, in a half-dozen years, from dilettante to scrupulous, publishing poet. In 1916, this scrupulosity had
earned him a special prize from *Poetry* for his verse play
Three Travelers Watch a Sunrise, and with his delight in rec-

---

[28] Introduction to Wallace Stevens, *Opus Posthumous,* ed. and with an
Introduction by Samuel French Morse (New York, 1957), p. xx.
[29] "Wallace Stevens, Bergson, Pater," *ELH,* XXXI (March 1964), 2n;
cited in Buttel, *Making of* Harmonium, p. 181n.

ognition had come also a greater assurance of pose. Shortly after receiving the prize—now a Pierrot-*parvenu*—he had written his wife from St. Paul:

Eminent Vers Libriste
  Arrives in Town
Details of Reception.
St. Paul, Minn. [June] 19, 1916. Wallace Stevens, the playwright and barrister, arrived at Union Station, at 10.30 o'clock this morning. Some thirty representatives of the press were not present to greet him. He proceeded on foot to the Hotel St. Paul, where they had no room for him. Thereupon, carrying an umbrella and two mysterious looking bags, he proceeded to Minnesota Club, 4th & Washington-Streets, St. Paul, where he will stay while he is in St. Paul. At the Club, Mr. Stevens took a shower-bath and succeeded in flooding not only the bath-room floor but the bed-room floor as well. He used all the bath-towels in mopping up the mess and was obliged to dry himself with a wash-cloth. From the Club, Mr. Stevens went down-town on business. When asked how he liked St. Paul, Mr. Stevens, borrowing a cigar, said, "I like it." (*L*, 196)

The effervescent gaiety behind this "dispatch" shines through the pieces that followed *Three Travelers,* two short dramatic experiments written for the 1917-1918 season of the Wisconsin Players. Both Carlos and Bowl, the title characters of these plays, are "cousins of Pierrot," as Buttel observes, "and equally ineffectual."[30] In the preliminary business of *Bowl, Cat and Broomstick*, Stevens describes Bowl as wearing "a gown falling below his knees":

It is black covered with a faded silver pattern. Flat hat. Jewel in the hat. Black stockings. Small silver buckles on his shoes. He is gaunt. He is reading aloud from a

[30] *Making of* Harmonium, p. 172.

book which is bound in yellow paper, like a French book.[31]

The incongruity of costume should not mislead us. Long before this play was published, René Taupin had recognized the Pierrot beneath Stevens' black-suited eccentrics.[32] To Stevens, in fact, both Pierrot and the dandy of the *dix-huitième* had always seemed two sides of the same elegant glove. In a letter of 1909, he had written to Elsie Moll: "Ought I not suddenly pull off my black wig and black gown and put on a white wig, full of powder, and a suit of motley—or maybe, the old costume of Pierrot?" (*L*, 134). Bowl mediates between both figures, revealing the fastidious eccentricity of the clown beneath the assurance of a foppish martinet. The "finical importance" with which he speaks, his "chilly diffidence" towards the dull-witted Cat, his Gallic refinement of taste and dress—all this suggests a spirit of self-burlesque quite close to that of *Harmonium*'s elegant showman. Yet in his way, Bowl is as piquant a figure as he is grotesquely mannered, and there are scraps of his discourse with Cat and Broomstick that deserve our serious attention.

A little past the middle of the play, for example, Bowl is reading titles aloud as he pages through his book of poems by "Claire Dupray":

Old Catamaran—an amazing thing in the way it designs the catamaran on the surface of the sea: one of the poems in which by the description of the thing seen, she makes an image of the greatest intensity. Nothing in nature could have revealed what her imagination and sensibility have revealed. . . . What an extraordinary effect one gets from seeing things as they

---

[31] All quotations of *Bowl, Cat and Broomstick* are from Wallace Stevens, *The Palm at the End of the Mind*, ed. Holly Stevens (New York, 1971), pp. 24-34.
[32] Taupin, *L'Influence du symbolisme*, p. 277.

are, that is to say: from looking at ordinary things intensely!

BROOMSTICK: But to look at ordinary things intensely, is not to see things as they are.

Here we catch sight of a new and arresting dimension of
the *fin-de-siècle* and black-frocked Pierrot. The Aesthete,
the scrupulous dandy *pierrotique,* enjoys the privilege of
seeing intensely and of feeling intensely what he sees; but
since his perceptions are refracted through an overrefined
sensibility, he changes reality: he sees things "not . . . as
they are." Like Prufrock and the Laforguean Lord Pierrot,
therefore, he inhabits a private and solipsistic world. Yet
compared with Prufrock's, the Aesthete's is quite livable;
for if it opens its doors to cosmic questions and women
talking of Michelangelo, the questions perforce are
piquant, the women invariably amusing. Even an insolent
fist of bananas can give the Aesthete keen delight—
provided, of course, the fruit is properly dressed:

> Pile the bananas on planks.
> The women will be all shanks
> And bangles and slatted eyes.
>
> And deck the bananas in leaves
> Plucked from the Carib trees,
> Fibrous and dangling down,
> Oozing cantankerous gum
> Out of their purple maws,
> Darting out of their purple craws
> Their musky and tingling tongues.
>   ("Floral Decorations for Bananas")

These pulpy lines might have been spoken by the
clownesque pedant of Stevens' third little play, Carlos, of
Carlos Among the Candles. An *"eccentric"* who "was always
affected by the grand style," Carlos makes his appearance
by a leap into a candle-lit decor *à la* Whistler—and begins

to pick his way, no less deliberately than the Pierrot of *La Peur*, through the furniture of his own exquisite mind. Yet, Aesthete that he is, he is certainly the gayer of the two *zanni*: the flickering of his tapers suggests "silks and fans . . . the movement of arms . . . rumors of Renoir,"[33] not the black, hanging shapes that haunt Margueritte's pallid clown. His impressions scintillate in dense, violet light, dyed by an overnice imagination; even the tall flowers outside the room *"are unnaturally large, of gold and silver."* ("A degree of artificiality in the flowers seen through the window is all that I am keen about," Stevens had written to the designer of the set [*L*, 200].) But as preciously delightful as this interior world may seem, it is as fragile as Carlos' crystalline metaphors. At one point in the play, a *"strong gust of wind suddenly blows into the room, extinguishing several of the candles on the table at the left"*; Carlos *"buries his head in his arms,"* then murmurs in desolate tones: "The night wind came into the room . . . The fans are invisible upon the floor." Inchoate experience, not always amenable to the rose-hued imagination, has threatened his close room of Self; and rather than yield to it, Carlos *"blows out all the candles that are still burning on the table."*

Yet the play ends somewhat ambiguously. After all the candles but one have been extinguished, Carlos *"opens the door at the right"*:

> [. . . *Outside, the night is as blue as water. He crosses the stage and opens the door at the left. . . . he flings aside the curtains. He extinguishes his taper. He looks out. He speaks with elation.*]
> Oh, ho! Here is matter beyond invention.
> [*He springs through the window. Curtain.*]

His exit appears to be a leap into experience, but it is probably a leap into a yet "profounder room" of the mind. The night, *"as blue as water,"* seems still to wear the color of his

---

[33] All quotations of *Carlos Among the Candles* are from *Opus Posthumous*, pp. 144-50.

imagination. In his elation before the unconfined world, in the joy of the leap itself, however, we sense a promise of invigoration—and of the change of the eccentric Pierrot from Romantic to "stiffest realist."

This change is the subject of "The Comedian as the Letter C," a poem that may be said to describe, in its six clickering cantos, the maturation of Pierrot. First published in 1923, this superficially difficult poem has been variously interpreted: as confession, autobiography, and—more recently, by Helen Hennessy Vendler—as a "strained Dionysian *tripudium*." Vendler's perceptive analysis uncovers gestures of "stressed physicality" in the poem, gestures beneath which Stevens' retreat before "the gross heterogeneity of the world" may be detected. And she concludes that "the Stevens of guzzling, rankness, and bluster disappoints and is false, except when he is engaged in such charming self-parodies as 'Bantams in Pine-Woods.' "[34]

That there is a perceptible shudder, a "recoil," before the world that the Comedian discovers is undeniable. In an essay "About One of Marianne Moore's Poems," published in 1948, Stevens remarked that to "confront fact in its total bleakness is for any poet a completely baffling experience."[35] And yet, since "Reality is the spirit's true center,"[36] the poet must come to grips with its grossness, at least if he is to assign to poetry the unsentimental, salutary values that Stevens always assigned it. It is not so much, therefore, that Stevens "disappoints" in 'The Comedian" as that he communicates his subtle aversion to a world that is neither warmed nor illuminated, in Kermode's admirable phrase, by "the light of the mind."[37] For the seagoing explorer of these blank-verse waves is not Stevens, nor has

[34] Helen Hennessy Vendler, *On Extended Wings: Wallace Stevens' Longer Poems* (Cambridge, Mass., 1969), pp. 52, 50, 54.

[35] In *Necessary Angel*, p. 95.

[36] "Adagia," *Opus Posthumous*, p. 177.

[37] Frank Kermode, *Wallace Stevens* (London, 1960), pp. 38-39.

he the profundity of his imagination. Like the avuncular Pierrot of "Le Monocle de Mon Oncle,"[38] Stevens here mocks himself in magnificent measure—and, in so mocking, creates an anti-self. Even as "annotator," the poet assumes a pose, a role. *"Voilà l'histoire d'un Pierrot écrite par un Paillasse,"*[39] wrote a hostile critic of Janin's *Deburau;* and the same could be said of Stevens' "anecdote." Pursued by the "whistling and mocking" (*L*, 352) of his chronicler's clownlike rhetoric, Crispin makes his way dumbly and meekly through the turbulent straits of the verse; and once at sea, he seems to want the rudder of his creator's articulate self-assurance. For Crispin is an "imperative haw / Of hum," a "lutanist of fleas," a "general lexicographer of mute / And maidenly greenhorns": he is, in other words, a clownesque ephebe, effeminate in his pretensions, immature in his knowledge of the world. He is *fin-de-siècle* Pierrot on the threshold of a palingenesis.

In a letter of January 12, 1940, in response to Hi Simons' article about the poem, Stevens concluded by appending a brief and interesting note, part of which reads:

> About the time when I, personally, began to feel round for a new romanticism, I might naturally have been expected to start on a new cycle. Instead of doing so, I began to feel that I was on the edge: that I wanted to get to the center: that I was isolated, and that I wanted to share the common life. . . . People say that I live in a world of my own: that sort of thing. . . . Of course, I don't agree . . .; I think that I am perfectly normal, but I see that there is a center. For instance, a photograph of a lot of fat men and women in the woods, drinking beer and singing Hi-li Hi-lo convinces me that there is a normal that I ought to try to achieve. (*L*, 352)

---

[38] See the discussion of the speaker of this poem as a "middle-aged conflation of Pierrot and the poetic dandy" in A. Walton Litz, *Introspective Voyager: The Poetic Development of Wallace Stevens* (New York, 1972), pp. 83ff.

[39] The remark was made by Félix Pyat; cited in Rémy, *Deburau*, p. 211.

The subtle, ironic recoil of that last sentence illustrates
Vendler's remarks perfectly; but the obvious lucidity with
which Stevens sees through the gross and the vulgar into
the "center" suggests what he felt the goal of his Comedian logically to be. As for the "normal" that he mentions
and upon which we have lightly, tangentially touched,
Stevens himself defined it as "the instinctive integrations
which are the reason for living"[40]—the integrations, I
would suggest, of the gross particles of reality by the refin-
ing but unfalsifying power of the imagination.

Before the integration, however, must come perception
of the "center"; and Crispin, "an every-day man who lives
a life without the slightest adventure" (*L*, 778), is the hero
through which the poet approached this center of the
"common life." He is "Crispin" rather than "Pierrot" because he is finally to be relieved of his Romantic *malheur*;
and to presage his recovery, the poet has resuited him in
"bellowing breeches, cloak / Of China, cap of Spain"—in
the vestments of a grittier, albeit fictive, comrade of *commedia dell'arte*.[41] But as the poem opens, with Crispin
("nincompated pedagogue") awash in "sea and salt," he
still seems cousin to Carlos, that pedantic eccentric *pierrotique*. His naïve, "domestic intelligence"[42] of a former
and healthier age is recalled:

> An eye most apt in gelatines and jupes,
> Berries of villages, a barber's eye,
> An eye of land, of simple salad-beds,
> Of honest quilts . . .

Yet after the Romantic disturbances of the last hundred

[40] "Imagination as Value," in *Necessary Angel*, p. 155.
[41] As Joseph M. Riddel argues convincingly in his book *The Clairvoyant
Eye: The Poetry and Poetics of Wallace Stevens* (Baton Rouge, La., 1965), Stevens' Comedian "owes the name of Crispin and perhaps little else to the
French comic valet, and similarly to Saint Crispin" (p. 95). He goes on to
say that Crispin "has many qualities, but no distinctive ones, of the many
masked harlequins [sic] of *Commedia dell'arte*" (ibid.); but there is no *commedia* mask, I should point out, that he resembles so closely in temperament at the beginning of his voyage as that of Pierrot.
[42] Fuchs, *Comic Spirit*, p. 34.

years (that "century of wind"), his vision has been somewhat impaired. By the opening of the narrative, his eye,
"confronted with the vastness of experience, has gone
obscurantist":[43]

> the eye of Crispin, hung
> On porpoises, instead of apricots,
> And on silentious porpoises, whose snouts
> Dibbled in waves that were mustachios,
> Inscrutable hair in an inscrutable world.

At the outset of his voyage, Crispin is adrift in a
"juvenile romantic subjectivism,"[44] which Carlos had earlier experienced "in effects so drifting, that I know myself
to be incalculable, since the causes of what I am are incalculable."[45] But because he cannot manage Carlos' selectiv-
ity of effects, Crispin is soon overwhelmed by reality, is utterly "washed away by magnitude." The "Ubiquitous con-
cussion" of the sea—"Polyphony beyond his baton's
thrust"—breaks the fragile globe of his pierrotish subjectivity, and there remains

> nothing of himself
> . . . except some starker, barer self
> In a starker, barer world . . .

This, then, is "the world without imagination" that gives
the canto its title—a comfortless world of impervious fact.
Crispin, "merest minuscule in the gales," seems now a
Peter Parasol deprived of identity as well as illusion. When
he becomes an "introspective voyager," it is not to return
to the silentious forms of his former subjectivity, but rather
to ingratiate himself with the "hoary darks / Noway re-
sembling his," with the "veritable ding an sich, at last."

---

[43] Ibid.

[44] Hi Simons, " 'The Comedian as the Letter C': Its Sense and Significance," *The Southern Review*, V (Winter 1940); reprinted in Ashley Brown
and Robert S. Haller, eds., *The Achievement of Wallace Stevens* (Philadelphia, 1962), p. 98.

[45] In *Opus Posthumous*, p. 145.

For the involuted eye with its profitless lunar evasions has
been made to turn its gaze outward upon the sea:

> The last distortion of romance
> Forsook the insatiable egotist. . . .
> Here was no help before reality.
> Crispin beheld and Crispin was made new.

As Crispin-Pierrot voyages epistemologically, so he
traverses—C-like—a very real globe: "Bordeaux to Yucatan, Havana next, / And then to Carolina. Simple jaunt."
Leaving his native country for a new, sailing "Into a savage
color," he is ineluctably changed in sensibility; and in
Yucatan, the old *aubadiste* of willowy white sleeves, "made
vivid by the sea," discovers complexities of his own temperament that a moon-pale *casaque* might otherwise belie:

> He that saw
> The stride of vanishing autumn in a park
> By way of decorous melancholy; he
> That wrote his couplet yearly to the spring,
> As dissertation of profound delight,
> Stopping, on voyage, in a land of snakes,
> Found his vicissitudes had much enlarged
> His apprehension, made him intricate
> In moody rucks, and difficult and strange
> In all desires, his destitution's mark.

After the discovery of this tougher, more difficult self, the
clown no longer seeks an "odorous bush" under an "Arab
moon" by which to frame pierrotishly expressive gestures;
rather he turns to "an aesthetic tough, diverse, untamed, /
Incredible to prudes, the mint of dirt, / Green barbarism
turning paradigm." But in his newfound earthiness, in his
delight in the jungle's "thick, cadaverous bloom," he feels
Yucatan and its gaudy splendors to be rather pungent, altogether too intoxicating for the neophyte of experience.
And so from Yucatan to Carolina—but before his leaving, a
word from the thunderstorms of the South. The thunder

("Tempestuous clarion") is "one / Of many proclamations of the kind," a proclamation of the discoverer's frail vulnerability in the face of natural force. As such, it is also an announcement of Crispin's subjugation to lordly fact, the stubbornness of which the clown will not wholly respect till his tale is brought to an end.

> The storm was . . .
> Proclaiming something harsher than he learned
> From hearing signboards whimper in cold nights
> Or seeing the midsummer artifice
> Of heat upon his pane. This was the span
> Of force, the quintessential fact, the note
> Of Vulcan, that a valet seeks to own,
> The thing that makes him envious in phrase.

In some measure enlightened by the experience ("His mind was free / And more than free, elate, intent, profound"), Crispin sails north to Carolina. But during the course of his voyage he is touched by a "mental moonlight," by "backward lapses" into romance, and he once again indulges in "an evasion" of the imagination, of his old subjectivity. Were he not a clown—not, moreover, "an aspiring clown"—the moonlight might effect a "liaison, the blissful liaison, / Between himself and his environment." But for the clownesque intelligence, by which the quotidian center of the "common life" is to be uncompromisingly routed out, the lunar influence seems

> Illusive, faint, more mist than moon, perverse,
> Wrong as a divagation to Peking,
> To him that postulated as his theme
> The vulgar, as his theme and hymn and flight,
> A passionately niggling nightingale.
> Moonlight was an evasion, or, if not,
> A minor meeting, facile, delicate.

For Crispin, the imagination is, indeed, a delicate meeting

with the world, since its precious hues seem still very much those of the Aesthetic sensibility. When he imagines the shores of Carolina, it is to see "a Carolina of old time, / A little juvenile, an ancient whim"; his fluctuations "between sun and moon," between the world of fact and the world of his imaginative apprehension, are sallies "into gold and *crimson* forms" (my emphasis), the moonlit shapes still being stained with illusive, purplish tints.

> But let these backward lapses, if they would,
> Grind their seductions on him, Crispin knew
> It was a flourishing tropic he required
> For his refreshment, an abundant zone,
> Prickly and obdurate, dense, harmonious,
> Yet with a harmony not rarefied
> Nor fined for the inhibited instruments
> Of over-civil stops.

And so to Carolina "He came. The poetic hero without palms / Or jugglery, without regalia." As he sails inland from the sea, the "moonlight fiction" disappears: Crispin embraces the "essential prose" of experience:

> He marked the marshy ground around the dock,
> The crawling railroad spur, the rotten fence,
> Curriculum for the marvelous sophomore.
> It purified. It made him see how much
> Of what he saw he never saw at all.

His voyage done, "Crispin in one laconic phrase"—"Nota: his soil is man's intelligence"—"laid bare / His cloudy drift and planned a colony." He relocates the roots of his intelligence, his imaginative capabilities, in earthy reality, and, in so doing, perceives more clearly than before his subservience to the natural world—perceives that upon the outer does man's inner weather often depend ("The natives of the rain are rainy men"). Now serving "Grotesque apprenticeship to chance event," he exults in his subservient

physicality and, bidding "the rabbit run, the cock de-
claim," records their clamor with keen and innocent eye:
"veracious page on page, exact."

But for all the integrity of his apprenticeship, Crispin enjoys a rather "haphazard denouement." In Canto V, *A Nice
Shady Home*, "there is a certain relaxation of Crispin's will,"
as Daniel Fuchs observes:

> No longer "the prickling realist" struggling with "was
> and is and shall or ought to be," he has given up the
> idea of actually forming a colony. A typically comic in-
> telligence, he has become too much the skeptic to plan
> even so modest a Utopia.[46]

Gradually, he is "infected" with a familiar languor; he "becomes subject," in Fuchs' words, "to the attrition of the
everyday":[47]

> Crispin dwelt in the land and dwelling there
> Slid from his continent by slow recess
> To things within his actual eye, alert
> To the difficulty of rebellious thought
> When the sky is blue. The blue infected will.

In a final subjugation to the enervating blue of the quotidian, he is humbled to ordinary reality:

> day by day, now this thing and now that
> Confined him, while it cosseted, condoned,
> Little by little, as if the suzerain soil
> Abashed him by carouse to humble yet
> Attach.

But although he is chastened by the knowledge of the
world's intractability, by its indifference to his quest, and
somewhat dispirited by the undramatic nature of its conclusion, Crispin,

> as realist, admitted that

---

[46] *Comic Spirit*, p. 54.   [47] Ibid.

> Whoever hunts a matinal continent
> May, after all, stop short before a plum
> And be content and still be realist.
> The words of things entangle and confuse.
> The plum survives its poems. It may hang
> In the sunshine placidly, colored by ground
> Obliquities of those who pass beneath,
> Harlequined and mazily dewed and mauved
> In bloom. Yet it survives in its own form,
> Beyond these changes, good, fat, guzzly fruit.
> So Crispin hasped on the surviving form,
> For him, of shall or ought to be in is.

The unheroic is-ness of reality inevitably leads him back to "social nature"; and this return "Involved him in mid-wifery so dense / His cabin counted as phylactery." For he takes to bed a young "prismy blonde" who gives him four "chits . . . for his jigging, bluet-eyed." Now the "indulgent fatalist" smiling upon a curly-headed brood, Crispin realizes that his quest has brought him back to the common simplicities, and, with them, the common perplexities. He accepts the identity of his quintessential self—of the plain man in a plain but opaque world—and thereby resigns himself to a bourgeois life:

> Crispin concocted doctrine from the rout.
> The world, a turnip once so readily plucked,
> Sacked up and carried overseas, daubed out
> Of its ancient purple, pruned to the fertile main,
> And sown again by the stiffest realist,
> Came reproduced in purple, family font,
> The same insoluble lump. The fatalist
> Stepped in and dropped the chuckling down his craw,
> Without grace or grumble.

And so "The relation comes, benignly, to its end," concluding, for Crispin-fatalist, somewhat "fadedly." Indeed, there is the suggestion that, "Prone to distemper" as he is, he may abate in his taste for the essential prose of the quotidian and,

> Fickle and fumbling, variable, obscure,
> Glozing his life with after-shining flicks,
> Illuminating, from a fancy gorged
> By apparition, plain and common things,

shove out once again upon romantic seas. But his annotator, wisely refraining from following him into such roiling, purplish waters, here cuts his history short.

So may the relation of each man be clipped.

"The real is only the base," wrote Stevens in "Adagia": "But it is the base."[48] In "The Comedian as the Letter C," the Pierrot of wan moonlight and evasion, of exasperating aloofness and lonely insularity, is brought back, in the person of Crispin, to the base of the world. Stevens, in having conducted his clownesque hero to the center of the common life, thereby metaphorically founds a *"point d'appui,"* in Vendler's words, "on which the immense structures of the imagination"[49] will later rise. Pierrot, for his part, may be said to have regained not only his classical respect for reality but the naïve, albeit cynical, intelligence that such respect naturally brings. In an important sense, of course, the intelligence yields little more than an admission of ignorance, since Crispin ultimately finds the world's turnip to be an "insoluble lump." But for Pierrot-Stevens himself, the quest has yielded much more: a poetic universe that is wholly solid but, at the same time, wholly his own. For while hero Crispin has discovered for both himself and the poet a "still new continent in which to dwell," the pose of his clownish chronicler has ensured Stevens' liberty to create a world.

Quite unlike his sober subject, who

> could not be content with counterfeit,
> With masquerade of thought, with hapless words

[48] *Opus Posthumous,* p. 160.   [49] *On Extended Wings,* p. 51.

> That must belie the racking masquerade,
> With fictive flourishes,

the "annotator" of Crispin's anecdote seems more than pleased—giddily gratified—by the word-favors dropping into his lap. Doubtless, part of his elation springs from the exhilarating, comic license of his language, for his own "flourishes" by no means preordain "His passion's permit, hang of coat, degree / Of buttons, measure of his salt," as Crispin assumes all language does. This mocker—a poser, a comedian of words, whose skill is in refracting not in reflecting the real—is free to skip from guise to guise in the execution of his performance. He, unlike Crispin, prefers gloss to text, likes palms, jugglery, regalia. We should see his exuberance as the opposing pole of Crispin's rather grim sobriety, his imaginative eccentricity as the anodyne to the fatalist's *ennui,* his solipsism that of an inverted Harlequin, while Crispin's clear-headedness is that of a Hamlet *renversé.* And the dance of the whole poem itself celebrates a rapprochement of the two. Neither in Crispin's uncompromising respect for the skin of things beneath their names, nor in his narrator's delight in the names of things in which they are clothed, resides what Stevens unabashedly calls "the truth." "Where was it one first heard of the truth?" asks a voice in "The Man on the Dump"; and the reply comes, cryptically, "The the." The truth is, as it must be, the flesh become word, the word become flesh. With this marriage in "The Comedian" of word and flesh, "intelligence" and "soil," earnestness and gaiety, the old Pierrot of self-sufficient imagination and a newer, stiffer realist join hands across the verse.

When Stevens again returns to the clown, many years later, after the appearance of Hoon and the shearsman of the blue guitar, he is attracted to the hero *pierrotique* at once by his ignorance and naïveté. The appearance is in *Notes*

toward a Supreme Fiction (1942), which opens, after several hymnic lines in praise of the poetic imagination, with an address to the initiate of experience:

> Begin, ephebe, by perceiving the idea
> Of this invention, this invented world,
> The inconceivable idea of the sun.
>
> You must become an ignorant man again
> And see the sun again with an ignorant eye
> And see it clearly in the idea of it.

But the idea to be most clearly perceived, the "major abstraction,"

>   is the idea of man
> And major man is its exponent, abler
> In the abstract than in his singular,
>
> More fecund as principle than particle,
> Happy fecundity, flor-abundant force,
> In being more than an exception, part,
>
> Though an heroic part, of the commonal.

"Major man," in other words, is abstract symbol, and symbol of the "commonal":

> The major abstraction is the commonal,
> The inanimate, difficult visage. Who is it?

It is not, again, in the white blouse and powdered face that this symbol becomes image: it is, rather, in the tight black coat, the sagging pantaloons, the yawning shoes of a tramp that it assumes resilient but diffident dimensions. It is as Charlot that the common man appears,[50] "in his old coat, / His slouching pantaloons, beyond the town. . . ."

Even before he (or his admirers) made his tramp into "a sort of Pierrot,"[51] Chaplin himself claims to have felt the

---

[50] For this suggestion I am indebted to Michel Benamou, *Wallace Stevens and the Symbolist Imagination* (Princeton, N.J., 1972), p. 32.

[51] Charles Chaplin, *My Autobiography* (New York, 1966), p. 224.

comic integrity and "commonality" of the character that
shuffles into Stevens' *Notes*. He describes the birth of his
famous derelict in these paragraphs of his *Autobiography*:

> I had no idea of the character. But the moment I was
> dressed, the clothes and the make-up made me feel
> the person he was. I began to know him, and by the
> time I walked onto the stage he was fully born. When I
> confronted [Mack] Sennett I assumed the character
> and strutted about, swinging my cane and parading
> before him. . . .
>
> . . . [Sennett] stood and giggled until his body
> began to shake. This encouraged me and I began to
> explain the character: "You know this fellow is many-
> sided, a tramp, a gentleman, a poet, a dreamer, a
> lonely fellow, always hopeful of romance and adven-
> ture. He would have you believe he is a scientist, a
> musician, a duke, a polo player. However, he is not
> above picking up cigarette butts or robbing a baby of
> its candy. And, of course, if the occasion warrants it,
> he will kick a lady in the rear—but only in extreme
> anger!"[52]

In the comic fluctuations of Charlot's character, from
poet to gleaner of gutter butts, we see, as if scribbled in
parodic relief, Stevens' image of the whole, "normal"
man. Neither given over exclusively to the indulgences of
romance nor succumbing completely to the indignities of
the pratfall, Charlot teeters along the middle ground between dream and macadam. His imaginative life is childishly naïve and the pavement he treads seems unaccount-
ably littered with banana peels, but it is in the very nature
of *le monde pierrotique* to burlesque the limits of normality.
Between these limits, Charlot-Pierrot makes his meek adjustments, occasionally abandoning himself to a Harlequinesque caprice or bowing under the austerities of the
Hamletic conscience, yet always finding between both ex-

[52] Ibid., pp. 148-50.

tremes the random consolations of a comically ordinary life.

With the tramp's brief appearance in *Notes toward a Supreme Fiction,* we come to the end of Pierrot's career, at least as it converges in Stevens and Chaplin. The death of Charlot or a shuffled exit from the *Notes,* however, does not, by any means, announce the *zanni*'s demise. As the flourfaced *naïf* of floppy white vestments, Pierrot is, assuredly, fast nearing death, lingering on fitfully in vestiges of the *commedia,* in fragments of a past, irrecoverable life. But no matter how deprived he may be of his former garb or how much his character suffers from its loss, we can still feel his presence, in one or another of his generic masks, about familiar but ruddy faces: about, for example, the face of Anthony Burgess' stool-ridden poet, or of Frank O'Hara's connoisseur of Manhattan lunch counters, or of any one of Samuel Beckett's wiry band of metaphysical *expulsés.* The list could be extended. The soft contours of Pierrot's mobile features may now seem to conform, in fact, to almost any physiognomy of a vaguely Laforguean cast. Indeed, Jean Starobinski, in his incisive *Portrait de l'artiste en saltimbanque,* suggests that it is the virtual facelessness of all modern clowns, their absence of definition, that is the source of their comic durability: "It is only at the price of this *vacancy,* of this initial *void* that they can *pass over* into the meaning that we have discovered in them. They have need of an immense reserve of non-sense in order to pass over into sense."[53]

The inexhaustible reserve of non-sense in Pierrot, his capacity to baffle the intelligence of his own heart and brain, is what enables him to endure his inescapable self-sufficiency. It is what, ultimately, ingratiates him with the popular consciousness—the consciousness of temperamentally ordinary people, whose discomforts of the body are relieved by an indulgence of the senses, and of the soul

[53] *Portrait de l'artiste en saltimbanque* (Geneva, 1970), p. 141.

by a naïveté of the mind. Pierrot has, as a consequence, a kind of moral indestructability that has always seemed to survive the guttering death of his candle; and until the book of moonlight is completely written and the comic imagination extinguished, he will continue to lend his voice and intelligence to the comedians of his world.

BIBLIOGRAPHY OF
PRINCIPAL WORKS CONSULTED

I. *Manuscripts*

The Larpent manuscript collection in the Henry E. Huntington Library, San Marino, California.

II. *Printed Works*

Adhémar, Hélène. *Watteau: sa vie—son œuvre.* Paris, 1950.

Adhémar, Jean. *Honoré Daumier.* Paris, 1954.

Aghion, Max. *Le Théâtre à Paris au XVIIIᵉ siècle.* Paris, 1926.

Alain-Fournier (Henri Fournier, called). *Le Grand Meaulnes.* Paris, 1964.

Albert, Maurice. *Les Théâtres de la Foire (1660-1789).* Paris, 1900.

————. *Les Théâtres des Boulevards (1789-1848).* Paris, 1902.

Arène, Paul. *Pierrot héritier, comédie en un acte, en vers.* Paris, 1866.

Attinger, Gustave. *L'Esprit de la commedia dell'arte dans le théâtre français.* Paris, 1950.

[Aubert, Mrs.] *Harlequin-Hydaspes: or, The Greshamite. A Mock-Opera* . . . London, 1719.

Auriac, Eugène d'. *Théâtre de la Foire: recueil de pièces représentées aux foires Saint-Germain et Saint-Laurent* . . . Paris, 1878.

Avery, Emmett L. "Dancing and Pantomime on the English Stage, 1700-1737." *Studies in Philology,* XXXI (July 1934): 417-52.

————. "The Defense and Criticism of Pantomimic Entertainments in the Early Eighteenth Century." *ELH,* V (June 1938): 127-45.

————. "Foreign Performers in the London Theatres in the Early Eighteenth Century." *Philological Quarterly,* XVI (April 1937): 105-23.

Avery, Emmett L. et al. *The London Stage, 1660-1800* . . . 5 pts. in 11 vols. Carbondale, Ill., 1960-1968.

Baldick, Robert. *The Life and Times of Frédérick Lemaître.* London, 1959.

Banville, Théodore de. *Mes Souvenirs* . . . Paris, 1882.

———. *Œuvres de Théodore de Banville.* 5 vols. Paris, [1889-1892?].

———. *Les Pauvres Saltimbanques.* Paris, 1853.

———. *Poésies complètes de Théodore de Banville, 1844-1854.* Paris, 1858.

Barberet, V. *Lesage et le Théâtre de la Foire.* Nancy, 1887.

Baschet, Armand. *Les Comédiens italiens à la cour de France sous Charles IX, Henri III, Henri IV et Louis XIII* . . . Paris, 1882.

Baudelaire, Charles. *Œuvres complètes.* Préface, Présentation, et Notes de Marcel A. Ruff. Paris, 1968.

———. *Petits Poëmes en prose,* ed. Robert Kopp. Paris, 1969.

Beaumont, Cyril. *The History of Harlequin.* London, 1926.

Behn, Aphra. *The Works of Aphra Behn,* ed. Montague Summers. 6 vols. London, 1915.

Benamou, Michel. *Wallace Stevens and the Symbolist Imagination.* Princeton, N.J., 1972.

Bernardin, N.-M. *La Comédie italienne en France et le Théâtre de la Foire et du Boulevard (1570-1791).* Paris, 1902.

Bonnassies, Jules. *Les Spectacles forains et la Comédie-Française* . . . Paris, 1875.

Bornecque, Jacques-Henry. *Lumières sur les Fêtes Galantes de Paul Verlaine.* Paris, 1959.

[Bradbury, Robert]. *Airs, Chorusses, and Business with a Description of the Scenery, In the New Pantomime of Harlequin and the Dandy Club; or, 1818* . . . [London], 1818.

Braun, Roger. *Adolphe Willette et son œuvre* . . . Paris, 1926.

Brenner, Clarence D. *The Theatre Italien: Its Repertory, 1716-1793.* Berkeley, Calif., 1961.

Brisson, Adolphe. *Nos Humoristes* . . . Paris, 1900.

Brown, Ashley and Robert S. Haller, eds. *The Achievement of Wallace Stevens.* Philadelphia, 1962.

Buttel, Robert. *Wallace Stevens: The Making of* Harmonium. Princeton, N.J., 1967.

Campardon, Emile. *Les Comédiens du roi de la troupe italienne pendant les deux derniers siècles: documents inédits recueillis aux archives nationales.* 2 vols. Paris, 1880.

———. *Les Spectacles de la Foire . . .: documents inédits recueillis aux archives nationales.* 2 vols. Paris, 1877.

Carré *fils,* Michel. *L'Enfant prodigue, pantomime en 3 actes . . ., musique de André Wormser.* Rouen, 1892.

Chambers, E. K. *The Elizabethan Stage.* 4 vols. Oxford, 1923.

Champfleury (Jules-François-Félix Husson, called Fleury, called). *Souvenirs des Funambules.* Paris, 1859.

Chaplin, Charles. *My Autobiography.* New York, 1966.

Chaponnière, Paul. *Piron: sa vie et son œuvre.* Paris, 1910.

Christout, Marie-Françoise. *Le Merveilleux et le "théâtre du silence" en France à partir du XVIIᵉ siècle.* The Hague, 1965.

Courville, Xavier de. *Luigi Riccoboni dit Lélio (un apôtre de l'art du théâtre au XVIIIᵉ siècle).* 3 vols. Paris, 1943-1958.

Cucuel, Georges. *Les Créateurs de l'Opéra-Comique français.* Paris, 1914.

Dancourt, Florent Carton. *Les Œuvres de théâtre de Monsieur Dancourt . . .* 8 vols. Paris, 1742.

Deburau, Gaspard and Charles. *Pantomimes de Gaspard et Charles Deburau, traduction par Emile Goby.* Paris, 1889.

Desboulmiers (Jean-Auguste Jullien, called). *Histoire anecdotique et raisonnée du Théâtre-Italien, depuis son rétablissement en France jusqu'à l'année 1769 . . .* 7 vols. Paris, 1769.

[———]. *Histoire du théâtre de l'Opéra-Comique . . .* 2 vols. Paris, 1769.

Description of the New Comic Pantomime, called, Harlequin from the Moon; or, The Magic Rose . . . Dublin, 1811.

Dibdin, T. J. *Harlequin and Mother Goose; or, The Golden Egg! A Comic Pantomime.* London, n.d.

[———]. *Harlequin in his Element; or, Fire, Water, Earth, & Air; A Favourite Pantomime . . .* London, 1808.

[———] and Kirby. *The Valley of Diamonds; or Harlequin Sinbad . . .* London, 1814.

Dick, Kay. *Pierrot*. London, 1960.

Disher, M. Willson. *Clowns and Pantomimes*. London, 1925.

Doutrepont, Georges. *L'Evolution du type de Pierrot dans la littérature française* . . . [Brussels], 1925.

————. *Les Types populaires de la littérature française*. 2 vols. Brussels, 1926-1928.

[Downing, George]. *The Tricks of Harlequin: or, The Spaniard Outwitted. A Pantomime Entertainment . . . Being the Comic Part of the celebrated Entertainment of Perseus and Andromeda*. Derby, 1739.

Dowson, Ernest. *The Poems of Ernest Dowson*, ed. Mark Longaker. Philadelphia, 1962.

Drack, Maurice (Auguste Poitevin, called). *Le Théâtre de la Foire, la Comédie-Italienne et l'Opéra-Comique: recueil de pièces choisies jouées de la fin du XVIIe siècle aux premières années du XIXe siècle* . . . Paris, 1889.

Duchartre, Pierre-Louis. *The Italian Comedy*, trans. Randolph T. Weaver. London, 1929.

Du Gérard. *Table alphabetique & chronologique des pièces représentées sur l'Ancien Théâtre Italien depuis son Etablissement jusqu'en 1697 qu'il a été fermé* . . . Paris, 1750.

Durry, Marie-Jeanne. *Jules Laforgue* . . . [Paris, 1952].

Eliot, T. S. *The Complete Poems and Plays, 1909-1950*. New York, [1962].

————. *Poems Written in Early Youth*. New York, 1967.

Enck, John J. "Stevens' Crispin as the Clown." *Texas Studies in Literature and Language*, III (Autumn 1961): 389-98.

Farley, Charles. *Chorusses, Recitative, and Dialogue, with a Short Description of the Business of each Scene, of the New Pantomime, called Harlequin Munchhausen, or the Fountain of Love* . . . [London], 1818.

————. *Harlequin and the Sylph of the Oak: or, The Blind Beggar of Bethnal Green; with a Sketch of the Story* . . . London, 1816.

————. *Harlequin Gulliver; or, The Flying Island* . . . London, 1817.

————. *The New Pantomime of Harlequin and Fortunio; or, Shing-Moo and Thun-Ton; with a Sketch of the Story* . . . London, 1815.

[————]. *Songs, Duets, Trios, Chorusses, &c. in the New Grand Comick Pantomime of Harlequin and the Ogress; or, The Sleeping Beauty of the Wood* . . . London, 1822.

[————]. *Songs, Chorusses, Recitative, and Dialogue, with a Description of the Scenery, &c. &c. in the New Pantomime, called Harlequin and Asmodeus; or, Cupid on Crutches* . . . London, 1810.

Favart, Charles-Simon, *Théâtre; ou, Recueil des comédies, parodies & opéra-comiques qu'il a donné jusqu'à ce jour* . . . 10 vols. Paris, 1763-1772.

Fielding, Henry. *Tumble-Down Dick: or, Phaeton in the Suds. A Dramatick Entertainment* . . . *Interlarded with Burlesque, Grotesque, Comick Interludes, call'd, Harlequin a Pick-Pocket* . . . London, 1744.

Findlater, Richard (K. B. Findlater Bain, called). *Grimaldi: King of Clowns.* London, 1955.

————, ed. *Memoirs of Joseph Grimaldi.* By Charles Dickens. New York, 1968.

Flaubert, Gustave. *Pierrot au Sérail,* in Vol. III of the *Appendice aux Œuvres complètes.* Paris, 1910.

Fletcher, Ifan Kyrle. "Italian Comedians in England in the 17th Century." *Theatre Notebook,* VII (1953): 86-91.

Florian, [Jean-Pierre Claris de]. *Œuvres de Florian.* 15 vols. Paris, 1805-1811.

Font, Auguste. *Essai sur Favart et les origines de la comédie mêlée de chant.* Toulouse, 1894.

Fournel, Victor. *Les Spectacles populaires et les artistes des rues.* Paris, 1863.

Fowlie, Wallace. *The Clown's Grail: A Study of Love in Its Literary Expression.* London, 1947.

Fuchs, Daniel. *The Comic Spirit of Wallace Stevens.* Durham, N.C., 1963.

Gautier, Théophile. *The Complete Works of Théophile Gautier,* trans. and ed. F. C. DeSumichrast. 12 vols. New York, 1910.

Gautier, Théophile. *Histoire de l'art dramatique en France depuis vingt-cinq ans.* 6 vols. Paris, 1858-1859.

———. *Souvenirs de théâtre, d'art et de critique.* Paris, 1883.

———. *Théâtre: Mystère, comédies et ballets.* Paris, 1872.

Gendarme de Bévotte, G. *La Légende de Don Juan: son évolution dans la littérature des origines au romantisme.* 2 vols. Paris, 1911.

———. *Le Festin de Pierre avant Molière.* Paris, 1907.

Gherardi, Evaristo, ed. *Le Théâtre Italien de Gherardi ou le Recueil général de toutes les comédies et scènes françoises jouées par les Comédiens Italiens du Roy* . . . 6 vols. Amsterdam, 1721.

Giraud, Albert (Albert Keyenberg, called). *Héros et Pierrots.* Paris, 1898.

———. *Pierrot lunaire: rondels bergamasques.* Paris, 1884.

Goldoni, Carlo. *Mémoires pour servir à l'histoire de sa vie, et à celle de son théâtre,* in *Tutte le opere di Carlo Goldoni,* ed. Giuseppe Ortolani. Vol. I. Milan, 1935.

Goncourt, Edmond and Jules de. *French Eighteenth-Century Painters,* trans. Robin Ironside. New York, 1948.

———. *Journal: Mémoires de la Vie littéraire,* ed. Robert Ricatte. 22 vols. Monaco, 1956-1958.

Gordon, Lyndall. *Eliot's Early Years.* Oxford, 1977.

Grannis, Valleria Belt. *Dramatic Parody in Eighteenth Century France.* New York, 1931.

Greene, Edward J. H. *T. S. Eliot et la France.* Paris, [1951].

Gueullette, J.-E. *Un Magistrat du XVIIIe siècle, ami des lettres, du théâtre et des plaisirs: Thomas-Simon Gueullette.* Paris, 1938.

Gueullette, T.-S. *Notes et souvenirs sur le Théâtre-Italien au XVIIIe siècle,* pub. J.-E. Gueullette. Paris, 1938.

———. *Parades inédites, avec une préface par Charles Gueullette.* Paris, 1885.

Guichard, Léon. *Jules Laforgue et ses poésies.* Paris, 1950.

Guitry, Sacha. *Deburau: A Comedy.* English version by H. Granville-Barker. London, 1921.

Harlequin Student: or The Fall of Pantomime, with the Restoration of the Drama; an Entertainment . . . London, 1741.

Harlequin, Tom, The Piper's Son. A New Comic Pantomime . . . London, 1820.

Hays, H. R. "Laforgue and Wallace Stevens." *The Romanic Review*, XXV (1934): 242-48.

Howarth, Herbert. *Notes on Some Figures behind T. S. Eliot.* London, 1965.

Hugo, Victor. *Œuvres dramatiques complètes / œuvres critiques complètes,* ed. Francis Bouvet. Paris, 1963.

Hugounet, Paul. *Mimes et Pierrots: Notes et documents inédits pour servir à l'histoire de la pantomime.* Paris, 1889.

——— and Félix Larcher. *Les Soirées Funambulesques.* Paris, [1890-1892].

Huysmans, J.-K. *Œuvres complètes de J.-K. Huysmans.* 18 vols. Paris, 1928-1934.

Jal, Auguste. *Dictionnaire critique de biographie et d'histoire* . . . Paris, 1872.

Janin, Jules. *Deburau, Histoire du Théâtre à quatre sous pour faire suite à l'histoire du théâtre français.* Réédité avec une préface par Arsène Houssaye. Paris, 1881.

Kenner, Hugh. *The Invisible Poet: T. S. Eliot.* New York, 1959.

———, ed. *T. S. Eliot: A Collection of Critical Essays.* Englewood Cliffs, N.J., 1962.

Kermode, Frank. *Wallace Stevens.* Edinburgh and London, 1960.

Klingler, Oskar. *Die Comédie-Italienne in Paris nach der Sammlung von Gherardi.* Strassburg, 1902.

Laforgue, Jules. *Lettres à un ami, 1880-1886* . . . Paris, 1941.

———. *Mélanges posthumes.* Paris, 1919.

———. *Œuvres complètes de Jules Laforgue.* 6 vols. Paris, 1922-1930.

———. *Poems of Jules Laforgue,* trans. Patricia Terry. Berkeley, Calif., 1958.

———. *Poésies complètes: Edition augmentée de soixante-six poèmes inédits.* Paris, 1970.

———. *Selected Writings of Jules Laforgue,* trans. and ed. William Jay Smith. New York, 1956.

———. *Stéphane Vassiliew* . . . Geneva, 1946.

Larcher, Félix and Eugène. *Pantomimes de Paul Legrand.* Paris, 1887.

Lea, K. M. *Italian Popular Comedy: A Study in the Commedia dell'Arte, 1560-1620, with Special Reference to the English Stage.* 2 vols. Oxford, 1934.

Lebègue, Raymond. "La Comédie italienne en France au XVIe siècle." *Revue de Littérature Comparée,* XXIV (January-March 1950): 5-24.

Lecomte, L.-Henry. *Histoire des Théâtres de Paris: Les Fantaisies-Parisiennes / L'Athénée / Le Théâtre Scribe / L'Athénée-Comique, 1865-1911.* Paris, 1912.

——. *Histoire des Théâtres de Paris: Les Folies-Nouvelles, 1854-1859, 1871-1872, 1880.* Paris, 1909.

——. *Histoire des Théâtres de Paris: Les Jeux Gymniques, 1810, 1812 / Le Panorama Dramatique, 1821-1823.* Paris, 1908.

——. *Histoire des Théâtres de Paris: Le Théâtre National / Le Théâtre de l'Egalité, 1793-1794.* Paris, 1907.

——. *Histoire des Théâtres de Paris: Les Variétés Amusantes, 1778-1789, 1793-1798, 1803-1804, 1815.* Paris, 1908.

Lehmann, A. G. "Pierrot and *fin de siècle,*" in *Romantic Mythologies,* ed. Ian Fletcher. London, 1967.

Léris, Antoine de. *Dictionnaire portatif historique et littéraire des théâtres, contenant l'origine des différents théâtres de Paris, le nom de toutes les pièces qui y ont été représentées depuis leur établissement . . .* Paris, 1763.

Lesage, Alain-René and Dorneval. *Le Théâtre de la Foire ou l'Opéra-Comique, contenant les meilleures pièces qui ont été représentées aux Foires de S. Germain & de S. Laurent.* 10 vols. Paris, 1724-1737.

[Lesclide, Richard]. *Mémoires et pantomimes des Frères Hanlon-Lees.* Paris, [1880].

Levy, Bernard. *The Unpublished Plays of Carolet: A New Chapter on the History of the Theatre de la Foire.* New York, 1931.

Lindsay, Frank Whiteman. *Dramatic Parody by Marionettes in Eighteenth Century Paris.* New York, 1946.

Litz, A. Walton. *Introspective Voyager: The Poetic Development of Wallace Stevens.* New York, 1972.

Magnin, Charles. *Histoire des marionnettes en Europe, depuis l'antiquité jusqu'à nos jours.* Paris, 1862.

Mallarmé, Stéphane. *Œuvres complètes.* Paris, 1945.

March, Richard and Tambimuttu, eds. *T. S. Eliot: A Symposium* . . . London, 1948.

Margueritte, Paul. *Le Printemps tourmenté.* Paris, 1925.

———— [and Victor]. *Nos Tréteaux: Charades de Victor Margueritte; Pantomimes de Paul Margueritte.* Paris, 1910.

Mauclair, Camille. *Jules Chéret.* Paris, 1930.

Mayer III, David. *Harlequin in His Element: The English Pantomime, 1806-1836.* Cambridge, Mass., 1969.

Mélèse, Pierre. *Le Théâtre et le public à Paris sous Louis XIV, 1659-1715.* Paris, 1934.

Mendès, Catulle. *L'Art au théâtre.* 3 vols. Paris, 1897-1900.

————. *Le Docteur blanc.* Paris, 1893.

Mic, Constant. *La Commedia dell'arte, ou le théâtre des comédiens italiens des XVIᵉ, XVIIᵉ & XVIIIᵉ siècles.* Paris, 1927.

Moland, Louis. *Molière et la comédie italienne.* Paris, 1867.

Molière (Jean-Baptiste Poquelin, called). *Œuvres complètes,* ed. Louis Moland. 12 vols. Paris, 1880-1885.

Morse, Samuel French. *Wallace Stevens: Poetry as Life.* New York, 1970.

Motteux, P. A. ("and other hands"). *The Novelty. Every Act a Play. Being a Short Pastoral, Comedy, Masque, Tragedy, and Farce after the Italian manner.* London, 1697.

Mountfort, William. *The Life and Death of Doctor Faustus, Made into a Farce* . . . *With the Humours of Harlequin and Scaramouche.* London, 1697.

Najac, Raoul de. *Souvenirs d'un Mime.* Paris, 1909.

Newman-Gordon, Pauline. *Corbière / Laforgue / Apollinaire* . . . Paris, 1964.

Nichols, Charles Washburn. "Fielding's Satire on Pantomime." *PMLA,* XLIV (1931): 1107-12.

Nicolini, Fausto. *Vita di Arlecchino.* Milan, 1958.

Nicoll, Allardyce. *A History of English Drama, 1660-1900.* 6 vols. Cambridge, England, 1952-1959.

Nicoll, Allardyce. *Masks, Mimes and Miracles*. London, 1931.

––––––. *The World of Harlequin: A Critical Study of the Commedia dell'Arte*. Cambridge, England, 1963.

Nouveau Théâtre de la Foire, ou Recueil de pièces, parodies & opéra-comiques représentées sur le Théâtre de l'Opéra-Comique, depuis son rétablissement jusqu'à présent. Année 1761. 5 vols. Paris, 1763.

Nouveau Théâtre Italien (Le) ou Recueil général des comédies représentées par les Comédiens Italiens ordinaires du Roi. 10 vols. Paris, 1753.

Oreglia, Giacomo. *The Commedia dell'Arte*, trans. Lovett F. Edwards. London, 1968.

Origny, Antoine d'. *Annales du Théâtre-Italien depuis son origine jusqu'à ce jour*. 3 vols. Paris, 1788.

Pandolfi, Vito. *La commedia dell'arte, storia e testo*. 6 vols. Florence, 1957-1969.

Pannard, François-Charles. *Théâtre et œuvres diverses de M. Pannard* . . . 4 vols. Paris, 1763.

[Parfaict, François and Claude]. *Histoire de l'Ancien Théâtre-Italien, depuis son origine en France, jusqu'à sa suppression en l'année 1697*. Paris, 1753.

[––––––]. *Mémoires pour servir à l'histoire des spectacles de la Foire, par un acteur forain*. 2 vols. Paris, 1743.

[–––––– and Godin d'Abguerbe]. *Dictionnaire des Théâtres de Paris, contenant toutes les pièces qui ont été jouées jusqu'à présent* [1st ed.: 1756] *sur les différents théâtres français et sur celui de l'Académie Royale de Musique, les extraits de celles qui ont été jouées par les comédiens italiens depuis leur rétablissement en 1716, ainsi que des Opéra-Comiques et principaux spectacles des foires Saint-Germain et Saint-Laurent*`. . . 7 vols. Paris, 1767.

Parodies du Nouveau Théâtre Italien (Les), ou Recueil des Parodies représentées sur le Théâtre de l'Hôtel de Bourgogne, par les Comédiens Italiens ordinaires du Roy. 4 vols. Paris, 1731-1738.

Péricaud, Louis. *Le Théâtre des Funambules, ses mimes, ses acteurs et ses pantomimes* . . . Paris, 1897.

Petraccone, Enzo. *La commedia dell'arte, storia, tecnica, scenari.* Naples, 1927.

Piis, de and Barré. *Théâtre de M. de Piis . . . et de M. Barré . . . contenant les Opéra-Comiques en Vaudevilles, et autres pièces qu'ils ont composées en société, pour le Théâtre Italien, depuis 1780 jusqu'en 1783.* 2 vols. London, 1785.

Piron, Alexis. *Œuvres complètes illustrées,* pub. Pierre Dufay. 10 vols. Paris, 1928-1931.

Pitou, Alexis. "Les Origines du Mélodrame français à la fin du XVIIIᵉ siècle." *Revue d'Histoire Littéraire de la France,* XVIII (1911): 265-96.

[Planché, J. R.]. *Doctor Syntax; or, Harlequin in London. A Pantomime . . .* London, 1820.

——. *Rodolph the Wolf; or, Columbine Red Riding-Hood. A Comic Melodramatic Pantomime . . .* London, 1819.

Ramsey, Warren. *Jules Laforgue and the Ironic Inheritance.* New York, 1953.

——, ed. *Jules Laforgue: Essays on a Poet's Life and Work.* Carbondale, Ill., 1969.

Rasi, Luigi. *I comici italiani, biografia, bibliografia, iconografia.* 3 vols. Florence, 1897-1905.

Ravenscroft, Edward. *Scaramouch a Philosopher, Harlequin a School-Boy, Bravo, Merchant, and Magician. A Comedy after the Italian Manner.* [London], 1677.

Reade, Brian. *Aubrey Beardsley.* Introduction by John Rothenstein. New York, 1967.

Reboul, Pierre. *Laforgue.* Paris, 1960.

Rémy, Tristan. *Les Clowns.* Paris, 1945.

——. *Georges Wague: Le Mime de la Belle Epoque.* Paris, 1964.

——. *Jean-Gaspard Deburau.* Paris, 1954.

Riccoboni, Luigi. *Histoire du théâtre italien . . .* 2 vols. Paris, 1730-1731.

——. *Observations sur la comédie et le génie de Molière.* Paris, 1736.

Richepin, Jean. *Braves gens: roman parisien.* Paris, 1886.

——. *Théâtre chimerique . . .* Paris, 1896.

Riddel, Joseph N. *The Clairvoyant Eye: The Poetry and Poetics of Wallace Stevens.* Baton Rouge, La., 1965.

Rivière, Henri. *Pierrot / Caïn.* Paris, 1860.

Rosenfeld, Sybil. *Foreign Theatrical Companies in Great Britain in the 17th and 18th Centuries.* London, 1955.

————. *The Theatre of the London Fairs in the 18th Century.* Cambridge, England, 1960.

Rostand, Edmond. *Pierrot qui pleure et Pierrot qui rit, comédie en musique.* Paris, 1899.

Ruchon, François. *Jules Laforgue (1860-1887): sa vie, son œuvre.* Geneva, 1924.

Sakari, Ellen. *Prophète et Pierrot: Thèmes et attitudes ironiques dans l'œuvre de Jules Laforgue.* Jyväskylä, Finland, 1974.

Salerno, Henry F., trans. *Scenarios of the Commedia dell'Arte: Flaminio Scala's* Il teatro delle favole rappresentative. New York, 1967.

Salvatore, Paul J. *Favart's Unpublished Plays: The Rise of the Popular Comic Opera.* New York, 1935.

Sand, George (Amandine-Aurore-Lucie Dupin, Baroness Dudevant, called). *Histoire de ma vie.* 10 vols. Paris, 1856.

Sand, Maurice (Jean-François-Maurice-Arnauld, Baron Dudevant, called). *Masques et bouffons.* 2 vols. Paris, 1860. (My citations are from the English trans. *The History of the Harlequinade.* 2 vols. Philadelphia, 1915.)

Schwartz, I. A. *The Commedia dell'Arte and its Influence on French Comedy in the Seventeenth Century.* Paris, 1933.

Sencourt, Robert. *T. S. Eliot: A Memoir,* ed. Donald Adamson. New York, 1971.

Sentenac, Paul. *Pierrot et les artistes: Mémoires de l'ami Pierrot.* Paris, 1923.

Séverin (Séverin Cafferra, called). *L'Homme Blanc: Souvenirs d'un Pierrot.* Paris, 1929.

Speaight, George. *The History of the English Puppet Theatre.* London, 1955.

Starobinski, Jean. *Portrait de l'artiste en saltimbanque.* Geneva, 1970.

Stevens, Holly. *Souvenirs and Prophecies: The Young Wallace Stevens.* New York, 1977.

Stevens, Wallace. *The Collected Poems of Wallace Stevens.* New York, 1954.

————. *Letters of Wallace Stevens,* ed. Holly Stevens. New York, 1966.

————. *The Necessary Angel: Essays on Reality and the Imagination.* New York, 1951.

————. *Opus Posthumous,* ed. and with an Introduction by Samuel French Morse. New York, 1957.

————. *The Palm at the End of the Mind: Selected Poems and a Play,* ed. Holly Stevens. New York, 1971.

Symons, Arthur. *The Symbolist Movement in Literature.* New York, 1958.

Taupin, René. *L'Influence du symbolisme français sur la poésie américaine (de 1910 à 1920).* Paris, 1929.

Théâtre des Boulevards ou Recueil de parades. 3 vols. Paris, 1756.

Thurmond, John. *Apollo and Daphne: or, Harlequin Mercury. A Dramatic Entertainment, after the manner of the antient Pantomimes* . . . London, 1725.

————. *Harlequin Doctor Faustus: with the Masque of the Deities* . . . London, 1724.

————. *The Miser; or, Wagner and Abericock. A Grotesque Entertainment* . . . London, 1727.

Vendler, Helen Hennessy. *On Extended Wings: Wallace Stevens' Longer Poems.* Cambridge, Mass., 1969.

Verlaine, Paul. *Œuvres en prose complètes.* Paris, 1972.

————. *Œuvres poétiques complètes.* Paris, 1962.

Weaver, John. *The History of the Mimes and Pantomimes . . . To which will be added, a List of the Modern Entertainments that have been exhibited on the English Stage, either in Imitation of the ancient Pantomimes, or after the Manner of the Modern Italians. . . .* London, 1728.

Welleford, William. *The Fool and His Scepter: A Study in Clowns and Jesters and Their Audience.* Evanston, Ill., 1969.

Wells, Mitchell P. "Some Notes on the Early Eighteenth-
Century Pantomime." *Studies in Philology,* XXXII (October 1935): 598–607.

Welsford, Enid. *The Fool: His Social and Literary History.*
New York, 1936.

Willette, Adolphe. *Feu Pierrot, 1857-19?.* Paris, 1919.

————. *Pauvre Pierrot.* Paris, [1885].

INDEX

Numbers in italics refer to illustrations

Frey, Max, 81n
Fuchs, Daniel, 167n, 181n, 186
Funérailles de la Foire, Les (Lesage
    and Dorneval), 41n
Fuzelier, Louis, 41n, 42n, 53

Galland, Antoine, 55
Garland for John Donne, A (ed.
    Spencer), 159
Garrick, David, 66
Gautier, Théophile, 3, 93, 94, 96,
    98, 101, 102, 103, 106, 108, 109,
    110, 111, 113, 114, 117, 122, 133,
    137
Gavarni, 110
Gefangener Pierrot (Captive Pierrot,
    Klee), 28
Gelosi (commedia troupe), 74
Génois (actor-tumbler), 76
Geoffroy, Charles, 13
Geratoni, Giuseppe, *see* Giaratone
Gherardi, Evaristo, 4, 18, 20, 21n,
    25, 28, 30, 31, 32, 40, 41, 49, 55,
    61, 71, 72, 83
Giaratone, Giuseppe, 18, 20, 23,
    25, 28, 30n, 32, 34, 40, 49, 51, 53,
    54, 60, 61, 64, 66, 67, 70, 71, 87
Giglio (stock type of Italian farce),
    76
Gille, 41, 66, 75, 77n. *See also* Gilles
Gille le Niais, 8, 75
Gilles, 27, 30n, 49, 54, 64, 74, 92,
    109, 115, 122, 123, 127, 145;
    compared with Pierrot, 76-77,
    136; contribution of character to
    nineteenth-century French Pier-
    rot, 96; eighteenth-century in-
    terpreters of, 76; eighteenth-
    century popularity of, 80-81;
    possible origins of, 75; role and
    character in *parades* of
    eighteenth-century French fairs,
    77-80. *See also* Gille
Gilles (Watteau), 9
*Gilles garçon peintre z'amoureux-t-et
    rival (parade),* 80
Gilles le Boiteux, 76
Gillot (marionette artist), 42
Giraud, Albert, 126, 127, 135,
    136, 137n, 138, 139

Giraudoux, Jean, 154
Goldoni, Carlo, 17
Goncourt, Edmond de, 118
Goncourt, Jules de, 118n
Granchio, Il (Corsini scenario), 15n
Grand Meaulnes, Le (Alain-
    Fournier), 136
Grand'mère amoureuse, La (Fuzelier
    and Dorneval), 42n
Gran Vittoria di Pedrolino, La
    (Croce), 1, 15
Gray, Dorian (character in Wilde's
    The Picture of Dorian Gray), 134
Greene, Edward J. H., 156n, 157n,
    159n, 160n, 164n
Griffin, Mr. (actor), 87
Grimaldi, Giuseppe, 104
Grimaldi, Joseph, 10, 81, 90, 91,
    104
Gris, Juan, 29
Gueullette, J.-E., 33n, 78n, 79n
Gueullette, Thomas-Simon, 14n,
    33n, 39, 61n, 77, 78, 79, 80n
Guichard, Léon, 154n
Guitry, Sacha, 105n
Guyon, Alexandre, 68n

Haller, Robert S., 182n
Hamlet, 69, 164; character of, 8-9;
    compared with Charlie Chaplin,
    191-92; compared with *commedia*
    stock types, 9-10; compared with
    Eliot's Prufrock, 165-66; com-
    pared with Harlequin, 7-8,
    72-73; compared with Pedrolino,
    72-73; compared with Pierrot,
    66-67, 73, 136-38, 153-55; com-
    pared with Stevens' Crispin, 189
Hamlet (Shakespeare), 8, 98, 99. *See
    also* Hamlet, Ophelia, Polonius,
    Yorick
Hamoche, Jean-Baptiste, 41, 54,
    58, 59, 64, 67, 88
"Hang up brave tapestries" (Ste-
    vens), 171, 173
Hanlon-Lees (mime troupe), 91n,
    119, 123
Hardy, Oliver, 25, 51
Harlakan, 82. *See also* Arlecchino,
    Arlequin, Harlequin

mockery in Stevens' poetry,
170-72, 176, 180; and Stevens'
Bowl, 175-76; and Stevens' Car-
los, 177-79; and Stevens' Cris-
pin, 181-89; and Stevens' Peter
Parasol, 173
"Pierrot" (Banville), 93
Pierrot (Picasso), 27
Pierrot (Rivière), 112n
Pierrot, Le (Rouault), 30
"Pierrot" (Stevens), 169, 170
"Pierrot" (Verlaine), 133-34, 136,
163
Pierrot, Le (Willette), 122
pierrotade, 110
Pierrot assassin (Richepin), 118, 123
Pierrot assassin de sa femme (P. Mar-
gueritte), 118, 119, 124
Pierrot au livre, Le (*Pierrot with Book*,
Gris), 29
Pierrot au Sérail (Flaubert), 111
Pierrot errant (pantomime), 101
Pierrot Escapes (Lipchitz), 31
Pierrot et Arlequin (*Pierrot and Harle-
quin*, Picasso), 32
Pierrot et squelette en jaune (*Pierrot
and Skeleton in Yellow Robe*, En-
sor), 24
Pierrot fumiste (Laforgue), 146, 154
Pierrot héritier (Arène), 117
Pierrot lunaire (Giraud), 126, 127n,
138n
Pierrot Marquis (Champfleury), 114
Pierrot Narcisse (Giraud), 136
Pierrot of the Minute, The
(Beardsley), 26
Pierrot of the Minute, The (Dowson),
26, 170
Pierrot partout (Charton), 101
Pierrot pendu (Champfleury), 114
Pierrot posthume (Gautier), 111, 117
Pierrot-Romulus, ou le Ravisseur poli
(Lesage, Fuzelier, and Dor-
neval), 42n
"Pierrots" (Laforgue), 151, 152
Pierrot sceptique (Huysmans and
Hennique), 18, 119, 145, 146
"Pierrots (*Scène courte mais
typique*)" (Laforgue), 151

Pierrot, valet de la Mort
(Champfleury), 114
Piis, Augustin de, 61
Piron, Alexis, 39, 55, 56, 58n, 77n
"Pitre, Le" (Verlaine), 66
Pluto, 48
Poe, Edgar Allan, 118
Poems of Ernest Dowson (ed. Sym-
ons), 170
Poetry (periodical), 172, 173, 174
Poinsinet, Antoine-Alexandre-
Henri, 81
Polichinelle, 3, 37, 44, 45, 49, 114,
125. *See also* Pulcinella, Punch,
Punchanello
Polonius (character in Shake-
speare's *Hamlet*), 9, 72, 164, 165
Pont-Neuf, 37, 75, 91
Portrait de l'artiste en saltimbanque
(Starobinski), 192
"Portrait of a Lady" (Eliot), 161,
162, 163
Pound, Ezra, 156, 158
Prencipe d'Altavilla, Il (Corsini
scenario), 15n
Prens-Tout (stock type of *parade*),
80
Princesse de la Chine, La (Lesage and
Dorneval), 55
Proserpine, 48
Proteus, 32, 118
Prufrock, J. Alfred (speaker of
Eliot's "The Love Song of J.
Alfred Prufrock"), 164, 166, 177
Puck, 80
Pulcinella, 4, 14, 116. *See also*
Polichinelle, Punch, Pun-
chanello
Punch, 87. *See also* Polichinelle,
Pulcinella, Punchanello
Punchanello, 87. *See also*
Polichinelle, Pulcinella, Punch
Pyat, Félix, 180n

Quattro finti spiritati, Li (Scala), 15
Queen's Theatre, 87
Quennell, Peter, 157n
Querelle des Théâtres, La (Lesage
and La Font), 41n

LIBRARY OF CONGRESS CATALOGING
IN PUBLICATION DATA

Storey, Robert F   1945-
    Pierrot: a critical history of a mask.

    Bibliography: p.
    Includes index.
    1. Pierrot.   I. Title.
PN57.P49S7   809.2'9'351   78-51194
ISBN 0-691-06374-5

809.29 S   99473

Storey, Robert F., 1945-

Pierrot :

809.29 S   99473

Storey, Robert F., 1945-

Pierrot :

DATE DUE	BORROWER'S NAME
FE 21 '84	Mary Meade
MR 6 '84	Renewed